THOSE
PHILADELPHIA
KELLYS

✤ WITH A TOUCH OF GRACE ✤

BY THE SAME AUTHOR

---

by ARTHUR H. LEWIS

THOSE PHILA- DELPHIA KELLYS

❖❖ WITH A TOUCH OF GRACE

WILLIAM MORROW AND COMPANY, INC.

NEW YORK   1977

Printed in the United States of America.

1 2 3 4 5 6 7 8 9 10

Library of Congress Cataloging in Publication Data

Lewis, Arthur H. (date)
      Those Philadelphia Kellys, with a touch of Grace.

      Includes index.
      1. Kelly family.   2. Grace, Princess of
Monaco, 1929-   3. Monaco—Princes and
Princesses—Biography.   I. Title.
CS71.K29   1977   929'.2'0973   77-5724
ISBN 0-688-03226-5

BOOK DESIGN   CARL WEISS

FOR

HERBERT M. ALEXANDER

ACKNOWLEDGMENTS

I am particularly indebted to Charles V. Kelly, Jr., who skillfully led me through the family labyrinth.

To Hobart Berolzheimer, Head, Literature Department, Free Library of Philadelphia, who once told me "somebody ought to write a book about the Philadelphia Kellys."

To Ms. Frances C. Ritchey for her editorial help.

To Robert D. Abrahams, Esq., for use of his island retreat.

To Ms. Geri Duclow, Librarian-in-Charge, Theatre Collection, Free Library of Philadelphia.

To Herb and Gwen Edwards for their patience, kindness, and desire to help me understand George E. Kelly.

To Ms. Marilyn Moody, for her research assistance.

To "Kathy" McKenna for her "interpretation" of Kell.

To Edward Pinkowski who generously shared his family research with me.

To B. Dale Davis, Executive Editor, *Philadelphia Bulletin.*

To Charles Martyn, Chief Librarian, Philadelphia *Bulletin.*

To Louis Rauco, Chief Librarian, Newspaper Department, State Library of Pennsylvania. To Digby Baltzel, Paul B. Beers, Ms. Leslie Bennetts, Mrs. Elaine Cruice Beyer, Miss Joan Blondell, Mrs. Frances Bolno, Mrs. Lillian Bregman, Miss Aleen Bronson, John Cain, Mrs. Marie Carton, Mrs. Ralph Greenleaf (China Doll), Mrs. Margaret Kelly Conlan, Brian Daly, Mrs. Mary Daly, Joseph X. Dever, Paul E. Devor, Jack E. Edelstein, Mrs. Kathryn Ferguson, Charles R. Fish, Jr., Tom Fox, Miss Grace Frommeyer, Miss Rita Gam, Francis Gowen, Taylor Grant, Stanley Green, Harry Hallman, Patrick Hayden, Bill Hegner, Mrs. Dorothy Hitchcock, Harry Jay Katz, Anne Kelly, Daniel R. Kelly, John B. Kelly, Jr., Mrs. Mary Freeman Kelly, Miss Mildred Kelly, Philip Klein, Wayne Knecht, Tommy LaBrum, Jules C. Lavin, Dom Legado, Mrs. Donald LeVine, Miss Betty Lewis, Phil Longo, Mrs. Amy Mc-Cauley, Daniel J. McCormick, Mrs. Mary McDonald, Willie Mosconi, Mrs. Mary Carol Anderson Mueller, Freddie Meyer, Ms. Kiki Olsen, Ms. Susan O'Neill, Miss Frances Peters, Joe Regan, Mrs. D. L. Reichard, D. L. Reichard II, Esq., William A. Reiter, Joe Rivkin, Louis Roth, Harry Rothstein, Dore Schary, Al Schmidt, Joseph Sharfsin, Esq., Si Shaltz, Miss Kate Shea, Mrs. Dorothea W. Sitley, Joe Smith (Smith and Dale), Mrs. Marion Cruice Smith, Miss Patsy Sims, Irwin W. Solomon, Mlle. Nano Stouroua, Rev. G. Hall Todd, Mrs. B. Shirley Turner, University of California, Los Angeles, Department of Special Collections, and Rosalind Salzburg, who interviewed George Kelly, Walter Williams, George Walter Zarn.

Morning Star
Nevis
Leeward Islands
British West Indies
October, 1976

CONTENTS

1

"THERE'S NEVER BEEN A GOOD KELLY MARRIAGE"

IT'S NOT EASY TO BE OBJECTIVE ABOUT THE PHILADELPHIA Kellys because you keep falling in love with them. The Kelly women are stunning, the Kelly men, handsome. They're amiable, gregarious, hospitable, and witty. I've met dozens of them and I can recall only a few exceptions and even these are not far from the family norm.

More often than not they win what they want to win against tough odds, whether it's in business, politics, or sports, and if they don't come in first, they're good losers. They can and do challenge the authority of their priests and, in one instance at least, the authority of the Holy Father himself. They can end unpleasant marriages by divorce; they can fail to attend Mass or make Confession and still be comfortable in the family brand of Catholicism and, I presume, die in the Kelly version of a State of Grace.

They can have cancer, be aware of it, and accept the inevitable. I know a Kelly who's been invalided for forty-three years yet welcomes each day with good humor and cheers visitors who come to cheer her.

And with appreciable bitterness, the Kellys are resigned to the fact that they won't be included in the *Social Register,* that they won't be invited to the Assembly, that their daughters will not be debutantes and that their sons aren't asked to join the First City Troop. This, despite the fact that in only four generations the Kellys have contributed more to Philadelphia than those tenth-, eleventh- and twelfth-generation Philadelphia gentlemen ever gave William Penn's "greene towne."

So it must be with a great deal of satisfaction ever since the family acquired a real, live Princess that the Kellys can cock a collective snook at the Biddles, the Cadwaladers, and the Drinkers. I suppose in fairness I should add that the Biddles, the Cadwaladers, and the Drinkers couldn't care less.

Considering all the Kelly pluses, and aware that I, too, am quite as unacceptable to the Bs, the Cs, and the Ds, I find myself itching to take sides and support the family no matter how many sins it has committed. Alas, of the latter there are multitudes.

As a starter, take Jack—John Brendan Kelly, Sr.,—holder of two Olympic gold medals and probably the greatest single sculler the world has ever known. I had a waving acquaintance with John B. back in the mid-Thirties when I was a lowly district reporter on the Philadelphia *Inquirer*. Kelly was a power in national, state, and city politics, a friend of FDR, and a close ally of George H. Earle, Pennsylvania's first Democratic governor in nearly half a century and in Harrisburg largely because of the political acumen of John B. Kelly.

I remember I'd finished the daily stint and stood in front of my aged Model A at Broad and Chestnut streets around 3:30 on a bitter cold winter morning gazing hopelessly at a flat tire, mindful of the fact that I carried no spare. I was frozen stiff; my crude manifold heater hadn't been throwing out much warmth that long night; besides I was almost out of gas. This was the nadir of the Great Depression; I had no money for even a gallon and I didn't dare run the motor merely to keep warm. There was just enough left in the tank to get me home, six miles to the north.

I debated what to do next. Should I walk back to the 19th District Police Station at 12th and Pine, wake up an irritable cop, and ask for help or leave the car and hitch a ride home? I didn't have to do either. Jack Kelly came to my aid. He pulled up beside me in his long black Packard and sang out, "What's the trouble, kid?" There wasn't much to explain; my plight was apparent.

Jack helped push my car to the curb, then drove me up to

6122 North Broad, where I lived. On the way there he poured a hot cup of coffee from a thermos, added a healthy slug of Old Overholt, and handed the mixture to me. Never before and I suppose never since have I drunk anything quite so welcome.

On still another cold night, some years later, I saw Jack once again come to the rescue. I was covering a fire near 25th and Taney streets, then, as it is today, a near-center city enclave for working-class Irish. Though there'd been no loss of life, one family was burned out completely; mother, father, and small children (including an infant-in-arms) huddled disconsolately across the street from their gutted home.

I was getting details from the Battalion Chief and the 25th Ward Republican leader. I don't know why Jack Kelly was present —probably he'd been the speaker at a charity affair in downtown Philadelphia, or maybe he'd been escorting one of his lady friends home. At any rate there he was, and as a former City Democratic Chairman he knew the exact constituency of the Taney Street neighborhood and was aware that a poor compatriot would be in need of help. Actually it wouldn't have mattered much to Kelly whatever the race, creed, or color of anyone in trouble. He didn't waste time. I don't recall if he even spoke to those who had been burned out. I do remember that he took a hundred-dollar bill from his wallet and handed it to the ward leader. I wouldn't have been so trusting; a hundred dollars was a hell of a lot of money in those days.

One more brief episode. Some twenty years ago I was in Pittsburgh plugging my first book in a department store, which had arranged an autograph party. There I was, an innocent in the ways of publishers' promotions, seated behind a desk piled high with my books, more than willing to sign copies all day long.

But after an hour of complete isolation it became apparent to me that nobody cared enough about my book to plunk down the cash or add $3.50 to his charge account. It wasn't that there weren't plenty of potential customers in the store that day—the aisles were filled with them. Yet, except for an occasional, amused glance from hurrying passersby, I was ignored.

I was ready to call it quits when I looked up and saw John B. Kelly walk along. He did a double-take and spoke to the men he was with. "Best book I ever read," he told them. "I'll take four more copies." He winked at me.

I followed his cue. "Give me your name, sir," I said, "and I'll autograph them for you."

Before he left, he'd twisted the arms of his friends, each of whom bought at least one copy. I also think he must have influenced others who'd heard his praise of a book he hadn't read and never would. Before that day ended I'd sold fourteen copies, establishing some kind of record for an autograph party given an unknown writer for a book discouragingly advertised as "inspirational nonfiction."

Nobody knows how many spontaneous acts of kindness John B. Kelly performed before he died in 1960; there must have been thousands. I do know that ironically while he gave much of his time to helping utter strangers, he messed up his only son's life by forging him into an instrument of personal revenge.

Furthermore, although John B. rose from hod carrier to millionaire and never lost the common touch, in a will of his own composition that could go down as one of the wittiest ever probated in Pennsylvania's Orphans Court, he didn't leave a dime to charity. I must note that the Catholic hierarchy didn't think Kelly's last testament the least amusing.

Although I knew who he was, I'd been around Philadelphia a long, long time before I met John B. Kelly, Jr., "Kell" to his Olympic friends all over the world, to his admirers in the Amateur Athletic Union, which he once headed, and to thousands of Philadelphians who thrice elected him to City Council, where I've seen him sleep through many a session. His late father, too, called him Kell and so do his sisters, cousins, and wife. I suppose the one exception is his mother, "Ma" Kelly. With more than a hint of asperity in her voice, she calls her fifty-year-old offspring "Junior" and didn't hesitate to spank him in public shortly after he'd attained his forty-sixth birthday.

Like most other Quaker City residents, at least those who read

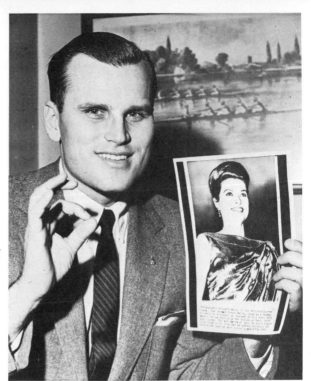

John B. Kelly, Jr., holding an AP wire photo of Princess Grace. The caption, dated March 19, 1962, announces her imminent return to the movies.

newspapers, listen to the radio, or watch television, I was aware that Kell divided his life into two major segments, girls and sports. I would estimate (and my opinion is buttressed by several local gossip columnists) there is a 50 percent slice of the former, 40 percent of the latter, and 10 percent for politics and public appearances. Kell loves Philadelphia just as much as his father did, and when he's not chasing the ladies—sometimes even then—can be counted on for a speech anywhere, anytime.

In apportioning Kell's time, I have taken into consideration neither the seven or eight hours he sleeps nightly, nor the five miles of jogging he does daily in Fairmount Park, all of which help him keep the superb physical condition he has always maintained. At this point I speak only en passant of Kell's macho. However, from the information I've garnered by talking to young ladies who have every reason to be knowledgeable, Councilman Kelly is, in this area, a master both of endurance and technique.

Almost everybody who knows Kell or reads about him in the sports pages or in gossip columns likes him even if most people don't understand why he suddenly tossed aside a lovely wife and six children as well as an almost assured political career. True, he does hold political office, but being a member of Philadelphia's City Council isn't much of a step up the ladder for a charming, internationally known athlete who not long ago before his precipitous action had the eyes of Democratic kingmakers upon him. Running as Councilman-at-Large, which means he had to attract voters on a city-wide basis rather than from individual wards, he finished ahead of Mayor Frank Rizzo. As I learned subsequently, Kell spent less than $500 on each of his three campaigns (1967, 1971, and 1975) or one-twentieth of what the other candidates invested.

When I got to know and grow fond of both Kell and Mary, his wife, after seven years of living apart (there's neither legal separation nor divorce) I asked Kell why he'd gone off on his own. His answer was that for him adolescence came twenty-five years late; that he was bored with monogamy; and that, unlike his father, he didn't believe in preserving an unhappy marriage by keeping up appearances. Furthermore, he didn't think the best way to deal with comment about extramarital affairs was to pretend they didn't exist. Mary has a far more conventional attitude toward wedlock and marital responsibilities.

While we're on the subject I might mention that in this one respect Kell has far outdistanced his father. A lady, always young, invariably stunning, usually blond, and often a beauty-pageant winner, can be seen by Philadelphia's jet set clinging to Kell's arm and looking up at him with both admiration and understandable expectancy every night in the week.

My formal introduction to John B. Kelly, Jr., came shortly after I decided to write a book on the family. Councilman Kelly's Administrative Assistant is Kathy McKenna, certainly one of the most photogenic blondes in Philadelphia. Kathy and her husband, Bill, are old friends of mine, so I had no trouble in arranging an appointment with Kell.

I was a bit early; Kathy and I sat talking in the Councilman's reception room while we waited for Kell, who was in his other office a couple of blocks away. He's president of Kelly for Brick-work, one of the largest contractors in the construction industry.

Kathy glanced at the tape recorder resting on my lap, sighed, raised her eyebrows, and shook her head.

"Jesus!" she breathed through tightened lips. "Take it easy, *please.* Remember Kell will respond to *any* question you ask and he'll give you an honest answer. He won't hedge and he's completely incapable of lying. That's his big trouble, Goddammit." She smiled ruefully. "If you want to find out how much he's worth or the size of his bank account, he'll more than likely show you his last ten-forty. All you have to do is ask and he'll hand you his current financial statement, then open up his wallet and let you examine what's inside."

I'm not sure, but I got the feeling Kathy was trying to put me on the honor system. I never did ask Kell how rich he was so I can't pass on that information. But there wasn't much else he didn't tell me. All I had to do in our subsequent conversations was steer Kell back on the road when he digressed. This didn't happen often; he knew what I wanted and he gave it to me without restraint. At times I was embarrassed by his frankness; he never was.

Kell's just as tall—six feet one—and as magnificently built as his father, the latter once called the "most perfectly formed American male." I can understand why many women find him irresistible just as ladies of the preceding generation felt drawn to John B. Kelly, Sr.

For the past two decades the best known member of the family has been Kell's Motion Picture Academy Award-winning sister Grace, now Her Serene Highness of Monaco. Princess Grace, born in 1929, is Jack, Sr.'s middle daughter. The twice-divorced Peggy, her father's favorite, was born in 1925; Kell in 1927; Lizanne in 1933.

Since, basically, my book is about other members of the family I won't dwell too much on this particular Kelly except to say I fell in love with her when I saw her playing opposite Gary Cooper in my favorite film, *High Noon.*

I was one of several hundred introduced to Princess Grace in the spring of 1976 at a so-called gala where Her Serene Highness presented Philadelphia's Free Library with a collection of manuscripts and memorabilia once belonging to her Uncle George, the playwright, John B.'s older, if not favorite, brother.

The presentation, in the form of a long-term loan (the family actually doesn't *give* much away), was made in the grand, high-ceilinged marble foyer of the main branch of the Library in Logan Square. The Library and its equally elegant neighbor, the Family Courthouse, resemble, architecturally speaking, those structures along the Champs Elysées which, shortly after World War One, were gazed upon adoringly by a one-time member of the City Council.

This Councilman, Charlie Hall, handed over ideas, plans, and contract for erecting the Library to a brother of John Brendan Kelly, Sr., Patrick, who went broke putting up this same building in which Niece Grace was to be the honored speaker a half-century later.

At the gala were a dozen or more members of the family plus scores of Philadelphians of all ages and sexes, some present because of their interest in books and others to see, be seen, rub elbows, and be photographed with Her Serene Highness. Even if most of the ladies were far more magnificently gowned and coiffed than Grace Kelly, it was Her Serene Highness, in a simple, dark green gown, her blond hair arranged in modest fashion, who stood out from all the rest.

The feature of the evening came when Grace walked down the brightly illuminated marble stairway and took her place at the head of the receiving line. She looked like the glamorous Hollywood star she once was, obviously retaining those qualities which, two decades earlier, had enabled her to win an Academy Award. Dutifully she greeted her adoring public, some of whom were not sure how to address the Princess—whether to curtsy or shake hands.

If a stage or movie director should typecast a queen, he wouldn't go wrong choosing Grace Kelly. It's just too bad that the "throne"

A studio portrait (Copyright 1955 by Paramount Pictures Corporation) *of movie star Grace Kelly.*

Her Serene Highness now sits upon is in reality only the caudal appendage to a high-class gambling joint. Nevertheless, Princess Grace is far more important to her adopted country and her subjects than Europe's few remaining rulers are to theirs.

There are excellent reasons why Monégasques love the American-born princess. For those who take Monacan history seriously it's important to recall that when Miss Kelly became part of the scene on April 19, 1956, the date of her marriage to Rainier, the Casino at Monte Carlo was playing to empty houses and tourism had declined to the vanishing point. Worst of all, His Serene Highness, although hardly a celibate, had been unable to furnish an heir. As a consequence, in accordance with a deal made years before between Monaco and France, the tiny country would revert to the Republic of France; all twenty-four thousand Monégasques would lose their tax and military service exemptions.

Then along came Grace, beautiful, fiscally sound and, best of all, fecund. The new Serene Highness accepted responsibilities that must have been pointed out to her. She shilled for the Casino and brought a return of those superrich gamblers who'd strayed to the competition in France and Italy; restored Monaco as the "in" place for Europe's and America's Beautiful People and, in rapid order, produced not one but three offspring.

Rainier's personal Confessor, Father Tucker, of Wilmington, Delaware, in Monaco by Papal appointment, had been understandably concerned about his charge's bachelor status. As so many members of the Grimaldi family had done in past centuries, young Rainier had developed a widespread reputation for fast living. Furthermore, grave doubts had arisen about His Serene Highness's potency, if not his virility. His mistress, lush French actress Giselle Pascal, known throughout Europe as "The Uncrowned Queen of Monaco," was barren after what must be assumed to have been a cooperative undertaking.

I once asked Grace's first cousin, Charles V. Kelly, Jr., who chairs the English Department at Philadelphia's La Salle College, whether it was indeed Father Tucker who arranged the famous Kelly-Grimaldi marriage.

Charles, a handsome and elegant intellectual (he admits to being a rarity in the family), shrugged his shoulders. "That priest always *said* so," his inference being that this Oblate Father may have been stretching a point. Dr. Kelly, who holds his degree in Latin and English from the University of Pennsylvania and who looks at life and people through wise, cynical eyes, has been my unpaid but willing guide on my journey into the lives and loves of the Kellys.

It was Charles who, as a guest of Cousins Grace and Rainier, once refused to eat in the Palace dining room unless a pair of dogs was removed.

Served their food in silver bowls, which first were passed from Prince to Princess for approval, the animals settled down in a corner.

Charles observed the ritual with disgust. "I told Grace either the dogs go or I go. I had no intention of eating *my* meal with a pair of slobbering beasts. The dogs went; I stayed."

This may be the proper time to consider certain stories that I judge were promulgated by envious ladies and frustrated gentlemen. I refer to Her Serene Highness's premarital virtue.

My authority is Charles Fish, Jr., a middle-aged Philadelphia realtor who has known Grace Kelly ever since she was an adolescent. Somehow or other Mr. Fish and I got on the subject of Princess Grace's chastity and I put the question to him.

"Absolutely not! And I don't think anybody could be closer to that situation than I was. Grace is a straight-arrow Catholic lady, and I'm a Protestant bastard. God knows I tried."

Before we leave the subject of Grace Kelly, temporarily at any rate, I do want to touch upon her marriage. Several years ago the Princess took an apartment in Paris ostensibly to watch over and perhaps restrict the social activities of daughter Caroline, who was attending school in the French city. However, for some time now, the former Miss Kelly has been doing more and more transatlantic and trans-U.S. travel without her Prince.

I would think that even if the couple has been separated de facto, if not de jure, their Serene Highnesses would go a long way to preserve the marriage. Each has too much to lose otherwise —Rainier, a beautiful, charming wife and devoted mother of his three children; Grace, a truly serene way of life unequaled in this increasingly troubled world.

There are times, though, when I have forebodings about a remark Charles Kelly once made to me. "There's never been a good Kelly marriage." Charles himself is a bachelor, the product, he admits, of a loveless union between his father, a brick contractor, and his mother, model for the title role in Uncle George's Pulitzer Prize-winning play, *Craig's Wife*.

George was born in 1887 of Irish immigrant parents, Mary Costello and John H. Kelly. There were nine other siblings, five boys and four girls. The playwright and brothers John B. and Walter C., the latter vaudeville's "Virginia Judge," were as well known in their day as is Niece Grace in hers.

George, a strange, brilliant mystic, seventh son of a seventh son, so he claimed, born in a cawl, anti-Semite and misogynist, was ashamed of his humble origin, which he altered to suit his elegant taste when the occasion required. He adored visiting the Palace with its pomp and ritual. "Of courts and cities I have known," he quoted, "this is my home."

He began his theatrical career in 1911 as an actor. He went on to write and direct six Broadway plays, all highly successful commercially and critically, between 1924 and 1929 and wrote nothing of fiscal or artistic value thereafter although he lived to be eighty-seven.

A tall, strikingly handsome homosexual, Kelly, after an episode that cost him several thousand dollars, remained, as far as I could learn, faithful to one man whom he kept, traveled, and lived with for at least four decades. As to his bigotry, it's difficult to comprehend why a man with George Kelly's high degree of intelligence, sophistication, and experience with and exposure to Jews in the arts would still believe in the totally discredited Protocols of Zion. According to Nephew Charles, he did, and no amount of argument could swerve Uncle George from his tenets.

George detested sports and often said that both Brother John and Nephew Kell wasted much of their lives rowing boats on the dirty Schuylkill River. A political reactionary, he once stalked out of a house in cold fury because his hostess served "Lady Bird Johnson" pie for dessert. George would have been more at home in the Union League than in John B.'s Democratic City Committee headquarters. Nonetheless, it was to this brother that George appealed for help to get him out of the army during World War One. Brother John succeeded.

George never smoked and didn't drink until he was past eighty. Even then he refused to admit that he liked alcohol; and when he wanted a daiquiri, his favorite cocktail, he'd ask his host or hostess to give him "one of those lemonade things." Usually his host knew exactly what George meant. Like others in the family he accepted death bravely and in his case with a gentle taunt at a niece. As he lay dying—and knew it—he turned to his sister

Mary's daughter, who'd come to bid farewell to the uncle she loved best of all.

"My dear," he whispered softly, "before you kiss me good-bye, fix your hair. It's a mess."

Walter, like Brother John, was not one of George's favorites, although they had much in common professionally. It was on the stage of Wilkes-Barre's Polis Theatre that I saw the Virginia Judge for the first of many times. My family had heard about Walter Kelly from Philadelphia relatives who enjoyed vaudeville as much as we did. We saw the Polis bill advertised in our newspaper, *The Mahanoy City Record,* and knew the famous monologist was not likely to play our town. So my father drove us to Wilkes-Barre and back the same night, a one-hundred-and-twenty-mile trip, which was a lot for a Model T but worth it.

This was in 1917; I was eleven years old and the "Judge" had been a headliner for fifteen years and would remain so for another dozen or until radio swept vaudeville into the past. He'd had top billing on two-a-day circuits all over the English-speaking world, in major and minor cities from New York to San Francisco, Montreal to Vancouver, London and the Provinces, Melbourne, Sydney, and Auckland.

What sort of stories did Walter tell, jokes that set audiences "rolling in the aisles"? Well, for one thing they were clean; he never used profanity on the stage. And for another, his jokes were ethnic, a small percentage Irish, but mostly Negro. He referred to blacks as "darkies" and their offspring as "pickaninnies." He fashioned his act from what he once heard in a Virginia courtroom and took his stage name from a witty member of the bench who dispensed justice to poor blacks charged with minor violations of the law.

The all-time favorite Walter Kelly story, which brought howls of laughter from people no matter how many times they'd heard it, is typical:

VIRGINIA JUDGE: What is the prisoner charged with?

POLICEMAN: Stealing chickens, Your Honor.

VIRGINIA JUDGE: What have you to say for yourself?

PRISONER: Jedge, Your Honor, I don' steal no chickens. May de Lord strike me dead if I stole 'em.

VIRGINIA JUDGE: All right. Stand aside for ten minutes and if the Lord doesn't strike you dead, I'll give you thirty days.

Before his near-hysterical devotees recovered from that one Walter went on with a "quickie":

VIRGINIA JUDGE (to an idler on the courthouse steps): Want to make a quarter?

IDLER: No, suh. I've got a quarter.

These *were* funny: I laughed at them and so did audiences of the day. But I should hate to be around now if the Virginia Judge told these dialect jokes in a Philadelphia, Chicago, New York, or Detroit theater. I'd want to get the hell out as fast as I could and I'm sure Walter Kelly would, too, if he were still around to tell them.

Just as Brother George had a few long-time Jewish friends— "Not the avaricious kind, you can be sure," he told Nephew Charles—so did Walter number among his intimates several blacks, Stepin Fetchit and Louis Armstrong, to name a couple. Furthermore, he did not hesitate to use the latter to promote Niece Grace's film career. However, if he could avoid it, he wouldn't play on the same bill with blacks and so instructed his agent, Rufus R. Le-Maire. I'd been told of this by members of the family and had it confirmed some months ago by George Roland, a retired vaudeville juggler, one of Walter's remaining contemporaries.

When the Judge was at home base his favorite spot was the Dugout, an East Falls restaurant where he'd meet and treat old cronies whose friendship dated as far back as the year Walter left school at age eight to work in Dobson's Carpet Mills. He quit Dobson's when he was twelve—on the day he lost the tip of his right forefinger.

Walter, unlike Brother George, was fond of the ladies, but he never married. Apparently there was one special woman in his life, identified only as "Ethelda M." in a faded, lovingly autographed picture Walter carried with him wherever he went and which was found among the Judge's effects when he died.

Almost everybody except Brother George liked Walter. Among his intimates the Judge counted some of the world's best known figures, Charlie Chaplin, George M. Cohan, and Sir Thomas Lipton. Walter, in turn, loved almost everybody with the possible exception of his maternal relatives, the Costellos. "Kissing a Costello," Walter once said, "is like embracing a concrete mixer."

Walter's favorites were Brothers "Jack" (John B.) and "P.H." (Patrick H.). It must have been a tough decision for the Judge to make when the family began a lengthy feud, Jack on one side and P.H. on the other, over the firing of P.H.'s son by Charles, Sr. Walter cast his lot with the former team; P.H., bereft of family support and a big spender besides, went down the financial drain and died broke. Jack, with promised aid from Walter, did make a last-minute attempt to assist P.H. but by then it was too late.

For two decades, the showplace of East Falls—"The Falls," as residents of that area call it—was the P. H. Kelly mansion at 3500 Midvale Avenue. It was a huge stone structure, built by P.H. himself, on half an acre of ground. There was a beautifully manicured lawn, a tennis court, a three-hole golf course, and a three-car garage. Inside were among others a dozen or more bedrooms, five baths, a capacious dining room, a ballroom, and a billiard room.

Although for many years they led the good life, the P. H. Kellys were not without great sorrows. Catherine, "Tap," the fifth of nine children, was stricken with polio in 1935 and has never left her bed since. George, the second son and fourth sibling, (whom I call the Other George to distinguish him from the playwright) became the National Pocket Billiard Champion by defeating the great Willie Mosconi but died an alcoholic, penniless and alone, in a Philadelphia Skid Row flophouse. P.H. must have cursed the day he bought the pool table and taught his son to play. P.H. himself was a champion and won the 1912 city-wide pocket billiard tournament.

Patrick, as did brothers Charles and Walter, began to learn the weaving trade at Dobson's Carpet Mills when he was nine or ten years old, an appropriate age to end school for children of poor immigrant parents. Like the rest of the family, he hated the millionaire English-born Dobsons who ran the neighborhood's largest industry, paid the lowest possible wages, sold shoddy blankets to Union soldiers, hired Irish biddies to do household chores, and, until the Kellys' ascendancy, ran The Falls.

P.H. was only five feet nine, taller than average for his generation but short for Kelly men. In middle age he grew portly but until then he weighed less than one hundred and fifty pounds. He was perhaps the best loved of all Kellys and his funeral in 1937 the largest the city had ever seen.

In addition to his overpowering love for his wife, Kitty, and their children—he wept when his sons and daughters married and left home—his tremendous affection was for the Knights of Columbus. The greatest moment in their father's life, his daughters told me, was in 1920 when he wrote and published privately an official history of that organization, a book praised by a Cardinal.

A man of strong likes and dislikes, he adored public speaking. In his day he was one of the most sought-after postprandial orators, not only because he came free but also because he was good. As a matter of fact he died of a heart attack in the middle of an after-dinner speech. "Tragic for us," recalled daughter Mildred, "but happy for Dad."

Generosity was another one of this Kelly's qualities and possibly an additional cause of his financial failures.

"P.H. was a soft touch," recalled Charles, Jr., "particularly when it came to the Church. One day our parish priest at Saint Bridget's asked P.H. for a fairly large quantity of bricks to build some kind of adjunct to the school.

" 'Of course,' agreed P.H., 'tell me just how many you need and I'll have them delivered to you.'

"Well, a month or so later the priest passed P.H. on the street and, to my uncle's shock, ignored him.

" 'What the hell's eating the Monsignor?' P.H. wondered."

Charles grinned.

"It was only after that they found out that my father, who worked for Uncle Pat, had sent a bill to the priest covering not only the cost of the bricks but delivery charges as well."

Pugnacious, fearless, overriding, hard-working, and merciless boss that he was, there are men and women who worked for him when he ran John B.'s Kelly for Brickwork Company who say unhesitatingly that Charles Kelly, Sr., was the backbone of the family and the prime reason for its financial success. They add that it was the beginning of the end for P.H. when Charles quit and went to work for Jack.

"He was a fabulous estimator, better even than P.H.," remembers Kate Shea, who has been with the firm for quite a number of years. "He also was a near-illiterate but he had an incredible memory, which compensated. When Charlie had to mark time sheets and couldn't spell employees' names he simply scrawled 'blue cote, nine hrs., or red jacket, eight.' "

The Charles Kelly family was small by Kelly standards. In addition to Charles, Jr., there was only one other child, Mary, now a handsome woman named for her mother.

"My father," said Mary, "was independent, colorful, and shy. He did all of Uncle John's dirty political work and he wasn't afraid of anybody except his wife [as Charles recalled]. He was more retiring than the rest of the Kellys but he had a saving sense of humor. He always watched the pennies and if he thought there were too many laborers on a job he didn't hesitate to fire the excess or what he *believed* was an excess."

Dan Kelly (no relation to the family), who runs his own competitive company, used to work for Charles, Sr.

"When Charlie walked on the job you didn't have to see him; you *knew* he was there because you could feel the tempo pick up. It was unbelievable. Yet there were some consuming peculiarities. He had a phobia about collecting paper. And he'd make all the labor foremen save paper cement bags."

Dan chuckled.

"Christ! It cost more money to save those paper bags than you could get for them. The foreman had to go round and collect them, fold them, and put them in neat piles. And if you threw away a paper bag, you could get shot."

His father's philosophy, averred son Charles, was "go out and fight for what you want."

He paused.

"I followed his precepts because I was forced to. I *wanted* to go to college and my father didn't want me to and he wouldn't give me the money. So I worked my way through, sixteen and eighteen hours a day, although there was no financial need for that. We weren't rich but we *certainly* weren't poor."

Charles shook his head sadly.

"You could hardly say my father's disposition was equable. His idea was to hit you first and then argue with you after he had established the fact. He was more vindictive than all the rest of the Kellys, a violent man.

"But he was extraordinarily dynamic; he lived at the run. Until the last years of his life food was totally meaningless to him. If my mother served peas every night in the week he'd never say, 'What! peas again?' It didn't matter to him that if Mother were out and he got in at six we didn't have dinner until ten. I never saw anyone less dependent on physical things than my father; he had no interest in life except work."

Mary Daly told me a story about her father:

"My cousin Peggy [John B.'s oldest daughter] was married to Gene Conlan. One time Gene came home from the South and said he'd met this guy at a service station pumping gas. The guy asked Gene where he was from and Gene told him he was from Philadelphia.

" 'What part of Philadelphia?' he asked and Gene answered, 'The Falls.'

" 'Do you know the Kellys there?' was the next question and Gene replied without telling him he was married to one of them, 'Why, yes. I know them very well.' The attendant then said, 'Did you ever hear of Charlie Kelly?' and Gene answered, 'Yes, indeed.'

"The guy went on, 'Well, I used to work for him. He was a tough guy. Do you know what happened when he died?'

"Gene shook his head.

" 'When they were taking his body to the cemetery and Charlie McIlvaine—he buries all the Kellys—was driving the hearse, Charlie said that all at once when they were going over a hill, Kelly sat up in the coffin and said, 'How many pallbearers do you have?' and Charlie said, 'Six.'

" 'Well,' says Kelly, 'lay off two of them.' ' "

Other members of the family have also added color to the monochromatic Philadelphia scene. One left home at fifteen to bear a set of twins. P.H.'s grandson, at age nine, won the All-City Junior Chess Tournament.

"Ma," John B.'s widow, although only a Kelly by marriage, fully qualifies for membership in the family. When son Kell announced his intention of running for mayor, Ma threatened not only to contribute to the opposition party but, so I am told, also pay for billboards on which citizens would be asked if they'd like to have a transsexual for their next first lady. Ma was referring to a blond nightclub entertainer whom Kell was dating at the time.

My story of the family really begins with Grandma, wife of John, mother of Patrick, Walter, Annie, John, (who died at age ten) Charles, Mary, George, John B., Elizabeth, and Grace. Said Grandma, who established the Kellys' supremacy in The Falls, a "woman's libber" a hundred years before her time, "If I had it to do over again I wouldn't have *any* children."

First, one brief digression. I was having dinner with Peggy, oldest daughter of Ma and John B., sister of Grace, Lizanne, and Kell.

"Whatever possessed you to write a book about the Kellys?" she asked. "*Every* large family is loaded with oddballs."

I thought for a moment before answering.

"True. But every large family doesn't produce so many champions."

2

"OH, FOR A MILLION MOTHERS LIKE MARY KELLY!"

THE ONLY CHILD OF WALTER COSTELLO, A POVERTY-STRICKEN tenant farmer in Ireland, Mary Anne emigrated to the United States just as the Civil War was drawing to a close. The girl, thirteen years old at the time, went to live with her paternal grandmother and a spinster aunt in Rutland, Vermont. In Ireland she had had to work, in America she was permitted to go to school.

"The one I went to in Rutland," she told William A. McGarry, author of "Oh, for a Million Mothers Like Mary Kelly!" in the September, 1925, issue of *American Magazine,* "was a mile from our house. There was a janitor; but I think he must have been a hibernating animal, for many a winter morning, after wading through a mile of snowdrifts, I've gone down to the schoolhouse cellar, gathered shavings and kindling, and started a fire to warm the building."

Her early and later struggles against cold and hunger had little effect on Mary Anne's well-being.

"In all the years of my life," she said, "I've never been sick a single day, except when my children were born. I had neither the time nor the heart to be sick! And that has more to do with it than we're willing to admit."

Reading, as all through her life, was Mary Anne's escape from harsh reality. By the time she was fifteen she was able to quote whole scenes from Shakespeare, something her son George did equally well, and often the pair would compete, one quoting the

Grandfather John H. Kelly was born in this tiny thatched cottage near Westport in County Mayo, Ireland.

UPI PHOTO

opening line of a scene and the other continuing with the rest. When she and her husband moved to Philadelphia she was the talk of Falls ladies, who used to stare in wonderment as she sat on the front porch rocking the cradle with one hand and holding a book with the other.

In 1869, when she was seventeen, Mary Anne met and married tall, black-haired John Henry Kelly, a six-footer two years her senior, whose life she dominated until a heart attack leveled him in 1917. The Kellys' first child, Patrick H., was born in Rutland in 1872. P.H. was his mother's acknowledged favorite to her dying day. Yet she didn't hesitate to banish him from the family when she felt he was wrong in his bitter quarrel with Brother Charlie when the latter, whom she didn't particularly care for, was right.

After Patrick's birth the family moved to Irontown in upper New York State, where Walter was born in 1873. John H., who worked on a railroad navvy gang, lost his job; he, his wife, and their two small children moved back to Rutland. There Annie was born in 1875. Nobody knows for certain why the Kellys left Vermont for Philadelphia, but about 1876 they rented and later bought a house at 3663 Midvale Avenue, between St. Bridget's R. C. Church and the post office.

"How much better off could you be?" Mary Anne used to say jokingly to granddaughter Marion Kelly Cruice Smith. "God on one side and the government on the other."

With moderate respect for R. C. caveats concerning connubial relations, along came John in 1878 (he's the son who died of croup in 1888), Charles 1880, Mary 1884, George 1887, John B. 1890, Elizabeth 1892, and Grace 1894, these last seven born in The Falls. Grandma had performed her duty to the Almighty, to the Holy Father, and to the pastor of St. Bridget's.

"I don't remember what this gentleman's name was," said Charles, my guide. "But I do know Grandma considered him pompous, stiff-necked and reactionary. In her presence the pastor was loudly condemning the actions of a parishioner who'd done something the priest didn't approve of. My grandmother believed that her pastor was totally unfair but she held her tongue till he finished his tirade. Then she let him have it."

" 'Thanks be to God, Father, there's a Higher Judge than you.' "

Charles laughed.

"I thought of another Grandma Kelly story. It was when they were building Saint Bridget's. My grandmother was sitting on the front porch, rocking one of the children and reading, I guess. The house, you know, was next to the church. Monsignor Walsh, a very kind, considerate, and gentle cleric, passed by.

" 'It certainly is an imposing edifice, Mrs. Kelly,' he commented.

"My grandmother stopped rocking and reading, shook her head, and looked down at the priest. 'It's a far cry from Bethlehem, Monsignor.' "

Nobody starved in the Kelly household, but there wasn't much for clothes and nothing for luxuries; so one after the other, as

soon as they reached ages nine, ten, or eleven, the children quit
school to work at Dobson's.

"I had to be cook, baker, laundress, scrubwoman, dressmaker,
milliner, valet, lady's maid, waitress, chambermaid," Mary Anne
related to writer McGarry. "I've been doctor, nurse, preacher, and
teacher. I've been a lawyer, for I laid down the code of justice in
the family: and I was the policeman that kept order, and the jury
that decided the cases, and the judge that handed out the punishment.

"Yes, and I've been the banker that received the money, the
accountant that kept the books—in my head—the cashier, and
the paymaster. I had to know groceries and dry goods, fuel and
light, plastering and papering and carpentering.

"That is what it means to be the wife of a poor man and the
mother of ten children.

"I tried to grow in knowledge. From the time I was a child
I had a hunger for books. I couldn't buy them but I begged and
borrowed them at every turn. All my life, I have kept up my reading . . . I was up at five o'clock in the morning and often it was
midnight before I went to bed. But I never stopped reading and
studying. I've stood by the stove hundreds of times, a baby under
my left arm and a book in my left hand, while I made pancakes
with my right one. And they were good pancakes, too."

Marion Smith smiled broadly when she recalled Grandma. "She
had such a sense of humor for her generation; she was a brilliant
woman. If you looked at her, she was a tired old lady—you were
aware she'd had ten children. But the brain!"

Marion shook her head in wonderment. "Shakespeare! She really
knew her Shakespeare. If, for example, you quoted a King of
England, whoever was King at the time, she could trace back his
family all the way. How they'd happen to be a Hapsburg or of
some other ancestry. As a child I'd be listening to all this and
drinking it in.

"Uncle George would be in New York and Uncle Walter
traveling around the world, but when they came home there

*The Kelly Clan. Standing, left to right: Sons Charles, George,
John B. and P.H. Seated, left to right: Father John H. and
Son Walter C.*

wasn't a thing she couldn't discuss with them whether it was
politics, religion, or art."

Marion and I were having lunch in her cheerful Bryn Mawr
apartment. She paused to refill our coffee cups, then went on to
speak of Walter Kelly's affection for his mother.

"He *adored* Grandma. Uncle Walter was a sort of dream uncle.
You see, I'm older than the rest of my sisters and I remember
things my sisters don't. He'd arrive on short trips to visit Grandma,

his mother. I can always see Uncle Walter getting out of the taxi and bustling in. He never was slow; he hurried. He always had a big cigar and a diamond ring and he was always smiling, like the world was his oyster.

"But after two days at home he'd be itchy. He'd be sitting with Grandma; they'd have breakfast and they'd discuss the family and where he'd been, the excitement he'd had and the important people he'd met. And then Grandma would look at him with those shrewd eyes and say, 'You're getting restless, aren't you, Walter? I *know* it; I don't expect it to be otherwise. I like having you to hear all the news. But this isn't your world.'

"Three days, like on the third day, he'd be packed and ready to go, New York or even Atlantic City. And then he was gone; maybe we'd see him at the Shore. Grandma and I would go to Atlantic City and stay at Haddon Hall while Walter would be at the old Dunlap on the Boardwalk."

Marion recalled that even after her Uncle Jack had left his mother and set up his own household he often came for lunch. "That was partly because he loved Grandma, partly because he was crazy about the cooking. He used to attribute his sculling success to two-inch steaks, a salad bowl, and cup custard. I can still see Uncle Jack coming to the table. He'd say, 'That's how I won the Olympics!' Grandma enjoyed this."

Before we take leave of Grandma I should mention the manner in which she defied the Dobsons, a courageous action in those days when the Dobsons ruled The Falls, and put bread into the mouths of the Kellys and other poor Irish men, women, and children. Before that, I should explain who the Dobsons were and even before *that* describe The Falls, its past, its present, and its citizenry, both past and present.

The Falls, it should be stated, and not merely in passing, played a most important part in the lives of the Kellys, from the time Grandma and her husband arrived there about 1885 or so, through the defeats and triumphs of Walter, George, John, Kell, the Other George, and Grace. It was at The Falls that they fought their battles, physical, moral, social, economic, marital, and ecclesiastic.

3

"YOU COULDN'T GET AWAY FROM THE GODDAMNED ENGLISH!"

IN ABOUT 1680 GARRETT GARRETTSON, A SWEDE, BUILT HIS home on the banks of the Schuylkill River, some two years before William Penn's ship, the *Welcome,* docked on the Delaware a score or so nautical miles south. No traces of Garrettson's cabin exist, but amateur East Falls historians say the site is just below the Falls of Schuylkill Bridge. Originally Garrett's settlement was called St. David's, then Falls of Schuylkill and finally East Falls, the name of a Reading Railroad whistle-stop.

The village grew slowly until it reached its current population of approximately twenty-eight thousand. It has been a part of the City of Philadelphia since 1811. Houses in The Falls, not including the projects, are 70 percent owner occupied; a large number of residents are blue-collar workers.

Coming up from center-city or driving south from Conshohocken, motorists who use the Schuylkill Expressway usually have plenty of time to gaze at what strongly resembles a deserted English town. All along the river are abandoned three- and four-story stone buildings, roofs with gaping holes, weeds growing from cracked walls, and windows blank except for scattered glass shards. These ruins are all that remain of the Dobson Mills, closed in 1927, but which during the Civil War and for several generations that followed, employed as many as six thousand men, women, and children, most of whom were Irish immigrants or their progeny.

As in Pennsylvania's hard-coal regions before the influx of Eastern Europeans, the English-born ran the show and ran it cruelly. Irish made up The Falls' work force. They were employed by English mill owners, to whom they paid high rents for the tiny, dilapidated row houses they lived in, were supervised by English foremen, and bought food and clothing from English shopkeepers.

As Jack Kelly commented more than once, "You couldn't get away from the goddamned English!"

The Dobson brothers, John and James, who owned The Falls' and other Philadelphia carpet and woolen mills, were typical. Both were born in Yorkshire—John, in 1827, and his brother in 1836. Both attended excellent English public schools, and after learning the textile industry in Yorkshire, both emigrated to the United States in 1848.

For two or three years the Dobsons were employed by others, but in 1851 they built the first of many mills.

By the time the Civil War ended they were wealthy men; in the 1870s their companies grossed more than twenty million dollars annually. James, the younger, built a mansion on his twenty-eight-acre estate at Henry and Abbottsford avenues, where in great luxury he raised five children, all girls. Ironically, the Dobson home, a Falls showplace, was razed in 1927 to make way for the Abbottsford Homes where seven hundred families, most of them black, now live. The Dobsons never knowingly employed a Negro.

According to the *Encyclopedia of Pennsylvania Biography,* "The record of John Dobson . . . is the narrative of the life of a stout-hearted man, who through honorable endeavor met adversity and prosperity with that unshaken equanimity and steadfast adherence to high ideals which indicate true greatness of soul."

No less fulsome was praise for the younger Dobson, "an outstanding figure who not only amassed a splendid fortune but in doing so has done what is of far greater moment both to himself and his descendants, he has built up an unblemished and unassailable business reputation."

Repeat these eulogies to a Falls Irishman and the comment you're likely to get will be both succinct and expressive—"Bullshit!" If there's any further comment, it goes like this, "The Dobsons? Why, those bastards got rich squeezing the guts of the Irish and selling shoddy blankets to the Union army."

I spoke to a couple of my old friends, Dan McCormick, a retired school official, and his close friend, John Cain, an accountant.

"My mother," said Dan bitterly, "used to tell me stories about what it was like to live in The Falls when she was a girl. She went to work at Dobson's when she was eleven years old and had to quit school in fifth grade. She worked from six-thirty in the morning until six at night for two fifty a week."

Grandma Kelly's sons and daughters, from Patrick through John B. (including George, who never admitted it) to Elizabeth and Grace, worked for Dobson's. By the time the last children were of employable age, nine, their brothers were earning enough money to keep these sisters in school.

"Even though most of the Kellys had to go into the mill when they were very young," said John Cain, "they read. I think that's what set them apart; they were different."

Dan McCormick is a fifth-generation citizen of The Falls. "I was born in the same house my mother was born in and the same house *her* mother was born in. It was right opposite McIlvaine's, the undertaker."

Dan smiled. "You don't get into heaven, you know, unless Charlie McIlvaine passes you through. He buries every Irish Catholic in The Falls."

Dan spoke of The Falls' isolation from the rest of Philadelphia. "The fact that we're so detached from the city is interesting and important, too, I think. It was, and I suppose still is, like an English town basically, with scores of lovely little streets that nobody seems to know about except those who live on them. And so many other places that are different.

"You can believe it or not, but until this particular generation dies out you'll find old residents of the Thirty-eighth Ward, which is The Falls, who haven't been to downtown Philadelphia more than a dozen times in their whole lives."

Social life for young Falls ladies a half-century ago centered around the dancing school run by Anna Kelly, P.H.'s daughter and not to be confused with Annie Kelly, P.H.'s sister. One graduate of the Kelly School of Terpsichore is Miss Frances Peters, who has been my friend these past thirty years and a friend of the Kellys much longer than that.

Frances, a librarian, lives on Midvale Avenue, in The Falls house where she was born and where her recently deceased mother was born ninety-seven years ago. The home is directly opposite Grandma Kelly's old place.

"It was quite the thing," said Frances, "for Falls children to attend dancing classes at the P. H. Kellys', and *all* The Falls children went. I remember that the Kelly house was one of *the* great Falls houses. My mother and I used to take Sunday morning walks and we'd pass the home; it was quite spectacular. They had a professional gardener who kept everything in wonderful order. Where the place once stood is the site of the Mifflin School.

"To go to the dancing class, we'd use the entrance to the house on the first level, then go to the lower level, which would be considered a basement, in our terms. It had been fitted up as a recreation room with hardwood floors. I can see it now; this huge room with benches all over. Anna Kelly was in charge. The more unmannerly of us would call her 'Ann.' However, the rest of us were taught to say 'Miss Anna.'

"Of course, there was Miss Babs, Miss Anna's sister, who played the piano, and their sister, Miss Mildred, who assisted in the lessons.

"The Kellys charged a half-dollar for each lesson, which took one hour and was given Saturday afternoon. I used to carry my money, a fifty-cent piece or two quarters in a little pocketbook, a faded blue one, which I still have. They taught us 'fancy' dancing.

"And Miss Anna—I marvel at her patience. We did Hungarian

and all sorts of other folk dances. Then once a year they would put on a grand show, and this was what we'd be working up to every week."

These annual performances, attended only by parents and other relatives, were held at a long-vanished landmark, Palestine Hall, or The Falls' Young Men's Literary Institute.

"One year," Frances went on, "I must have been nine or ten. In the big annual performance Miss Anna starred my girlfriend, Martha Kendall, and me. We were in a presentation called 'Two Little Girls in Blue' and were dressed exactly alike, in blue gowns and blue paper hats. But when we got on stage I forgot everything and didn't know what to do.

"Miss Anna kept shouting from backstage, 'One, two, three jump! Frances, *jump!*' But I stood on stage like a stick: I couldn't budge. Miss Anna was absolutely furious."

Not long afterward the Misses Kelly gave up their dancing school, although Frances does not hold herself at fault.

The Kellys—P.H., Charles V., Sr., Anna Kelly Cruice—were The Falls' most popular hosts during Frances' growing-up days. Her preference, however, was for the C. V. Kellys. Theirs was the only Falls home where sandwiches were served to children, one on each child's plate.

Dancing school, children's parties, construction of the P. H. Kelly showplace, other signs of family affluence and the rise to fame of Walter, George, and John, and, of course, Princess Grace occurred long after the poverty-stricken John H. Kellys were struggling to get money for food, clothing, and shelter. Yet it was then that Grandma Kelly took her stand and, while other Falls Irish trembled in fear of the Dobsons, thumbed her nose at the rich English brothers.

John Cain, my accountant friend, tells the story.

"You have to remember that the Dobsons were kings of The Falls, actually harsh despots. Even if you hated them, you did what they said, never crossed them, and followed their orders to a tee. It was that or else . . . Whenever a Dobson girl was married— James had five daughters, I think—Mary, their mother, grandiloquently gave a penny or two to Falls Irish kids for which they were ordered to line the path and cheer the bridal party as it went into the church."

John grinned.

"The church was Saint James the Lesser, Anglican, naturally, and hardly popular among Falls Irish. The particular wedding I'm talking about was a Whitney of the New York Whitneys. I don't know how she was related to the Dobsons nor why they gave her the wedding, nor why she was married in The Falls. But she was.

"So along comes the elegant Mrs. James Dobson, tossing pennies to the kids and ordering them to line up. Among those who got their orders were at least four of Grandma Kelly's brood, probably Grace and Liz, Jack and maybe George, too—these were the youngest. The Whitney wedding was around the turn of the century and by then Pat, Charlie, and Walter would have been too old.

"Now I don't know if the Kellys were already lined up in front of Saint James the Lesser, or on their way there with other Falls youngsters; whether Grandma saw pennies being tossed to them, or if she stopped the kids in their tracks."

With a smile Dan McCormick picked up the story. "No matter what, this was the first time the Kellys asserted themselves, and it's remembered by Irish families here to this day.

"According to the most popular version, the children *were* lined up. Grandma heard what was going on, ran down the street to the church, yanked her kids out, some by the ears and some by the arms, and within earshot of the bridal party, shouted, "To hell with your pennies! No Kelly's going to stand up in front of a Protestant church and cheer the Dobsons, now or *ever!*"

4

"TO BE A MILLIONAIRE
WAS SOMETHING!"

PATRICK H., GRANDMA KELLY'S OLDEST, WAS THE FAMILY'S FIRST
success and almost its only financial failure. He was named in
honor of his father's brother, a schoolteacher in rural County
Donegal, a revolutionary and the editor of a small weekly newspaper. P. H., as did most of his brothers and sisters, quit school at
about age nine, and went to work for the Dobsons. This would
have been about 1881, shortly after the John H. Kellys moved
from Vermont to The Falls.

P.H. was at the Dobsons' for only a few years, but before he
left to learn the building trade, he was placed in charge of one
section of the mill's color charts and corresponding dies. His
daughter Marie, "Babs," recalled being told about the time that
P.H. got pneumonia. His foreman came to the Kelly home in a
horse and carriage, took the boy out of his sickbed, wrapped him
in a blanket, and drove him to Dobson's. Apparently, he was the
only person able to straighten out a confused color problem that
had closed an entire section of the mill. He was rewrapped and
driven back home. Babs doesn't know what Grandma Kelly said
nor whether P.H. was docked because he hadn't worked a full
day.

While learning the building trade, P.H. went to night school at
Peirce Business College, where he won first prize for penmanship
and mental arithmetic. Then, with funds borrowed from Brother
Charles, he went into the contracting business for himself; Charles

came with him, not as a partner but as outside foreman. This was five years before the turn of the century. Walter had already left home to work in shipyards near Norfolk, Virginia; George, his apprenticeship at the mill ended, was a draftsman for a bridge-builder; John J. was dead; Annie, Mary, and John B. were at Dobson's, and the two youngest were at school.

With Charlie handling the labor crew, success came quickly for P.H. and by 1897, even though he'd been giving a good portion of his earnings to his parents, he had enough left over to get married and set up his own Falls home, near Midvale Avenue above Ridge. His bride was a redheaded Falls girl named Catherine, "Kitty" Loughlin.

Within thirteen years of their marriage at the old St. Bridget's —Patrick built the new one—the P. H. Kellys had nine children.

According to nephew Charles (my Charles), "The P. H. Kellys never were on time for anything. Notwithstanding, my Uncle Pat was the first East Falls Irishman who made lots of money. The Dobsons, of course, were rich—they were Protestants and it could be expected—but no one thought anybody Irish could make it. P. H. broke the pattern.

"He said one day, and I heard him, 'I'm a millionaire.' And for an Irishman to be a millionaire in those days was something!"

In any case P.H. and Kitty didn't hang on to their million, or perhaps millions, much after World War One ended. With Charles, Sr.'s resignation from the firm, and diminishing business, the P. H. Kelly Company, Incorporated, at 1713 Sansom Street, Philadelphia, was forced into receivership in September 1923.

But during the intervening years, between marriage and acquisition of great wealth and the building of the Falls mansion, the P. H. Kellys had a comparatively happy life and a far more luxurious one than any other member of the family. This was some time before George (the Other George) went off the deep end.

Two of Patrick Kelly's daughters, Mildred and Babs, were talking to me in their home, a large stone house, surrounded by a well-kept lawn and with a two-car garage.

Mildred, who retired not long ago as a court stenographer, showed me a picture of the Midvale Avenue mansion. The photograph, in fading sepia, must have been taken in warm weather; P.H., Kitty, and eight of their children are dressed in summer attire of the day—circa 1910—posing on the lawn off from the tunnel that led from garage to house.

"That's where we grew up," Mildred said, "and where we lived happily for twenty years. But 1929 was a bad year for us. We'd be driving along the parkway and pass the Library there. My father would stop, look at it, and say, 'That's my mausoleum.' We sold the house and got one in Highland Park, out in the Sixty-ninth Street section, which isn't even Philadelphia, let alone The Falls. We all went to work."

Mildred smiled.

"But we didn't stay away very long, only until 1931. We *had* to come back to The Falls. My father then bought a house at twenty-eight oh three Queen Lane, which is just about the very end of The Falls, and we were living there when father died of a heart attack on January twentieth, 1937. My mother survived him less than five months. They were both sixty-five."

Babs spoke of her father's love for being in the public eye. "He adored making speeches and I think he was better in front of an audience than my Uncle Walter."

Our conversation was interrupted for a few moments by the appearance of a handsome young man who, I thought, resembled his cousin Kell.

Mildred introduced us. "This is Patrick H. Hayden, my sister's youngest of five. P.H. is my father's namesake. He's a fine chess player; won the city championship, once, didn't you, Pat?"

P.H. grinned. "Oh, that was a long time ago—1960."

"Show Mr. Lewis the picture," his Aunt Babs said, and P.H. reached over to a table and removed a framed clipping, which he handed to me. It was from the *Sunday Inquirer* and the caption read: "Here is Chess Champion, Patrick H. Hayden, of School House Lane, concentrating on playing at the Mann Recreational Center where he won the Pee Wee Tournament. Patrick, represent-

*Still another champion: Chess Champion Patrick H. Hayden,
grandson and namesake of Patrick H. Kelly, at the age of nine.*
THE PHILADELPHIA INQUIRER

ing the Water Tower Center, defeated Bahdan Makro, the title-
holder."

Mildred and Babs seem to have only fond recollections of their
father's brothers. Both women, as well as their surviving siblings,
were invited to Grace's wedding at Monaco; accepted the invitation and, in Mildred's words; "had a ball."

They did recall, however, some family criticism when their
father, after donating twenty-five hundred dollars to St. Bridget's
Building Fund, complained that other Kelly kin had not contributed in accordance with their financial ability. Those others
complained that P.H. himself got the contract to build the new
church.

5

"POOR GEORGE!
HE WAS SUCH
A BEAUTIFUL MAN"

ON A HOT JULY NIGHT IN 1950 A COATLESS DERELICT STAGGERED
into the Palace Hotel, a dirty, crumbling flophouse at 824 Race
Street in Philadelphia's Skid Row. He plunked down fifty cents
for lodging, climbed to the third floor, threw himself on a cot
in a tiny cubicle and went to sleep. He never woke up. This was
how George P. Kelly, the "Other George," spent his last night
on earth.

Next morning his body was removed to the morgue. A yellowed
clipping preserved in foil, found in the dead man's pocket, gave
police sufficient information to call John B. Kelly and tell him
that his nephew, George P. Kelly, was deceased. Uncle Jack made
formal identification; Charlie McIlvaine handled funeral arrangements; and after brief, private services at St. Bridget's the Other
George was buried in the family plot at Westminster Cemetery.

Only seventeen years before, George had won the national
pocket billiards crown by defeating the great Willie Mosconi
125-119 in Minneapolis after a spectacular run of 95. Willie, later
to gain the world's championship by defeating Ralph Greenleaf
and Frank Taberski, "the Peaceful Pole," recalled the Minneapolis
tournament. Mosconi abandoned billiards in favor of golf, and
shoots in the low seventies. We were talking in the Bala Club,
where he is a member.

"Since I was six years old I'd been playing pocket billiards,"
Mosconi reminisced. (I learned quickly that you *never* say you

"shoot pool" or call a poolroom anything but a billiard parlor or academy.) "I used to play in my South Philadelphia neighborhoods but I moved uptown to the Fox Billiard Academy near Sixteenth and Market streets.

"This is one of the places George Kelly frequented and where the top competitors came. At the time the Billiard Congress of America was scouting for young players and new faces. And that was the first year I came in contact with George Kelly. This would have been 1933.

"But in 1931 George had gotten into the finals and finished second to Ralph Greenleaf. The following year I don't know how George did but evidently not too well because, in 1933, he had to qualify for the championship event, the same as I had to do and I was just beginning tournament play."

Willie paused to order coffee for me, for himself, and for three members of his foursome who sat with us. A short, sunburned, rugged man in his midsixties, Mosconi glanced at the chit before signing it, then continued.

"George and I rode out from Philadelphia by bus. We'd both won the Sectional and I'll tell you how that went. Each city had what they called a Divisional and if you were one, two, or three in the Divisionals, you qualified for the Sectionals with all the Divisional winners. *Then* if you placed first, second, or third you went out to Minneapolis for the National Championship. If you wound up one, two, three there, you got into the World's Championship.

"Anyway, George and I went out to Chicago in a Greyhound and somehow or other I lost my cue stick on that bus. It might have slipped down a seat or somewhere but anyway neither George nor I could find the darn thing. Well, George knew a cuemaker in Chicago by the name of Rambeau—he was the most famous craftsman of his time. George took me there; he made me a cue right on the spot that day. The day we went to Minneapolis.

"That was the start of big-time competition; I was just nineteen and George was kind of a steadying influence on me and much more experienced than I. I tied with a Syrian whose name, I think,

*And still another champion: George P. Kelly—"The Other
George"—winner of the national billiards crown, 1933.*

was Charles Scabach or something. I beat him, but in the playoff
George beat both of us and won the National Championship."

Apparently George, after winning in Minneapolis, got loaded
and was in no shape to play in the World Championship the following week in Chicago, where he finished near the bottom of
the list.

"George always did drink," Willie went on. "After that tournament in Minneapolis I didn't see him very much. I traveled for
the Brunswick Company and I'd run into George every once in a
while when I came back to Philadelphia. And whenever we would
play matches at Allinger's [Philadelphia's most famous billiard
parlor until it went out of business about ten years ago], George
would stop in and say hello.

"I played George again in 1937, at a place on Thirteenth Street;
there's a dentist's office there now. Anyway, in this match with
George I beat him twelve games in a row. There weren't many
people came in to see us play and we had to depend on gate
receipts for our money. Times were tough for me.

"But with George—I don't know, he seemed to go the other way. My family never had much and I had to get out and work. Even in those days George's parents had money, they still had some even in the Thirties. George drove around in a beautiful automobile. He'd always lived well. I think that the reason he went the way he did was because his father gave him everything he wanted."

The waiter refilled our coffee cups. Willie's companions looked at him impatiently and regarded me with something akin to hate, but the former World's Champion grinned and calmly went on.

"The old man would give him everything he wanted. We'd call him 'spoiled.' George could have any kind of car he asked for to race through them. He had easy access to bootleggers and that started him drinking.

"When we played matches or tournaments in those days they'd put a curtain across the room and block off the back part of it; they were trying to get admission, you know. Well, that time I was telling you about at Ramsey's on Thirteenth Street, after the twelfth game, we all went up to the coffee counter. Suddenly, we wondered, Where's George? We hadn't seen him.

"The next thing you know we see smoke coming up from the back end of the room behind the curtain. What do you think George had done? He'd gone around the room and collected all the paper and stuff he could find, put them underneath that pool table and lit a match to it. He was just that temperament; hotheaded. He *never* got mad at any other person, but he did get mad at himself for playing so badly and was going to burn that table up because he couldn't win on it. Of course, he'd been drinking."

Willie shook his head.

"I always liked George; everybody did. But he'd never been trained to do anything except maybe billiards and if you drink you can't play. Finally, George accepted jobs in billiard rooms and even got to manage one down at Eleventh and Market, where the Earle Theatre used to be. But he never could hang on to the jobs very long; first thing you know, he'd be drinking heavily.

"After 1933, he really went down. He knew the game, of course, but some of the young players who'd come up during that era were playing a lot more and got the chance to learn more from the great players like Greenleaf and Ponzi. Whereas George was at a standstill.

"It took me from 1933 to 1941 to win the World's Championship. Maybe George could have made it; he was good. I worked for Brunswick for twenty-eight years; I don't know how long George worked for them, but they paid big money. I got six hundred a month and all expenses when George beat me back in 1933. He could have done the same."

We talked a bit more; then Willie shook hands, said so long, and with his restive companions shouldered his clubs and took off. Just as he walked out of the room Mosconi turned to me. "See Phil Longo; he must have known George well. Phil's got a billiard parlor near Fifth and South. He's the oldest operator in the city. He knew them all, Greenleaf, Ponzi, Rudolph—Greenleaf in particular; he was a great drinking companion of George."

Greenleaf, the World's Pocket Billiard Champion fourteen times until Willie Mosconi wrested the title from him on the fifteenth try, died in Hahnemann Hospital, Philadelphia, March 16, 1950. The cause of his death was listed as an internal hemorrhage, but those who knew Ralph say he died of acute alcoholism. Ralph and his wife, "China Doll," the latter a retired vaudevillian, were two of the Other George's best friends. The Doll lives alone in a West Philadelphia row house. Phil Longo, who told me Mrs. Greenleaf had been one of the prettiest girls he'd ever met, set up the date for me.

No longer a girl, Mrs. Greenleaf, a tiny woman, is in her eighties. The Doll has retained some of her youthful good looks and, I'd hazard to guess, most of her charm. We sat drinking tea out of huge cups in Mrs. Greenleaf's battered kitchen while her obese tomcat, Algernon, looked on.

"I met George Kelly at Allinger's Billiard Parlor in 1925, I think it was. He was in his early or midtwenties, I'd say, an absolutely handsome young man."

The Doll's features—cheeks, chin, and mouth—were blurred by wrinkles, her coloring a kind of off-white, and only from the almost undetectable slant of her jet black eyes, could I tell she had some Oriental blood.

"I had to work, so I tried out and got a job with B. F. Keith. I really hadn't much of a voice, actually a peculiar one, but I had one big advantage. I was the only Chinese vaudeville singer in the whole world."

She smiled.

"Well, they billed me as 'The Chinese Nightingale,' but Phil Longo and George Kelly always called me 'China Doll.' I had no operatic training; I sang anyway—if you could call what I did singing—and if I couldn't reach the high notes, I talked them. I was a single on B. F. Keith from 1917 to 1927."

I asked the Doll if she'd ever met Walter on the circuit.

Her eyes lit up. "The Virginia Judge? Yes, indeed! Many times, all through Mr. Delmar's Southern territory. I remember playing with Walter in Norfolk. He was a great entertainer, but he never stayed around to chitchat. As soon as he did his act he disappeared. He was off to be with friends. He had friends in every city he ever played.

"And while I didn't know George, the famous playwright, I'd heard of him. The George Kelly that Ralph and I knew was his nephew. A remarkable family, the Kellys. Makes me believe in reincarnation."

I listened as the Doll went on.

"In 1924 I was playing at Keith's Theatre in Philadelphia and met Ralph then.

"Ralph, he was a champion, the World's Champion, and we ran off to Elkton, Maryland, to be married. That was the marriage mill in those days. We were having some kind of belated wedding supper at Ferraro's Restaurant after my act, and George Kelly walked in. He was a very sweet man and Ralph was his idol. Ralph always had a feeling for young players.

"The next day they were having a tournament at Allinger's and I went along with Ralph. He wasn't playing in this one and was there kind of acting as the Kelly kid's backer. The place was jam-packed and George got a bit nervous when he saw so many people watching. I remember George was wearing a green velvet jacket, sort of a tuxedo, and everybody was laughing at him. This was George's first big-time match.

"Well, before they got started, Ralph put an arm around George's shoulders and said, 'Kid, just forget everyone. Play your game; ignore the crowd and pretend you're playing somebody for two dollars.' Which is exactly what George did, and he won."

The Doll spoke of another tournament that followed shortly afterward. This time the world's great had entered, Rudolph, Taberski, Greenleaf, and a few others. George competed and to everyone's surprise came in second, beating Rudolph, who merely placed. As a result of this, George Kelly was hired by Brunswick.

"George and Ralph traveled all over the country together, playing everywhere, and Brunswick paid their expenses. Kelly was a mild soul but when he got drinking sometimes, when he talked about his family, he grew violent. He was a two-fisted drinker and when he was loaded, he'd sing. He had a wonderful baritone voice and his favorite song was 'Mandalay.' The way he sang it would bring chills up and down your spine. But he sang it only when he was drunk. Ralph and George and I had a lot of good times together."

The Doll sighed.

"Poor George! He was such a beautiful man and he had such wonderful chances. He went from bad to worse, drinking, drinking. He could have been anything; he had such talent. Ralph wasn't going with George anymore. But we went up to Allinger's, where there was some kind of unimportant tournament to watch. George was there; he looked pretty seedy—he didn't even place. He'd been drinking but he said hello to Ralph and me. That was in 1938. It was the last time I ever saw George Kelly."

George married a Philadelphia girl, not from The Falls but Germantown, shortly after he came in third in his first really important match, held at Allinger's, December 4, 1931. The family was on hand to cheer him. On one side sat Uncles John B. and Charles V., and on the other, his father, P.H.

Devotees and historians of the game will be familiar with George's competitors. They, and their interim scores, appear at the top of a full-column story in the *Evening Bulletin,* December 5, 1931:

THE STANDINGS

	W.	L.	HIGH RUN.	BEST GAME.
Erwin Rudolph	3	0	83	ᵥ 14
Ralph Greenleaf	2	0	85	2
George Kelly	3	1	38	11
Frank Taberski	2	1	53	8
Andrew Ponzi	2	1	70	9
Bennie Allen	2	2	51	8
Onofrio Lauri	1	2	85	10
Marcel Camp	1	2	36	13
Johnny Layton	1	2	29	15
Al Miller	1	2	29	16
Spencer Livsey	1	3	50	12
Robert Lindblom	0	2	15	—

The Other George's marriage was not a happy one. After living with him a dozen years more or less, his wife and their two children moved to California. George's drinking companions of that era, and a surprisingly large number are still alive, recall Mrs. George Kelly's frequent attendance at the tournaments, not to see her husband play but rather to see if she could get money for her own support and that of their young sons. George's old pals also recall that Mrs. Kelly rarely collected.

Almost everyone, particularly members of the family, preface their comments on this son of P.H. Kelly with "Poor George." Before the conversation ends, invariably they tell me how beautifully he sang "Mandalay." His first cousin, Miss Grace Frommeyer, daughter of Grandma Kelly's oldest girl, Annie, was no exception.

"Poor George!" this handsome Kelly spinster said, "he got too much, too soon. His father spoiled him; gave him what he wanted and would take him around at night to show him off at friends' houses where they had billiard tables or in poolrooms. I know Grandma Kelly didn't like that at all. George's success must have gone to his head but our family was proud of his achievements; my Uncle Pat certainly was. But George's marriage was unsuccessful.

"Once I went out to visit them; they had a house in Ardmore. George wasn't around; his wife, who was a very nice person, asked me please not to speak about George or ask where he was in front of the children. Of course I didn't. Then, when George got out of the army after World War Two, he didn't return to his wife and sons. So she and the boys moved out to the West Coast. I doubt if they ever saw him although one of the sons came to his father's funeral."

By prowling around what few are left of Philadelphia's once numerous billiard rooms—Allinger's, the Fox, the Hudson with its one hundred and twenty-five tables have long since vanished from this one-time capitol of the billiard world—I was able to round up a baker's dozen of the Other George's friends in bygone days. Of billiard parlors in the great tradition, only Longo's at 5th and South streets remains.

Mr. Longo is a gentleman of the old school. He's short, slightly built, never raises his voice, and certainly is in his midseventies. But he maintains the kind of order in his Academy as, I would guess, Mr. Chips did in his classroom. Mr. Longo knows all of the players, most of whom are young, and calls them by their Christian or their nicknames, and they, in turn, address him as "Mr. Longo," although an occasional older person will call him "Phil."

There's an air of peace about this establishment that has been in the same location for half a century with Phil and his pretty wife, who's from Shenandoah, Pennsylvania, owners and operators. When you enter, all you hear is the click of the ivories, and subdued voices, and, as you stand by the Longos' front desk, all you see in the dim cavern to the rear is a series of shaded lights and tobacco smoke rising over the Academy's sixteen pocket billiard tables.

Mr. Longo, as did the other twelve gentlemen, expressed much the same opinion of P. H. Kelly's son, that George was a gentleman, that he played the game superbly, that he never got angry with anyone except himself, and that when drinking, which was most of the time, he sang "Mandalay."

I was fortunate, indeed, to receive a visit at my house from Mr. Walter Williams, one of those thirteen. Mr. Williams, a well-preserved and well-tanned gentleman of uncertain age, is a horse player. Except for occasional exhibitions in private homes, where he does trick shots, he has given up the game that brought him together with the Other George, an association that lasted four decades.

Mr. Williams speaks in the slightly stilted vernacular of the late Damon Runyon and easily could have stepped from the cast of *Guys and Dolls.*

"I resided," said he, "at two oh oh seven East York Street, in the city of Philadelphia. I became interested in billiards when I was around fourteen years of age at the Seaman's Institute, which was then located at Front and Queen Street. I participated daily in this neighborhood club.

"When I met Mr. George Kelly, I played very well; in fact, Mr. Kelly played only a little better than I did. We became very dear friends. The gentleman and I would be hustling together when we weren't visiting a neighborhood bar consuming a beer or whiskey. The gentleman couldn't play unless he was partially intoxicated.

"I don't care to make this kind of a statement in regards to the gentleman, but the gentleman, to I, was nothing but a habitual sot. This all came about when the gentleman was married. His wife didn't care about him participating in this pocket pool [my gentleman caller *said* it] and naturally she had him arrested several times for nonsupport, and he was without sufficient funds. He couldn't pay her any support, and that's why the gentleman used to go out on the road."

Did Mr. Williams see Mr. Kelly frequently during that long association?

I put that question to my guest, who nodded. "We were just like husband and wife; we couldn't wait until we saw each other the next day." Mr. Williams sighed. "Well, one night Mr. Kelly didn't have any money, which for that gentleman was not an unusual situation. So I gave Mr. Kelly three dollars of which sum he could pay his entrance fee where he was residing at the time. I said, 'George, when you get up in the morning, you'll have money for your breakfast.'

"Anyhow, I went to the billiard room the following day to see if Mr. Kelly was available. He was not available and the gentleman did not show up. I didn't think anything about it, but when Mr. Kelly did not show up the second day I thought something occurred, you know, because the neighborhood where Mr. Kelly resided in was nothing but a lot of derelicts and a lot of bums and what have you, I ask?"

The question was rhetorical.

"Shoplifters and boosters, whatever you care to add yourself to that conversation. The following day I made it my business to go over where he resided. They found him dead. They made funeral arrangements; you couldn't see his body; it was a closed casket.

"I was sorry about that because I would have loved to have viewed his face."

Mr. Williams seems to have found a measure of consolation elsewhere.

"I will say this," the gentleman said in conclusion, and his comment could have been a non sequitur. "As far as myself is concerned I do possess a lot of willpower and, in fact, I buy two cases of beer a week and a carton of cigarettes a week. And when I come back from the racetrack where I go every day I stop into the neighborhood taproom where I reside."

6

"LINE MY GRAVE
WITH BRICKS"

CHARLES V. KELLY, JR., AND HIS SISTER, MARY, WERE HAVING
dinner at my home one evening.

"Did I ever tell you the one about my father's theory of the
proper way to lay bricks?" Charles asked, and when my wife and
I shook our heads he went on.

"Of course you know it's backbreaking work, picking up those
bricks; I speak with authority. Bricks are laid in a line with men
on both ends and men in between. Anyway my father, rather
strategically, would put an awfully good bricklayer on each end
of the line. I remember one, Louie something or other."

Mary interjected. "Louie Vasilotti."

Charles nodded and went on. "Louie was very fast and very
sure and my father put him on the one end and a bricklayer,
equally good, on the other end. This meant that all the people in
the middle had to work faster to keep up. And my father would
always be saying, '*Get* that line up: *get* that line up!' That was
because the faster the line went up the more bricks got laid and
the more money the company made.

"Well, after a backbreaking day came near to a close, one of
the bricklayers in the middle stopped and groaned, 'Jesus Christ,
Charlie! Rome wasn't built in a day.' My father replied without
a moment's hesitation, 'I wasn't the foreman on that job.' "

Mary had something to add. "Speaking of bricks, my father's
will was quite specific. His grave had to be lined and faced with

brick. 'That's the only way I can be sure I'll be warm,' he stated in a codicil.''

We adjourned to the patio for coffee.

"My father," Charles said, renewing the conversation, "was afraid of nothing."

Mary interrupted. "Oh yes he was. Funerals, flowers, and false faces."

Her brother grinned. "You're right, but that's a couple of other stories. Let me get on with this one.

"One Sunday morning, a new little priest, wearing his biretta and robes, got up on the pulpit and denounced 'you legions of the devil who refuse to accept the guidance of the Mother Church and set yourselves up as authorities on what should be.' He was denouncing, like the Last Judgment, you know, lambs on the right and goats on the left."

(I should say that whenever Charles and Mary told stories where dialect was appropriate, they used it. And I don't believe the Virginia Judge could have done better.)

"Across from St. Bridget's, which was on Calumet Street, you could sit on the porch steps and see inside the church and, of course, hear what was going on, as you could this particular day. There was a little Scotchman on our stoop, not missing any of the action."

(Here Charles goes into Scotch dialect.)

" 'Hey!' he says. 'What's goin' on in there?'

"And Barney Kelly, who wasn't a member of the family at all, didn't want the Scotchman to know there was friction in the church. My father wasn't taking any nonsense from the priest and shouting back. So Barney says [and the accent is Irish], 'Oh, they're on'y havin' a bit of a debate.'

"So the Scotchman, who'd recognized my father's voice, nods and says, 'I know yon booger'll win.' "

Mary, who'd been patiently waiting for her turn, entered the conversation.

"I said before that my father was afraid of funerals; he wouldn't go to them or wakes and he wouldn't look at a corpse.

And he didn't like flowers and wouldn't have them in the bedroom. He was afraid of masks and he had a fit if he saw anybody in one. He wouldn't let me wear a false face on Halloween."

Charles nodded. "I remember once when my father took Mary and me down to the Benjamin Franklin Hotel for some affair. We were standing in one room and he came to the door. He whispered, 'Come out of there quick!' Apparently there was a peculiar light in that room, which made our faces look green and corpselike; he actually yanked us out, he got absolutely panicky.

"When Jim Kelly, who was his best friend, died, he wouldn't go into his house. Just stood on the porch. Another person he loved was Dan McCormick."

"That's right," Mary added. "He liked Danny very much and everything he did was right, no matter what."

Charles had said previously that his mother and father did not get along, and we talked about that again. I asked our guests if there was any specific reason for this state of affairs.

Charles thought for a moment. "Aunt Margaret [John B.'s widow] often says, 'It's very difficult being married to a Kelly.' "

We wound up the evening with a final story about Charles V. Kelly, Sr.; Charles V. Kelly, Jr., told it.

"One day my mother came into town to meet my father in his office. Since she didn't go there often and never went out on my father's jobs, naturally no one knew who she was. She sat there waiting and some laborers came in. This was in the days when blacks constituted the whole labor force and, in general, were uneducated.

"On the wall in the waiting room was a picture of the whole family. One of the laborers knew the family, while the other apparently did not. The one was pointing out various figures in the photograph to the other.

" 'That's Mistuh P.H.,' "—the accent was Southern black—
" 'that's Mistuh G'eoge, that's Mistuh Waltah, and that's Mistuh Chollie.' At this the other Negro said, 'That's Mistuh Chollie, all right. I never will fo'get that man. God damn!' "

7

HE WAS AFRAID
OF HIS MOTHER'S LEFT

A VERY ELDERLY GENTLEMAN TO WHOM I HAD JUST BEEN introduced picked up the microphone of my tape recorder and, with an air of complete confidence and a cheerful grin, opened our session at the Percy Williams Residence for Retired Actors in Englewood, New Jersey.

"I'm Joe Smith," he said, and waited for the next question.

"And what did you do in the theater, sir?" I continued, having been told by my busy hostess, a former Follies girl, only that the gentleman I was about to interview had known Walter C. Kelly.

Mr. Smith regarded me with patience although he had every reason to think I was being impertinent, or stupid, probably both.

"I'm the Smith of Smith and Dale, the 'Avon Comedy Four,' you know." He smiled.

I nearly dropped the recorder. This was one of the three most famous names in vaudeville. Smith, his partner, Charles Dale, and the Virginia Judge. I'd watched Smith and Dale at least a score of times and laughed loudly and long at each appearance. Besides, scarcely a week before I came to Englewood, I'd seen *The Sunshine Boys*, Hollywood's takeoff on the personal and professional lives of this team, for which Mr. Smith, aged ninety-seven, had been a technical advisor.

After an hour or so of priceless (for an old vaudeville fan

like me) variety-show recollections, we finally reached the subject of my current research. Mr. Smith had forgiven me.

"It must have been about eight or ten years after Charlie and I put our act together that I met Walter C. Kelly. We were on a bill with him at Hammerstein's New York Victoria. This would have been around 1909. I remember talking to him after the show—we'd gone someplace to eat—and asking him where he got his material. He told us it was from some Southern judge. I think he said his name was Crutchfield."

One of the jurists immortalized (if he ever existed) by Kelly was named John Dudley Brown, although Walter on different occasions referred to a certain Judge Crutchfield.

"Well," Mr. Smith continued, "one day Charlie and I played Roanoke and I kept thinking about Walter Kelly's judge. So Charlie and I called on him.

" 'Your Honor,' I said, 'I'm Joe Smith and this is my partner, Charlie Dale. We're good friends of your good friend, Walter C. Kelly. He built his act on you and said you were a very funny man. So we came to see just how funny you are.'

" 'Well,' says the judge hospitably, 'you gentlemen sit down and listen.' So Charlie and I sat down in the courtroom to see what kind of material His Honor was furnishing Walter with.

"We gathered one that day for Walter. A colored couple came into the courtroom and stood in front of Judge Crutchfield. This woman was saying that the man came into her yard and stole a lot of wash that was on the line.

" 'Who is he?' His Honor asks.

" 'I don't know him, Jedge; I never seen him before, Jedge, and I don't know where he come from, Jedge.'

"So the 'jedge' says, 'Well, I don't know where he 'come' from, but I know where he's going. Six months!' "

Smith chuckled.

"After court was over, we took Judge Crutchfield to the theater to catch our act. I said kiddingly, 'Judge, you weren't so funny. We didn't get as much stuff as Walter did.'

"He laughed and said, 'If my clients don't do a good straight,

Walter C. Kelly—"The Virginia Judge."

I can't be funny.' For Walter Kelly the judge performed, and Walter became a great monologist on that material."

Mr. Smith called for coffee; it was served us in fine style. My host continued.

"Just to let you know how big Walter was in the profession I'll tell you about once in Cleveland. Again, we were on the same bill with Walter at the Hippodrome. There was another vaudeville circuit at the time called Klaw-Erlanger. They were bitter rivals of the Keith circuit, which Walter, Charlie, and I were booked in.

"So the big war between the two 'enemies' was on and Walter was Keith's big gun. The critics wrote it up just like it was a battle, something like: 'The manager of Klaw-Erlanger fired the first shot with a dancing act and Keith's retaliated with another strong dancing act, and so on with jugglers, dancers, trick riders. But the final shot was fired by Walter C. Kelly for Keith's and the Virginia Judge mowed Keith's rivals down.' "

He shrugged his shoulders.

"I'm kind of busy and I got to hurry over to New York; I'm doing an hour show for CBS. But I've just got about enough time left to tell you how Walter ended his act."

Mr. Smith rose, looked around the porch where we'd been sitting, and picked up a small metal vase.

" 'Well, George,' Walter would say, and pound his gavel on the table. [Mr. Smith used the vase to demonstrate this action.] 'Get me my fishing line. Court's adjourned.' "

With this, Mr. Smith, who like Walter Kelly was a "money spot" performer, walked offstage.

I was Mrs. McCauley's luncheon guest. George Roland, seated on my left, had been, until arthritis forced his retirement, a performer in circus acts and on the vaudeville stage for fifty-five of his ninety-three years. Mr. Roland juggled cannonballs, three of them, on the back of his neck. "Now," he says, shaking his head sadly, "I can't even *lift* one."

Mr. Roland knew Walter Kelly.

"I wouldn't say I was his *friend*. I'd rather put it I was a kind of low-caste acquaintance of Mr. Kelly's for a long, long while.

"I'm colored, you know," he said by way of explanation. "I was on the bill with the Virginia Judge five or six times. At the Broadway Theater in Camden, New Jersey, and at Young's Million Dollar Pier in Atlantic City. I was on the bill with him again at the Polis Theatre in Wilkes-Barre, Pennsylvania."

I told Mr. Roland I'd seen the Virginia Judge on the stage of this upstate theater.

"You might have seen me there, too. I played the Polis several times. I was on the bill with the Judge in Scranton, and I worked with him lots of other places. First time, I guess, was in 1907. I remember his act very well. I can see him walking onstage, picking up his gavel, and saying, 'Ohdah in de Co'tt room. You niggahs get out of the window and let some air come in.'

"In those days, white and colored didn't mix; didn't associate with each other. Walter Kelly treated me nicely though and saw that others treated me likewise. But I will tell you something that Walter did and it did make people angry. This happened in New York at Hammerstein's. I wasn't on the bill but I saw it. Besides Mr. Kelly, the stars were Avery and Hart, a colored team. They were very famous. Some folks in show business said the Virginia Judge was jealous of them when he was on their bill.

"Avery and Hart's song—I guess you'd call it their 'theme song'—was, 'I Care Not for the Stars that Shine.' It went something like this."

Here Roland sang his own rendition of the Avery and Hart theme song.

"Well, that usually brought down the house. Then when the team came out to take their bows and there was the few seconds of silence you get in between, suddenly everybody in the audience and onstage heard Walter Kelly's voice coming from the wings, 'I Care Not for the *Shines* that Star.' "

The family has much to tell about Walter C. Kelly, nearly all of it in Walter's favor and, I thought, some of it amusing. For my benefit, Mary Daly summoned relatives, including Brother Charles, to a lunch in her Falls home. Among others present were Mary and her three children, Catherine, Bryan, and Moira, as well as cousins Marion Cruice Smith and Elaine Cruice Beyer.

"I must have been twelve or thirteen," Marion said, "and Grandma was dying. Uncle Walter loved her dearly. When I look back and think, if he was only *walking* through the room and Grandma was sitting there in her favorite rocker, something spicy would come out from his lips. He'd shock her maybe, wink, then she'd realize what he'd said, it was so funny.

"Well, at any rate the entire family was there. Monsignor Bonner, the young curate at St. Bridget's which was next door to our house where Grandma was living, was kneeling at her side.

"I said the *entire* family but that wasn't quite true. My Uncle Walter had been notified but hadn't arrived yet. Everybody else was kneeling—the floor was covered with Kellys wall to wall— praying and weeping. Suddenly he came in from New York; he still had his overcoat on when he entered the room. The priest was giving last rites; he heard the door open, looked up, and saw Walter."

The other Kellys were listening intently although they must have heard the story a hundred times.

"All of us realized it was the end for Grandma; many tears were being shed, there was deep sadness, and we could all feel the tension as she lay there so still. Father Bonner raised his head and beckoned to Uncle Walter.

" 'Come here,' Father Bonner told him. Walter walked all around the others, then knelt down to pray.

" 'Come closer, Walter,' Father Bonner said, 'over to the bed.'

"My Uncle Walter shook his head. 'Not on *that* side, Monsignor. I've always been afraid of my mother's left.' "

Marion's audience was appreciative; Sister Elaine took the floor.

"My Uncle Walter always *was* funny at funerals, telling stories. And my mother, his sister, used to get furious at him saying he was a disgrace to the family because at wakes and all, he kept telling one hilarious tale after the other.

"At these Kelly wakes and funerals my mother would be trying to keep a proper face. If the house had a basement, my Uncle Walter would get all the men down there and suddenly you'd hear them all laughing when they were supposed to be walking around very pious. He was a cutup wherever he went.

"But he was a real doll; he made you feel terribly important."

"And don't forget," Marion added, "he never failed to hand each of the four Cruice kids a twenty-dollar gold piece every time he came home. That was *something!*"

Charles, too, was a beneficiary of the Virginia Judge. "He'd say, 'Here, kid,' and hand me a dollar. 'Run down to the corner store and get me a couple of cigars.' I'd get the two cigars for him with the change and he'd say, 'Keep the change.' This was in 1920 and the dollar was worth five then.

"I'd go to my father and say, 'Look what Uncle Walter gave me.' And my father would say, 'What did he give you that for?' And I'd tell him. Then he'd say, 'You take that money right back to him. You don't take money from your Uncle Walter for

going down to the store to get him cigars. You do that as a *duty*.'
So I'd have to go back and return the money.

"My Uncle Walter was a big spender and when I'd do what
my father ordered, he'd say, 'Keep it!' and I guess maybe I did.
My Uncle Walter always was the maverick of the family. The
other brothers and sisters would abide by the decisions made by
their mother and father but he would fight against it. He was the
individual who would not conform."

Elaine also spoke of the Judge's generosity.

"He was always giving money away. That was his downfall,
I think. He supported every old crony he ever knew in his lifetime; hadn't any idea of how to say no. He was so open; everybody's friend."

After dessert at Mary Daly's we sat around the table, talking.

"My Uncle Walter," Charles said, "was different from his
brothers. He was the hail-fellow-well-met type. Up with the big-
wigs; always loving to have his picture taken with the rulers and
the shakers of the country. That kind of thing.

"I wouldn't want to make the claim that this had anything
to do with the contrast between my Uncle Walter's disposition
and my father's but . . ."

Charles paused to laugh.

"My Aunt Annie told me—she's Grandma's oldest daughter,
Grace Frommeyer's mother—and I won't vouch for its accuracy,
that when *her* mother was carrying my father, Grandma and
Grandpa Kelly were feuding and hadn't talked to each other for
weeks. Apparently, when Grandma was carrying Walter, my Aunt
Annie's predecessor, Grandma and Grandpa were on speaking
terms."

Marion recalled one of the internationally famous people whom
the Judge was able to call a friend.

"My Uncle Walter used to travel on the Lipton yacht with
Sir Thomas; they were very close. And he was a good friend of
Jackie Coogan and Louis Armstrong."

I mentioned the Judge's feeling toward blacks.

Elaine shook her head. "Not all of them. There were some he

didn't like. He used to call that kind 'The Flip and the Forward.' But he had many colored friends. Marion mentioned Louis Armstrong; he was a *very* good friend of my Uncle Walter's."

"You're right, Elaine," Mary agreed. "That's how Grace got into *High Society,* the movie, you know. Grace did become friendly with Louis herself, but the family connection was Walter. I'm sure my Uncle Walter didn't think of Armstrong as colored or anything else except being an actor."

Charles nodded in agreement. "It's like the story they tell about some baseball fan who saw Willie Mays on the field for the first time and complained indignantly, 'How come they put a nigger on the team?' The answer reached him quickly from the guy seated next to him, who said, 'That ain't no nigger; that's a ball player.' "

I asked the assembled Kellys, since the pair were in the same profession, if Walter and George were close. There was comparative silence for a couple of seconds. Then Charles gave his answer.

"No, I don't think so. The Kellys are essentially righteous, puritanical, and moral people. We're always expressing moral judgments. And my Uncle George, as you know, in all his plays deals with moral issues. 'This is right; this is wrong; this is true; this is false; this is good; this is bad'—that kind of thing.

"My Uncle George always *said,* 'I am not the judge'—he wasn't referring to his brother—'and I am not the law giver.' Nevertheless he was passing judgment all the time. I don't believe he approved of my Uncle Walter's drinking and playing cards. And the fact that Uncle Walter didn't invest his money sensibly and lived up to his income also annoyed my Uncle George.

"The fact that my Uncle Walter left the family before he became so successful and 'rejoined,' also had something to do with the cleavage between the brothers. Actually, Uncle Walter got his start in vaudeville because he was a maverick, wouldn't obey his parents. One evening when he was twenty-one and his father said, 'Be in the house by eleven o'clock,' and he wasn't, Grandfather locked the door and Walter couldn't come in. So he ran away to Newport News, Virginia, to begin a new career."

There are, not surprisingly, several versions of how Walter C. Kelly spent his time between that spring evening in 1895 and the start of his theatrical career. But whatever he did in that period there is complete agreement that his rise to international fame on the vaudeville stage was fast.

In his breezy, accurately titled autobiography, *Of Me I Sing,* written in 1938 but unpublished until 1953, and then posthumously, the author says that during the years 1891 and 1895 he worked at the Baldwin Locomotive and Midvale Steel Companies. No doubt his experience there got him a job at Old Point Comfort, Virginia, where, Kelly wrote, he helped build the battleships *Kearsarge* and *Kentucky,* then under construction.

For a couple of ensuing years, the succession of events in the life of Walter C. Kelly gets fuzzy. The author says he stumped the Dominion for William Jennings Bryan and he himself ran for U. S. Congress on the Republican ticket. It is no surprise that neither the would-be President of the United States nor the candidate for the House of Representatives won. As Walter told Brother John B., "There didn't seem to be any Republicans around," an experience members of the same political persuasion have suffered before, during, and since.

Walter lived in a boarding house at Phoebus, a Virginia town no longer in existence. A gregarious young man who enjoyed the company of both sexes, drank heartily, and usually picked up the check, Kelly made many friends in the area. A few of these, one in particular referred to by Walter solely as "Eddie," were on Kelly's private dole in the coming years. Some popped into his dressing room when, as the Virginia Judge, he played Norfolk.

Whether what I am about to say was a case of nature imitating art or the reverse, I'm not prepared to offer warranty. However, the Dominion State, at the end of the last century and during the first several decades of this one, seemed to have a plethora of judges who competed with each other in the courtroom histrionically.

Each one apparently counted on a visitation from a performer, impresario, or newspaper reporter, who might catch this daily show, spread the word, and thus make the judge immortal. Prisoners were blacks, summoned before the benches of these members of the minor judiciary to plead their cases without benefit of counsel. This handicap naturally placed them in a position where they had to play any role assigned to them, usually that of straight man.

Visitors, some of whom came from afar—all white, of course—were welcome courtroom guests. Aware of what audiences had been promised, judges fitted punishment not to the crime but to the chance for a bon mot. I daresay many a defendant spent extra time in stir because his innocent answer to the Court's planned question afforded the latter a chance for a riposte.

For example, another of the Virginia Judge's classic jokes concerned a Negro who'd stolen—what else could it be but—chickens? Asked by His Honor how long he'd been circulating in the area, the prisoner, after being informed what *circulating* meant, replied, "Sixty days." Whereupon the Court, in his role of endman, responded with, "Well, you won't be circulating for the *next* sixty days." You wonder if the reply had been, "Thirty days," would that have been the sentence?

Walter C. Kelly must have spent a good many hours in those Virginia courtrooms. Without conscious intent, the future Virginia Judge was gathering material that, in less than a decade, would make him an internationally famed monologist, perhaps the best in the world of his day. I *heard* him and, I repeat, he *was* funny. I don't know who said, "I don't care *what* makes me laugh as long as it *makes* me laugh"; but as far as I'm concerned, this is my defense.

Sometimes I'm persuaded that Judge Brown was a figment of Walter C. Kelly's fertile imagination or perhaps he was a composite, because I find no record of his existence. However, an Associated Press dispatch, under a Richmond, Virginia, dateline, notes the passing of Judge Crutchfield.

"John Jeter Crutchfield," reported this wire service on November 22, 1929, "whose witticisms delivered as Justice of Police Court for thirty-two years made his court nationally known as 'Justice John's Court' died yesterday at the age of seventy-six. . . . His court was a regular stopping place for tourists."

Walter, in the family's eyes, had been a ne'er-do-well. He never came home, rarely let his parents know what he was doing, and communicated only with Brother Patrick, and then merely to negotiate temporary touches in small amounts. These loans, I discovered, were returned a thousandfold when P.H. needed cash.

Sometime in 1899 or 1900 Walter left the Norfolk Navy Yard and headed for New York. One version of Kelly's success story has it that shortly after his arrival in Manhattan he was in a lower Seventh Avenue saloon where he entertained newly found companions with the Kelly interpretation of what went on in a Virginia courtroom. It so happens, in this rendition, that a famous booking agent is present socially, hears the former Falls young man, and laughs so heartily that he signs up Kelly forthwith.

Another interpretation of the theme told more often by Walter himself goes like this, and I quote from a 1935 issue of the New York *Theatre News:*

"At a political rally here in 1900, Walter Kelly met Big Tim Sullivan. In the course of the evening Mr. Sullivan extended to him a casual invitation to attend the anniversary celebration of his Bowery political club. Kelly went. He evidently had given Big Tim the impression that he had been quite a political figure down Virginia way because during the evening he was called upon for a speech.

"Taken by surprise, he rose and, by way of having at least something to say, told a few of the stories he had heard in Judge Brown's courtroom. He stopped the show. The next day a variety impresario asked him whether he wanted to play a Sunday night at the Grand Opera House for twenty-five dollars. The sum staggered him. He accepted and played several similar dates.

"An actor who heard him on one of these occasions invited him to a dinner at the Green Room Club. There he told his stories again and had no sooner finished than he was approached by no less a worthy than A. L. Erlanger. Would Mr. Kelly be interested in becoming a real actor? He would. Well, then, he was to report Monday morning for rehearsals."

The play in which Walter Kelly made his first professional appearance was a musical adaptation of *Huckleberry Finn.* Kelly played the role of Mr. Doughton, a temperance lecturer. Despite the fact that a local resident, Mark Twain, helped with direction, the play folded after three weeks of road tryouts. However, area critics liked Kelly's performance and, as a result of good notices, he did make a few more appearances on the legitimate stage in 1901, playing one-night stands in western Pennsylvania, eastern Ohio, and northern West Virginia in *The Price of Honor,* a melodrama.

I don't believe, though, that the success or failure of *Huckleberry Finn* or *The Price of Honor* would have mattered a whit to Walter C. Kelly. As the Virginia Judge, he was on his way skyward and by 1904 an almost instantaneous success in variety houses. He was in big-time vaudeville. In theatrical history, particularly that of vaudeville, there's hardly anyone who reached the top as fast as Grandma Kelly's second son.

For the week commencing June 5, 1905, Walter C. Kelly, "The Inimitable Comedian" (not to be billed as the Virginia Judge until later that year), had the "money spot" at the Alhambra, Seventh Avenue and 126th Street, owned by the Orpheum Company and managed by Mr. Percy G. Williams. On the same program were "Gillette's Clever Canines," Clement D'Leon, the Billiard Ball Manipulator, "and other star acts." In addition the Alhambra management proudly announced "the first appearance in Harlem vaudeville of Jacob Adler, the Famous Jewish Tragedian in Scenes from *The Merchant of Venice* supported by an English Company." As an "extra feature," Mr. and Mrs. Sydney Drew presented a one-act comedy, *When Two Hearts Are Won.*

As a basis for comparison, the preceding week's money spot at the Alhambra had been held by Mr. Conway Tearle, supported by Miss Charlotte Ives, Miss Maud Knowlton and Mr. Henry

Mortimer in *Fancy Free,* a comedy by Stanley Houghton.

The former Falls resident's next two most important appearances were both in Philadelphia. Here he played a two-a-day at B. F. Keith's and visited the Midvale Avenue home of his parents. Walter, the prodigal, was the first of John H. and Grandma Kelly's children to become famous. This was nearly three-quarters of a century ago and no member of the family then alive is extant, so I can't offer any firsthand report on Walter's triumphant return. But I don't doubt for one moment that his parents, brothers, and cousins—as yet neither nephews nor nieces had been born—held orchestra seats for as many performances as they cared to attend.

From that time on, and for the rest of his life, the Virginia Judge was "at liberty" only when he chose to be. Collectors of theater memorabilia will find Mr. Walter C. Kelly's name in the top place on bills at every variety hall of any consequence from coast to coast. By skimming through these you get an idea of his theatrical activities.

In 1921 he played every one of B. F. Keith's thirty-five variety houses from Boston to Indianapolis, then picked up Western and Southern circuits for a total of forty-eight weeks. He played with the top performers vaudeville offered and never had to relinquish his demand for star billing. His picture adorns the covers of a thousand theater programs. He was the best there was; he knew it, his audiences knew it, his agent, Rufus R. LeMaire, knew it, and so did owners of vaudeville circuits, who paid accordingly.

The Virginia Judge, in 1907, went abroad for the first of many appearances in England and on music hall stages in other parts of the English-speaking world—Australia, New Zealand, Egypt, and South Africa. In those moments before he appeared behind the footlights of London's Coliseum that year, he told Brother John, he was scared to death. For Walter, this was indeed an unusual confession.

"I didn't think the English would know what the hell I was talking about. Who in the British Isles ever met an American darkie and listened to him talk?"

But when he concluded his act, switched "gavel for fishing line" and "adjourned court," he knew by the tremendous applause that he'd made it; his English audiences not only understood what the Virginia Judge was talking about, but loved it, and loved Walter C. Kelly as well.

After London he toured the rest of the British Isles, heading bills everywhere he appeared. He met Sir Thomas Lipton in Bristol, where the Virginia Judge was in the usual spot at the "Hippodrome, Tramway Centre, St. Augustine's Parade, in Association with the London Coliseum, which proudly presents, week of Monday, June 9, twice nightly at 6:20 and 8:30, Walter C. Kelly, the Virginia Judge." Walter was then thirty-three years old, and the world *was* his oyster.

Walter's promotion throughout the British Isles was handled by Mr. Ernest Edelsten, 5 Lisle Street, Leicester Square, London. " 'Tis not in mortals to command success but I've done more,—deserve it"—with apologies to Addison, this became the modest caption for similar advertisements Mr. Edelsten placed in newspapers prior and during his client's appearances.

Following his return from a triumphant fourth tour abroad, Walter was the prophet with honor in his native Falls. On Wednesday, August 16, 1911, two hundred and twenty-five prominent Philadelphians in such fields as politics, law, medicine, bench and business gathered to pay homage to the Virginia Judge at a testimonial dinner held at the New Turf Villa, Falls of Schuylkill, Philadelphia, Pennsylvania.

Among those present were a dozen Kellys, including John H., the honored guest's father, who a mere quarter-century before had, in effect, told the wayward Walter "never to darken my door again." On the dais with John H. sat brothers P.H., Charles V., George E., and John B. Other nonfamily Kellys sat elsewhere as did a pair of Costello cousins, George and John J.

One representative of the political arena was William S. Vare, outstandingly crooked even in a city that takes pride in venal politicians and frequently rewards them with high office. Mr. Vare, a Republican, after being duly elected to the United States

Senate, was denied a seat there by members of that body who, surprisingly, didn't like the way their would-be colleague had bought his victory.

One of the legal profession's representatives was William A. Gray, Esq., probably the highest paid and the most successful criminal lawyer in the Commonwealth. For the bench there was the Honorable Hugh T. McDevitt of Common Pleas Court Number One. For business there was wealthy, German-born brewer, John Hohenadel.

Unfortunately, since the dinner was strictly stag, Grandma Kelly was not around to enjoy Son Walter's triumph in The Falls, from which, as he once told Nephew Charles, "I was tossed out on my ass."

8

"REFORMERS ARE
DYSPEPTIC MEN
AND HOMELY WOMEN"

THINGS DID NOT ALWAYS RUN SMOOTHLY FOR WALTER C. KELLY despite his enormous popularity and substantial earning power. As for the latter, Kelly in 1920 was getting as much as five hundred dollars for a single appearance and two thousand dollars a week, which guaranteed star treatment and included first-class travel, hotel suites, and all other expenses. By 1927, Agent Le-Maire had upped his client's ante to one thousand dollars for a single appearance and doubled his weekly pay.

In the summer of 1920, during the height of Atlantic City's tourist season, Walter got into a nasty brush with the Protestant clergy of that vacation spot. At the time the Virginia Judge was headlining a bill at B. F. Keith's Garden Pier Theatre.

According to a Philadelphia *Evening Bulletin* correspondent's dispatch filed from Atlantic City, July 23, 1920, "The Reverend Henry Merle Mullen, President of the City Ministerial Union, issued a statement today excoriating Mayor Bader and his three organization associates in the City Commission.

"The minister blames the Commission for permitting Walter C. Kelly, known in vaudeville as 'The Virginia Judge' to insult committees of men and women representing five thousand church members, during a sensational hearing preceding the passage of the 2 A.M. jazz curfew.

"The bill adds an hour to the after midnight 'open season.'"

The debate grew acrimonious; Walter did not hold his tongue.

"Kelly," the newspaper continued, "in a tirade directed at citizens pleading for conservatism, who maintained the former ordinance fixing a one o'clock deadline was liberal enough for any reasonable person, averred the opponents were a lot of 'reformers' and said, 'Reformers are dyspeptic men · and homely women whose love affairs have been blighted.' "

The ministerial spokesman was equally insulting, even hinting at violence.

" 'A real "Virginia Judge" would have ordered this man out of the room and a Southern body of public-spirited men would have sent him helter-skelter out of town for so gross an insult, not only to ladies present at the City Hall hearing but to the womanhood of Atlantic City,' said Mr. Mellon today.

" 'This man should be ordered out of town and he should be given to understand that whatever may be our differences on local issues we are not in the habit of submitting supinely to insults offered our women in public.'

"Mr. Mellon thought Kelly's friends would do well to urge him quietly to leave Atlantic City."

It should be recorded that the bill passed with only one dissenting vote; Atlantic City's places of amusement were permitted to operate until 2 A.M.; and Walter C. Kelly played to packed houses at the Garden State Pier. I saw him perform there myself, although I don't recall if it was during the week of July 23, 1920.

Before he began his fall tour Walter sailed for Antwerp, Belgium. There he watched Brother John win the Olympic single sculls and on the same day saw John and Cousin Paul V. Costello win the pairs.

After he returned from Europe, Walter extended himself from a double- —vaudeville and legitimate theater—to a triple-threat entertainer by signing a contract to make phonograph records for Victor of Camden, creators of "His Master's Voice." That company's announcement of the event came in the form of national newspaper and magazine advertising plus a widely circulated brochure distributed June 8, 1921. A smiling Judge adorns the cover. The brochure follows in part:

"Walter C. Kelly is one of the historic entertainers who have carried into every accessible country of the world, the National American reputation for clean and honest humor. He is known to the stage of Europe, Africa, Asia, Oceanica [sic] and the two Americas—chiefly in his character of 'The Virginia Judge'—by which title, perhaps, he is almost as well known as by the name bestowed on him by Fortune and his parents."

I presume the author of Victor's promotional pamphlet was referring to Walter's family, not Christian name. As far as the record shows, the Virginia Judge appeared neither in South America nor "Oceanica."

"Mr. Kelly," the pamphlet continued, "is a versatile and accomplished artist. With only an empty stage, with no 'props,' no scenery to speak of, he can create human character, chiefly crusted character, in many forms. His characters are just as much alive as if they stood around him, filling the proscenium wtih their visible as well as their audible presences.

"Not everyone knows that the original 'Virginia Judge' whose presentation has contributed much to Mr. Kelly's fame as an entertainer, was a real living personage, known and carefully studied at first hand. He was Justice John D. Brown, of Tidewater, Virginia, who died at a ripe old age. He became famous throughout the whole of the Middle South as a swift and accurate dispenser of justice, a certain appraiser of men, and withal, a singularly sweet and lovable human character beneath his assumed crabbedness. . . . His court became known as 'Justice John's Court.' "

This last statement certainly should have been, if it wasn't, protested by Justice Crutchfield, who claimed *his* was "Justice John's Court," which would label as imposters all others making the same claim. But since background material for the pamphlet must have been furnished by Victor's newly contracted star, I think this was exactly the kind of character our Judge thought he had portrayed. It wouldn't matter much whether the act was developed

in Tidewater, Virginia, Richmond, Virginia, or elsewhere; or
Media, a town in suburban Philadelphia, where a magistrate with
similar ideas of the law as applied to "darkies" once dispensed
justice.

"Mr. Kelly," said Victor's anonymous copywriter waxing
poetic, "does not lecture; he gives an hour of life, the sunshine
and the merriment of it, and something, too, of its tragedy and
pathos. And an evening with him no more exhausts his repertoire,
or his full stage knowledge, than a cupful of water exhausts the
contents of a mountain well."

Wow!

I am not a collector of phonograph records; I've long since dis-
posed of nearly all of my old monaurals. But I did manage to
preserve one of Walter Kelly's historic disks, probably because
this was my father's favorite as well as mine. It is labeled "Virginian Judge (Southern Court Scene—Second Session) Part I and
Part II No. 45202." I don't understand why, after all the buildup,
Walter, in the eyes of Victor, became the "Virginian" not the
"Virginia Judge." I don't remember when my father bought it,
perhaps after our return home from the family excursion to
Wilkes-Barre's Polis Theatre. Neither do I know how much he
paid for it—it may have been a dollar and a quarter or half—
nor how much Walter C. Kelly added to his income from sales
of the Virginia Judge recordings and, later, Irish dialect jokes
told on Victor disks. I do believe the amount was substantial. As
I recall, every one of my companions of the twenties, at least those
whose phonographs displayed the famous "His Master's Voice,"
had at least one Kelly record.

While Kelly had friends, male and female, almost everywhere
he played, his favorite city was Los Angeles. There he hobnobbed
with movie stars of the Twenties. In a letter to Brother John
dated January 2, 1925, the Virginia Judge relates with great satisfaction a New Year's Day dinner held at the home of Jackie
Coogan, a "great little fellow."

It always was Walter's claim that it was he who urged Chaplin
to try his luck in the United States after seeing the comedian

perform in England about 1907. This may well have been the truth although I found nothing in Chaplin's biographical data to confirm the Judge's boast.

Few, if any, people realized it then, but in 1926 radio entertainment was beginning to become popular and big-time vaudeville had, at best, only three more years to live. A minuscule portion of Walter's competition, fleeting though it was, yet indicative of the trend, came from members of the family. It was in 1926 that Walter's niece Ann and her brother, the Other George, children of P.H., broadcast a daily half-hour program of "songs with words and music" from Philadelphia's radio station WEAF.

Vaudeville, which had withstood silent movies, was unable to survive radio and the "talkies." One by one, all over the country variety houses were closing; some would be converted to motion picture theaters, some would become retail stores or warehouses, and some would be razed to make parking lots.

Walter C. Kelly's final "live" appearance in Philadelphia as the Virginia Judge—he did return six years later as the star of a film bearing that name—came the week of March 18, 1929, at the Earle Theatre. Even with the top-flight cast, he led the program but received supplemental support in the form of a movie. This last, in itself, certainly was prophetic.

"Walter C. Kelly, famed and favorite as 'The Virginia Judge' . . . won a hearty and enthusiastic reception when he appeared as the headliner at the Earle Theatre," wrote the Philadelphia *Inquirer*'s entertainment critic.

"Judge Kelly has a whole new crop of 'cases' about the Southern darkies which he puts over in characteristic drollery; the material is so diverting that it makes his appearance seem all too brief."

Others in the show included Signor Friscoe, "that dexterous player of the xylophone," the Chew Hing Troupe of Chinese Wonder Workers, who displayed quite a variety of stunts and great dexterity, and "Mazie Clifton and Billie DeRex, who are quite entertaining in a knockabout comedy."

It's difficult to comprehend why a bill of such diversity and talent required supplemental nurturing but obviously the Earle's management thought so.

" 'Stolen Kisses,' " the *Inquirer* continued, "a Vitaphone picture, is a snappy feature with May McAvoy and Hallam Cooley in the leading roles. It tells of a hectic jaunt to Paris by a lively young couple and its consequences. The cast included Claude Gillingwater, Edna Murphy and Reed Howes."

Walter C., instead of bemoaning the Fates, added another dimension to his career. In 1932 Howard Publications signed Kelly to write a syndicated weekly newspaper column. I don't know why his column didn't last more than a few months; what he had to say sounds great even today.

A half-dozen or so of these columns suggests that what the Virginia Judge produced was a combination of a contemporary whom he admired, O. O. McIntyre, and those pundits who appeared in print then or would appear later—Walter Winchell, Heywood Broun, and Cholly Knickerbocker. There are even bits that H. L. Mencken would have applauded. For example:

"The Reverend Harold Davidson, Pastor of the Church of England at Stiffkey, Norfolk, has recently been convicted of gross immoral ties with various London streetwalkers; and following that comes the conviction of Dave Hutton, a baritone ram and chief stud of Aimee Semple McPherson's choir loft in Los Angeles. Dave's evangelistic fervor so impressed Miss St. Pierre that she had to repair to a maternity hospital and the jury smacked a ticket on Dave for five thousand Vanderbilt buttons.

"Upon hearing the verdict, Sister Aimee did a fainting number, and upon her recovery we may look for a full week's revival in Aimee's temple, during which the congregation of Iowa hog-callers and Kansas corn-huskers will pay for Dave's buck jumping. Amen."

I think Winchell and his readers would have approved of this next item:

"*Karl: You have been so good to me. I am sorry to end it all. The baby is not growing right and I am going to take her with me. Martha.*

"In all the sordid welter of political, theatrical, foreign, sporting, financial news of last week, the above tragic farewell of a distracted nineteen-year-old mother made me pause long enough to pay the tribute with a sigh. Although not overly sentimental and rather vague in my faith as regards streets of gold and hell fire, I would really like to believe that this tired and hapless little soul with her first born will on some farther shore find full compensation for her brief and tragic earthly journey."

But for the last and characteristic phrase, O. O. McIntyre might have accepted the following:

"King C. Gillette, inventor of the safety razor, passed away recently at his estate in Calabasas, California. He well deserves a place among the immortals. For many years I enjoyed the friendship of this kindly gentleman and while barbers will not erect monuments to his memory, it can be truthfully said that he prevented more bloodshed than all the peace conferences ever assembled and practically disarmed the Negro race."

9

"KELLY DROPPED INTO THE
WHITE HOUSE FOR A CHAT"

WALTER C. KELLY WAS AWARE OF VAUDEVILLE'S DEMISE EVEN though he still was in great demand as a single at conventions and social gatherings and received fifteen hundred dollars for an hour's performance. As early as 1927 he was paid one thousand dollars for an appearance on the National Carbon Company's program at the Radio Industries Banquet held in New York's Astor Hotel. But transcontinental tours as such were over.

So the Virginia Judge returned to a career he had abandoned in 1901 after those one-night stands on the stages of western Pennsylvania, eastern Ohio, and northern West Virginia theaters. Not completely forsaking the character that made him famous, Kelly appeared as Judge Totheride in Vincent Youmans' *Great Day,* which opened October 18, 1929, at New York's Cosmopolitan Theatre.

Though we're still singing, whistling, playing, humming, or listening to the show's hit tunes, "Without a Song" and "More Than You Know," this musical comedy starring Mayo Methot and Allan Pryor was by no means the usual, anticipated Youmans success.

"Only the elimination of a soggy and pointless book and the substitution of something more nearly befitting several of the tunes that Mr. Youmans has provided could conceivably make 'Great Day' a Broadway dance-and-tune fiesta. . . . The dry humor of Walter C. Kelly, vaudeville's Virginia Judge, and the

Walter C. Kelly in 1935, the year he made his first talkie,
McFadden's Flats.

comedy of Maude Eburne are of slight service, and querulous
antics of the blackamoor comics, Miller and Lyles, only a little
more so," said *The New York Times.*

In 1931 Kelly took time out from conventions, club dates,
and Broadway to make his first motion picture, *The Seas Beneath,*
a class B if there ever was one. Under the Fox flag it featured
the heavy-handed acting of George O'Brien supported by John
Loder. Except in hometown dailies and an East Falls throw-
sheet, wherein Kelly's name led all the rest, his performance in
this, his film debut, was largely forgotten.

The Virginia Judge was more impressive in his return to Broad-
way, where he played the thoroughly engaging role of Solomon
Fitzmaurice in Maxwell Anderson's Pulitzer Prize-winning play,
Both Your Houses. Speaking only of the play, *The Times'* Brooks
Atkinson said, "Of all the theatrical attacks upon the depravity
of representative government Maxwell Anderson's 'Both Your
Houses' is most stirring and direct. It is not only an angry crying

of names and cases but an excellent play that will interest those to whom it is convincing."

Above all the rest of the cast, which included Morris Carnovsky, Jerome Cowan, Jane Seymour, and J. Edward Bromberg, each of proven star quality, Walter C. Kelly was singled out to be praised by critics on Broadway, in Philadelphia, and wherever else this Guild presentation appeared.

"As Solomon Fitzmaurice," Atkinson continued, "he is blissfully unscrupulous as he beams over his spectacles and turns the blandishments of soft words and brotherly love against every eruption of honesty."

"Mr. Kelly," said Richard Lockridge of *The New York Tribune,* "enriches the play with his portrait of Solomon Fitzmaurice, one of the few characters to come alive." Otherwise, Lockridge doesn't think too much of the play.

They really loved Walter in Philadelphia.

Said the *Inquirer*: "Walter C. Kelly . . . in the role of Fitzmaurice, is the very spirit of lively cynicism as he laughs, cajoles, wisecracks, and even preaches his gouging way, playing the game according to his idea of the rules."

Said Arthur B. Waters of the *Public Ledger*: "Mr. Kelly's magnificent performance as Sol, wisest and probably most graft-incrusted of all the group, lifts the play up again and again."

Said Jeff Keen in the *Daily News*: "Walter C. Kelly, both by virtue of capturing the best lines spawned by Maxwell Anderson, and a type of acting admirably suited to the role, reaped the largest crop of bouquets."

Both Your Houses had a long and successful run.

Two seasons later Kelly returned to Broadway to play the role of General Philoman Smallwood in a Civil War fantasy written by the Lewises, Sinclair and Lloyd, the latter a Chicago drama critic and unrelated to his collaborator. The star of the show was Fred Stone and it was to this actor that critics gave their attention, Kelly receiving not much more than brief notices. Even in Philadelphia, a tryout town, where the play was presented at the Garrick, October 22, 1934, the Judge fared little better than he did at New York's Cort Theatre.

Except for a single venture on Broadway in 1936, the Judge's decision now was to spend his remaining years in Hollywood, there to make movies and enjoy life with friends. He had no trouble finding work. In 1935 he made two low-budget films for Paramount, *McFadden's Flats* and *The Virginia Judge*. Of the first, a *Times* critic, André Sennwald, had this to say:

"Obviously Walter C. Kelly believes in 'McFadden's Flats.' The Virginia Judge of blessed vaudeville memories is surely the classic McFadden. Broad of figure and plain of face, he plays his part as though it were a privilege. He revels in McFadden's invincible democracy, his trademarked Irish humor, his dislike of sham. Even when the gags are . . . cobwebbed . . . Mr. Kelly recites them eagerly and well . . . This homely neighborhood folk tale has all the qualities which caused 'Abie's Irish Rose' to confound the cynical gentlemen of the press."

Kelly's second movie that year was *The Virginia Judge*, which the *Hollywood Reporter* gave a near-rave review on September 14, 1935:

"For nearly thirty-five years Walter C. Kelly has been playing The Virginia Judge in vaudeville and uncounted millions of Americans have laughed at the famous southern court scene and have been touched by its humanity. The picture, as a whole, is episodic but its abundance of laughs and its folksy flavor, besides Kelly's enormous personal following, should sell it to the lesser localities. . . . The Judge's weakling stepson is excellently played by Robert Cummings . . . To the plot has been added some laughable Negro material with Stepin Fetchit singing as he seldom has before.

"The star, himself, is credited with having written the story in collaboraton with Octavus Roy Cohen and they have uncovered a rich vein of colored comedy. . . ."

Walter lived the good life those final years. "When the Judge isn't engaged in a picture," said the *San Fernando Valley Magazine,* "he may be found presiding at the Lakeside Round Table where fellow celebrities come from near and far to listen to the rare reminiscences and bon mots of the prince of story tellers."

The Judge's last motion picture was made not by Paramount but Republic Productions, which signed a fifteen-hundred-dollar-a-week contract with him. He was to play the role of Pat Kelly in *Laughing Irish Eyes*. For those who cherish the Judge's memory, what the critics reported about this film is better left unsaid.

In the autumn of 1936 Kelly returned to Broadway, where, at the Mansfield Theatre, he played the lead in *Lend Me Your Ears!*, a purported comedy by Philip Wood and Stewart Beach. The play opened October 5, and closed after eight performances.

Atkinson, of *The Times,* was unusually acerbic. "By exercising great ingenuity the authors of 'Lend Me Your Ears!' . . . have contrived a comedy without a sense of humor. Philip Wood and Stewart Beach have written a burlesque of politics that passes the time in a state of complete sobriety. Being loyal to his authors, Leo Bulgakov [who did the staging and was coproducer] has admirably sobered up his actors and put laughter out of countenance. For consistency in point of view, 'Lend Me Your Ears!' deserves a grimace of praise. . . .

"In the cast you will find Walter C. Kelly, the guileful jedge of ole Virginny, who is funnier than the play he is temporarily wrestling with. . . ."

Between a return from this less than successful venture on Broadway and his death about two years later, Kelly did little professionally although he was in demand at conventions, lodge meetings, and dinners and still was able to command fees ranging from one thousand to two thousand dollars for a performance. But the great days of the variety stage had passed.

On December 8, 1938, the Judge tried to cross a Hollywood street, stepped back on the curb to avoid a speeding truck, fell, and struck his skull on the concrete. Physicians in Los Angeles called Kelly's injuries serious but certainly not critical. However, it may come as no surprise for nonmedics to learn that this was an incorrect diagnosis. Walter, too, believed his head injuries would respond to treatment, but despite his host of Hollywood friends, he wanted to come home to Philadelphia. John, in answer to his older brother's urgent plea, flew to California to get him.

"John B. Kelly, city Democratic leader, returned from Hollywood today, with his injured brother, Walter, known on the stage as the Virginia Judge," said the Philadelphia *Public Ledger*, December 12, ". . . the party arrived at North Philadelphia Station of the Pennsylvania Railroad at 7:55 A.M., twenty minutes late, and the train was delayed another fifteen minutes while the injured man was lifted through a window and placed on a stretcher.

"Greeting the party at the station were Mrs. Margaret Kelly, John's wife . . . and Dr. John F. McCloskey. About a hundred curious persons watched the proceedings. The veteran actor appeared cheerful as he was lifted from the train and joked with photographers. 'I wish I could pose for you, boys, but I'm not able to.' "

On January 18, Kelly succumbed to his injuries in Women's Medical Hospital, less than a half-mile from the house from which he'd been driven forty-one years before. At his bedside when death came was Brother John. Services, attended by fifteen hundred, were held at St. Bridget's, with Father Curtin handling the spiritual and McIlvaine's the business end of the funeral. Burial was in the family plot at Westminster Cemetery.

"Kelly," said the Philadelphia *Bulletin,* "knew personally all the Presidents of the United States from Theodore Roosevelt to Herbert Hoover, and always dropped into the White House for a chat when he played Washington. Woodrow Wilson was a particular fan of the Virginia Judge."

Even though he'd earned millions, Walter died broke. The funeral tab was shared by surviving Brothers Charles V. and John B. In an old Sante Fe cigar box found in Walter's trunk were his baby picture, a pair of glasses, a glass case, that photograph of Ethelda M., and a note reading: Finder return to W. C. Kelly, Friars Club, 110 West 48th Street, New York, N. Y.

10

"JUST IN CASE
I MEET MAGGIE"

IF A MEMBER OF THE FAMILY OFFERS YOU THAT THIRD MARTINI
or seconds on the mashed potatoes and you say, "I don't really
want it but I'll take it," then pause and add, "Just in case I meet
Maggie," you'll get a laugh. A Kelly will ask you how you know
because this is a genuine "in" joke; it might bring a chuckle even
in Monaco. Before we let Charles Kelly, Jr., tell us how and when
the phrase was invented I'd like to take you to Evacuation Ambu-
lance Company No. 67 somewhere in France. The year is 1918,
the month, February. Master Sergeant John B. Kelly has the
floor:

"I'm going through a battlefield picking up casualties and I
stop for chow at another company's mess. I haven't had anything to eat for maybe twenty-four hours and I'm hungry. I'm
piling up my plate and shoveling it in, perhaps more than they
can spare, when one of the guys turns to another, grins, looks in
my direction, and says, 'Just in case he meets Maggie.'

"I almost jump out of my skin; I stare at him and say, 'Where
in the hell did you hear that?' He laughs, 'Oh, we got a kid in
our company, he's in the field hospital now, and he's always
saying that, Sarge.'

"What's his name I ask, and he says, 'Kelly, same as yours.'

"Well, do you know his first name?

"The guy shakes his head but a corporal answers, 'George,
I think.'"

All of us were sitting around John B. Kelly's table in the Esquire Bar of the Penn Harris Hotel in Harrisburg. Thomas "Tip" O'Neill, political reporter for the old Philadelphia *Record*, Gerson "Lefty" Lush, who did the same job for the *Inquirer*, Duke Kaminsky from the *Bulletin*, and a half-dozen other Harrisburg correspondents, including myself, then doing features for the now defunct Pittsburgh *Sun-Telegraph*.

We listened avidly. Jack never failed to attract the press, not just because he was newsworthy and invariably had a story to tell but, what was rare among politicians, he never tried to use us.

Kelly went on. "I got shipped over in 1917 and I knew George was around somewhere; he'd come over a year or so after I did. I hadn't seen or heard from him during that time but I knew he was in France, my mother wrote me that. But whoever said that bit about Maggie *had* to be my brother or some other Falls kin." The ex-sergeant laughed. "I must say George was as glad to see me as I was to see him." Kelly shook his head. "George didn't like the army and I wouldn't have been surprised if the feeling was mutual. He wanted to get out; I pulled some strings, had him transferred to my company, where I could watch over him, and finally got him out. But that's another story."

If ever there was a military misfit it was George E. Kelly. He hated the discipline; he hated the lack of privacy; he hated the food; he hated the camaraderie. But most of all he hated the shocking waste of time the army took away from his writing. Even so, Kelly managed to write the first draft of *The Show-Off* somewhere in France before he got his honorable discharge and came back home to the theater he loved. He had been away for eleven months as a result of his unwanted but uncontested call to arms.

I'm saving the story of what strings Sergeant Kelly pulled to get his older brother out of the service, meanwhile permitting Nephew Charles to tell how "Just in case you meet Maggie" came into being.

"You'll have to realize," Charles said, "that until comparatively recent years, the Maggie business was supposed to be within the

Playwright George E. Kelly at the time he wrote The Show-Off.

NICKOLAS MURAY, NEW YORK

family perimeter exclusively. So, what an astonishing moment it must have been for my uncle to hear it spoken by a complete stranger; the realization that my Uncle George was close by and Grandma Kelly's last words to my Uncle John ringing in his ears.

"What she said, I think, is important for a better understanding of her attitude toward these sons."

I nodded.

"My grandmother didn't believe in displays of emotion," Charles continued, "so when my Uncle John and my Uncle George went to World War One, she merely shook hands with them. She would always say, 'I was worried about our poor George over there, going off to face the war,' and my Uncle John would ask, 'Why didn't you worry about me?'

"Grandmother would laugh; 'John, I always knew that if there was one warm blanket in France, *you'd* have it. But poor George isn't able to fend for himself that way.'

"And so to Maggie. There was a woman in the Falls named

Maggie Costello; she was a first cousin of my grandmother. She made some Johnny-cake—that's a kind of shortbread—and sent it to our house. Dinner was over but my Uncle George came in late and was eating by himself when the Johnny-cake arrived. My grandmother was sitting down keeping my Uncle George company while he was eating."

Charles said his grandmother was quite annoyed.

" 'Wouldn't you know,' she complained, 'that Maggie Costello would send this Johnny-cake *after* dinner was over. It's always like the Costellos to be late and here's this lovely cake and our dinner is over and we can't enjoy it.' And all the time she was berating Maggie she was cutting up bits of the cake, buttering and eating them.

"And my Uncle George said, 'Why, Mrs. Kelly, for one who seems so upset by the late arrival of the Johnny-cake, you seem equally able to enjoy it.' So Grandma thought for a moment and said, 'George, that's only in case I meet Maggie.' And there you have it."

We both laughed.

"So," Charles continued, "this has become a kind of family statement and if any member takes too much of anything at the dinner table, more than his or her share, someone sitting beside him will say you know what."

With an honorable discharge in his possession, George Kelly returned to the United States in 1918 to resume his theatrical career. Walter was then at his peak; John was still in the army. As for Niece Grace and John B., Jr., they wouldn't be born until the late Twenties.

"I'll tell you this about John B., Walter C., the Princess, and Young Kell," Charles predicted. "A hundred years from now they'll be long forgotten. But my Uncle George won't. College students working for doctorates will pore over his plays in libraries and wherever else literature of the 1920s is preserved."

George Kelly's career, like that of his brothers and sisters, began at Dobson's, an unpleasant episode he refused to admit ever happened to members of the family. He preferred to allow people to think he'd been born into a household of wealth, where cooks, butlers, maids, and chauffeurs could be summoned by ringing a bell, and high tea was routine. His plays reflect this myth; servants are always entering the scene, toting glasses of water on silver trays and being ordered about by their masters and mistresses. There is a definite "Upstairs-Downstairs" feeling in so many Kelly sets; he was a staunch believer in the caste system.

A niece, Mrs. B. Shirley Turner, née Jeanne Cruice, speaks of her uncle's presumption that high tea was a normal, everyday function in the house.

"Every time George came East he spent at least a week with me in Westport. He and Ann Harding, his friend, always came for high tea and the pair would have fun reminiscing about the good old days and the current decline of the theater. When they met first he had two hit shows playing on Broadway and Ann was making her professional New York debut.

"At any rate, I always arranged to have help when he was my guest. He wouldn't deign to use paper napkins and he would be highly insulted if I did. Of course, I couldn't *possibly* have a napkin ring because he didn't approve of them."

Jeanne, still another stunning Kelly woman, laughed.

"I had to have fresh napkins for *every* meal; I'm sure when he was housekeeping he had enough help and someone there to keep the linens coming. But for me, it was a production! When George was my guest we had to have the best silver and china, sparkling all the time. Fresh flowers and much entertaining. It would annoy him if things were not running smoothly so before he arrived I always made sure I had plenty of assistance. At that time I had only a day worker who came in twice a week, but when Uncle George was my guest I always hired a colored man who was on the spot to fetch and carry for him."

Mrs. Turner now lives in Middleburg, Virginia, a Washington, D.C., suburban community. Here, too, George was an unusual guest.

"After tea," said Jeanne Turner, who doesn't appear to take life or herself very seriously and has a superb sense of humor,

"Uncle George would sit on the patio which overlooks the Little River. He'd comment, 'I don't understand why when I spent all my life looking for this place, the likes of you end up getting it finally and I think *I* should have it.'

"I always was under the impression that he *really* wanted me to give him my house in Virginia for nothing. I don't know if I was his 'favorite.' I know he always stayed with me, perhaps because he felt that he could push me around as he couldn't the other girls. He would not hesitate to tell me what he liked and what he did not like. He really had me running! Trying to please him and he was *always* correcting me. I was *always* making horrendous mistakes!"

Jeanne and I were having lunch in a Washington hotel dining room. I didn't see any necessity for it—she's quite slender—but she was careful when she ordered. She was amused when I suggested a rich dessert.

"Not even for Maggie," she said. "This is how I keep my weight down. But we were talking about Uncle George and how he was always finding fault with me. My pronunciation, for example; he was a purist. I'd say 'Am*u*rrican' for American [there Jeanne did a typical Philadelphia accent for a couple of sentences] and wouldn't be aware of what I'd said.

"George would always lecture me then for five minutes. He would embarrass me about my accent, about my pronunciation; he had a very sensitive ear and many times he was right, you know.

"I suppose that's fine when you're twelve years old, even up to sixteen. But for me, it was too late; he upset me. However, I loved him and he got away with it. He did approve of me because I had only two children and he thought that was very civilized. He *hated* anybody with large families."

Jeanne smiled.

"He was, you know, one of ten children and when I reminded him of that he'd say, 'My poor mother; the opportunities she had but she was given no chance.' But he was very generous and if I didn't have the right thing to wear and I was going out, he would say, 'Jeanne, tomorrow just go out and buy; don't look at the price tag.' He was so generous I never let him know that I wanted or needed anything.

"The only time I wished to take a trip—it was to the Virgin Islands and I was living in Westport—my husband was upset because we had a mortgage on our house and he wanted it paid off. So George gave, or loaned, my husband the money.

"But those teas! George loved them. And sometimes in Middleburg I'd take him to our neighbors', Tom and Betty Furness' [again!]. Tom's very bright, Master of the Hunt, *very* old family. At first glance George would be stiff and terribly proper. Then, all of a sudden, he'd feel comfortable, and if he liked someone, he would relax and tell the most delightful stories. The Furnesses had very lovely high teas."

What Niece Mary Daly remembers best (and with a shudder) is George Kelly's predilection for tea and his contempt for the American method of preparing it.

"My God! If there's anything my Uncle George detested, it was a tea bag. He'd go into a tizzy if I ever tried to use one. You see, he loved not only the ceremony of high tea but he loved tea itself."

For one raised on coffee and indoctrinated by a mother who believed tea should be used only as a gargle for sore throat, I find it difficult to comprehend anyone actually enjoying that other beverage. However, as a reporter, I know I must not permit his peculiarities to mar my judgment of George E. Kelly. The fact that he was an eccentric should not, and I trust won't, color my honest appraisal of his talents.

George Kelly was, I truly believe, one of the best and certainly most successful playwrights of the Twenties, when American theater was great.

11

"THAT'S MY UNCLE GEORGE!"

BECAUSE HE WAS ASHAMED OF HIS EARLY LIFE, EMBARRASSED that his parents were poor, that he had nine siblings—only immigrant Irish were capable of such prolificity—and that he quit school in fourth grade, George Kelly invented any number of fictions to conceal the truth about his upbringing. For example, he claimed he was educated by private tutors, a complete fabrication.

We can assume that he worked for Dobson's because that's what his brothers and sisters did and weren't trained for anything better than was George, despite their mother's knowledge of Shakespeare. Once, when requested by the Philadelphia *Record* to fill in a few blanks in his biography for a piece that newspaper was preparing, Kelly said that for a period of time he had worked as an apprentice draftsman in a Philadelphia bridge building firm. He mentioned no specific years, but if true, this probably was after 1905 and before 1910.

Theatrically speaking, George Kelly is first heard from in 1910 when, like Brother Walter, he barnstormed western Pennsylvania on one-night stands. According to biographical data prepared by the Free Library of Philadelphia prior to a "Princess Grace Gala," held in March of 1976, George Kelly's initial stage performance was in Mrs. Henry Wood's *East Lynne* and "other old favorites." Foster Hirsch, of Brooklyn College, who wrote the definitive critique of the Kelly plays, published by Twayne in 1975, supports this.

In 1913, according to Hirsch, Kelly played in a national touring company of *Live Wires*; in 1914, *The Common Law*; and in 1915 went on the variety stage playing the lead in Paul Armstrong's "Woman Proposes." The following year Kelly wrote, acted, and directed "Finders-Keepers," a comedy sketch. With this, George Kelly was launched into big-time vaudeville for a career that lasted for seven years. As a headliner, although certainly not of the Judge's star quality, he played on many of the stages Brother Walter had been dominating for eleven years. Neither brother makes mention of crossing paths although there must have been many near-misses. It would almost seem as though they tried to avoid each other.

"This was my first one-act play," George told the University of California's Rosalyn Salzburg in a taped interview at Kelly's Sun City, California, home, less than a year before the playwright's death.

Perhaps because it was his first success, "Finders-Keepers," of all the many and far more widely known plays, was his most cherished. Those who in later years even remembered Kelly's one-acter were objects of the author's gratitude and those few who actually produced it could become a Kelly friend.

Irwin W. Solomon, a former newspaper colleague of mine and currently Director of Public Relations for the Annenberg Theatre at the University of Pennsylvania, recalls the development of such a friendship.

"It must have been 1965 or 1966," Solomon said, "when the Philadelphia Arts Council was planning a celebration to honor local artists who'd made good in their particular fields. George Kelly was one. We sat down and talked. I said I knew his play, 'Finders-Keepers,' and that really got to him. He said, 'You know, Mr. Solomon, that was the first thing I ever wrote and I was then an actor, doing vaudeville.'

"Mr. Kelly was so pleased that anyone still remembered this

and that I actually produced and acted in it, just as he, himself, had done some fifty years before.

"Well, after we'd discussed 'Finders-Keepers,' and he got so warmed up over that and how I'd done it myself, he started to discuss directing in general. He began to tell me about a play he'd written and directed himself; I forget which, but Ina Claire was the star. He had one particular scene in mind and said, 'Now, I'll show you how that should be done.' "

Solomon recalled that in Kelly's apartment, between the living room, where they were seated, and an adjacent dining room, there was an ugly, dull green curtain hung from a heavy, old-fashioned rod with large hoops. Kelly walked into the dining room.

"A few moments later," Irv went on, "his hand came through; he pulled the curtain apart a bit, then the whole curtain, and he walked into the room. He was no longer George Kelly, he was Ina Claire, and I'm not saying this in a pejorative sense. He had just assumed all the postures of the woman in his play. And he did some lines from it—this was totally astounding. Then he reverted to George Kelly."

Solomon thought for a moment.

"Mr. Kelly was a very quiet, interesting man with a great deal of charm and a high degree of sensitivity. He and I corresponded for many years."

A playlet, "The Flattering Word," written in 1922, probably was what one of his nieces saw during her uncle's last year in variety.

"I was a very young girl, seven or eight years old," Marion Smith recalled, "when I saw my uncle act on Keith's stage in Germantown. I can remember calling out loud to friends who went with me to the Orpheum, 'That's my Uncle George!' It was fascinating, the very tone of his voice, the timbre! It just made me shudder, it was so very exciting."

Marion shook her head slowly then sighed.

"He was *so* handsome. Six feet one, perhaps even a bit taller than my Uncle Jack but he was slender, and Jack, you might say, was robust."

In the Theater Collection of Philadelphia's Free Library there's an undated photograph of George Kelly taken, I would guess, when he was in his early thirties. His hair is jet black and parted in the middle, his forehead is high, nose straight, chin firm, lips full, ears small and set close to his head. Of all the Kellys I've met, I think his nephew, Charles, Jr., bears the closest resemblance to George.

That year, 1922, was a prolific one for Kelly and marked a turning point in his career, with the Broadway production of *The Torch Bearers*, his first full-length play and a hit. Prior to this, in the same year, he'd written a half-dozen other one-act vaudeville sketches. According to Foster Hirsch, these included "The Flattering Word," "Poor Aubrey," "The Weak Spot," "Mrs. Ritter Appears," "One of Those Things," and "Smarty's Party."

But it was "Mrs. Ritter Appears" that lifted the talented Kelly from vaudeville to Broadway. "This one-act play," wrote Douglas Gilbert in *American Vaudeville*, ". . . that opened in a Keith Circuit House in Jamaica, Long Island, was so funny that the management withdrew it at once for an all-star presentation. Such a production did not come about, so Kelly, irked by the delay, rewrote it as the full-length production, *The Torch Bearers*, which opened in New York, August 29, 1922, at the Forty-Eighth Street Theatre."

The play was an immediate success. Most of New York's critics gave it reviews ranging from "good" to "raves," and the thirty-five-year-old Kelly became a much sought-after playwright.

The Torch Bearers is concerned with the little-theater movement in America. Kelly's loathing for anything that smacked of amateurism on stage, his contempt for women, his deep-seated morality, and his refusal to be vulgar are all imbedded in his first Broadway success. He would follow these concepts and prejudices for the balance of his career, never yielding to "popular demand" and never sacrificing principles for expediency.

As a result, Kelly's plays remain of the 1920s. He was a superb technician and what in men of lesser talents might have become lifeless, stilted diatribes, in Kelly became amusing, frequently hilarious, and until changing times outdistanced him, good solid theater. His decade of acting, writing, and directing vaudeville skits, plus a few preceding years of one-night stands, had given Kelly not only staging skills but also a keen sense of what it took to hold his audiences, what brought them to laughter and tears. His finely honed scalpel could dissect character, expose weakness, venality, and ego, yet make the revelations sound funny to victims of his surgery.

For almost a decade making a good living had been no problem for George Kelly. While *The Torch Bearers* was not as great a financial success as the two plays that followed, *The Show-Off* and *Craig's Wife*, his first Broadway production did enable Kelly to leave the road and live in New York. He took an apartment on Thirty-sixth Street, east of Fifth Avenue, furnished it expensively, hired a houseman, and shared his newly earned wealth with his mother and his widowed sister, Mary A. Cruice.

Though the former Falls boy's success is due basically to his own gifts, much of the credit must go to agent and producer Rosalie Stewart, who represented Kelly from variety stage through theater, in triumph and disillusionment, through joy and bitterness, battled his enemies often without her client's knowledge, and squeezed as much money as she could from those who bought Kelly's talent.

Even during the last decade of the playwright's life, which included the final few years of her own, Miss Stewart was loyal to Kelly, entertained him, made his train reservations for him, endured his foibles, shared her California secretary with him, and tolerated his male "companion."

"Rosalie Stewart," recalled Kelly to Nephew Charles, "was a woman of great integrity. During all the years she represented me and produced my plays we never had a contract in writing, merely her word and mine. This was sufficient."

12

"IF WE DON'T LIKE
A PLAY WE ENDURE IT
OR WALK OUT"

ORIGINALLY THE FIRM WAS STEWART AND FRENCH BUT AFTER the death of Bert French in 1923, Miss Stewart took over the operation, which included representing several top-flight variety hall acts, although not that of The Virginia Judge. Miss Stewart's own background was vaudeville; her father, a Texan, managed a chain of theaters in that state and when his sight failed, his daughter became her father's eyes.

She'd met French, a dancer, in 1914 or 1915. He was sick of travel, wanted to stay in New York. Miss Stewart felt the same way and together they formed a theatrical agency. Both had vaudeville connections all over the country, and within a year they represented a score of acts.

"It is because so much trite delicatessen has appeared in the public printeries that the real achievements of Rosalie Stewart may have been obscured," wrote an unnamed correspondent for *The Morning Telegraph* of New York, shortly after the opening of Kelly's play *Craig's Wife* in 1925.

"Her fame rests not upon her youth, neither does it rest on the United States currency she has managed to snare her way. If it must be known, and I proclaim this in as stentorian a voice as I can muster in drab eight-point type, her fame rests in the fact that she unearthed George Kelly."

Miss Stewart was introduced to Kelly in 1917. There are several versions of this meeting, some told by Miss Stewart herself, who enjoyed playing down her own importance, and a few related by Kelly. Whatever the true version, the fact is that they did meet and subsequently were associates for nearly half a century.

Miss Stewart saw merit in that one-acter, "Mrs. Ritter Appears," which B. F. Keith failed to turn into a full-length Broadway production. She'd already represented Kelly and sold, as well as produced, several of his previous sketches and had great faith in his future if not in long-time continuance of vaudeville, at least in the form of the playlet.

"When George came back from the war in 1918," Miss Stewart told Herman L. Dieck, of the Philadelphia *Record*, in November of 1925, "I had an idea. I told him he simply must write a play and this was 'The Torch Bearers.' When this was completed I urged him to write another. He did 'The Show-Off' and, as you know, it was an enormous success.

"George took a successful vaudeville skit, completely revised and vastly amplified it, with the result that the public had its comedy treat. We did well with 'The Torch Bearers,' but 'The Show-Off' was a tremendous hit from the start.

"Bert French, my partner, died five days before the play came into New York and that rather cast a gloom upon us all. Mr. Kelly had chosen the actors, staged the play and written it. That was the way I wanted it, too. I have great faith in his artistic judgment and knowledge of the stage."

There is almost complete unanimity among the critics that George Kelly's new play had everything for a smash hit although I do think the correspondent from the *Evening Ledger*, Kelly's hometown paper, hedged a little.

New York's critics whipped up more enthusiasm.

"Best of all American comedies—an authentic nugget in this, the golden age of the American Theatre," said Heywood Broun.

"An extraordinary comedy of Philadelphia folkways, a genuinely indigenous play of American life, salty, humorous, true," said Alexander Woollcott.

"The season's comedy topnotch, without any exception," reported Alan Dale.

Kelly made his first trip abroad the following year when he directed the London presentation of *The Show-Off* at the Queens Theatre. It opened on October 20, 1924, with an all-American cast the playwright himself selected and he and Rosalie Stewart accompanied across the ocean. The English venture was not a financial success.

"Nor was it a failure," Miss Stewart told the New York *Review* on Saturday, December 10, of that year upon her return from Europe. "The reviews were excellent but the play never really had a large enough audience to get started. Critics liked it and highly extolled the cast. The public . . . failed to respond."

What distressed Miss Stewart and Kelly, as well, in their first joint European venture (this was not Miss Stewart's initial production abroad) was the attitude of London audiences.

"They take their theater too seriously," the agent said. "Here, in America, if we don't like a play, we very politely endure it or walk out. In London, they hiss and boo, and sometimes use language not of the very best. Quite fortunately, 'The Show-Off' received the plaudits of all on opening night, and not only that, but they were so pleased that they demanded a speech from George Kelly."

There's no record of what Kelly said in his response but I imagine the event was quite distasteful to him. After the New York opening of his play he was nowhere to be found. He'd left the theater as soon as the curtain was rung down on Act Three; stood unrecognized on the pavement listening to comments; then walked to his apartment, where Miss Stewart reached him by telephone. He refused to return to greet the happy performers and told his agent that whatever suggestions he had to make would be held in abeyance until a cast meeting scheduled for noon the following day.

"It was not that my Uncle George was without ego; his was tremendous," recalled Jeanne Turner. "Several times he'd be reading a play to me and I'd say, 'Don't you think you should use a modern word'—and he'd be using an old-fashioned phrase —and he'd turn on me. 'Now don't *you* be telling *me*!'

"I think that this ego of his stood in his way. I do believe he would have made ten times as much money if he had been willing to compromise. But he was an absolute martinet about that, *never* changing anything he wrote."

Jeanne smiled.

"I was so relieved when I read Uncle George's will, to find that he did not specify that his scripts couldn't be changed."

Yet, without the change of a single line, *The Show-Off* has been revived time and time again in every major city in the United States on both professional and amateur stages including the straw-hat circuit.

The Show-Off was the opener for what *Billboard* labeled "Arena-style Broadway legit" on May 31, 1950, twenty-six years after its premier. Martin Manulis did the staging and Lee Tracy starred in the title role.

"*Show*-wise," reported critic Bob Francis in that publication, "the Kelly play still stands up as a sardonically amusing portrait of a flatulent braggart who raises hob in a middle-class Philadelphia family by marrying its youngest daughter."

As recently as 1967 and 1968 *The Show-Off*, with Helen Hayes in the role of Mrs. Fisher and Clayton Corzatte as Aubrey Piper, was a hit in New York, where it opened on December 6, 1967. It toured the country, playing at Philadelphia's Walnut Street Theatre for three weeks beginning October 17, 1968.

"With the unerring skill in the selection of plays that has always done the A.P.A. Repertory Company credit, it came up with a beautifully timed—in every sense—revival of George Kelly's 'The Show-Off' at the Lyceum Theatre. This is unquestionably the best American play seen on Broadway for some seasons. . . ." wrote critic Clive Barnes in *The New York Times*.

"Forty or so years is a tricky age for a play, for while in one sense it is a period piece, its ideas and concepts are not yet historically frozen . . . 'The Show-Off' survives magnificently, partly because it is a good, well-written play, but much more because Mr. Kelly's dramatic situations—and even more his characters—are timeless and, in that sense, classic."

13

"OH, MY GOD!
UNCLE GEORGE IS HOME"

WITH THE PRAISE OF CRITICS RINGING IN HIS EARS AND PLENTY
of money in the bank, George came home to Philadelphia, where,
in the peace and quiet of the Falls, he would work on his next
play. Marion Smith remembers.

"I must have been about nine or ten. Uncle George had moved
to a lovely New York apartment at 101 West Fifty-fifth Street.
This would be in 1924 and he was arriving from New York. It
was very quiet on Midvale Avenue then, not many cars moving;
they were few and far between.

"I was sitting with Grandma and a Yellow Cab was due; we
were aware of it coming. And Grandmother said to me, 'You go
out on the sunporch—and you look right down Midvale Avenue
and watch for the cab and when you see it, hurry and tell me.' "

Marion sighed at the recollection.

"Now, when you think how much it meant to Grandma, it was
very touching. As soon as I saw the cab I ran into the living room
and said, 'Here he comes!' And she put on her Victrola in the
corner of our living room and played 'Boy of Mine.' It was like
a stage set and as he climbed up the steps and into the room the
record was playing and Grandma weeping."

(From one who Charles Kelly, Jr., claimed did not believe in
"displays of emotion," Grandma Kelly's sentimentality, as seen
through the eyes of the child, Marion, is a bit difficult to accept.)

"He and Grandmother had a wonderful relationship. My uncle

was just precious, warmhearted, an absolute angel. I loved him so much; everybody did. I don't think there was one person in the family who didn't."

Niece Elaine Beyer's recollections of Uncle George's home-comings were not quite so pleasant.

"Even though I adored him—we all did—I used to dread it when he came home. That was because you had to tiptoe around the house because he would write at all hours and sleep whenever he felt like it. So when you had friends in, you'd have to whisper to them, 'Uncle George is home. We'll have to be quiet.'

"It got to the point where his return to work was known all over the Falls. I went to Cecilian Academy and everybody, includ-ing the nuns, my playmates, and their parents would say, 'Oh, my God! Uncle George is home.'

"He'd be writing and mother would say, 'You must be very, very quiet and after school, be sure to tiptoe in. He used the type-writer—that's all you heard, the clicking of the typewriter and then my Uncle George pacing back and forth."

For still another niece, Grace Frommeyer, daughter of George's sister Annie, this was a familiar scene.

"I remember so well when I was a child and my Uncle George used to compose his plays right on the typewriter in the Falls."

Miss Frommeyer laughed.

"On summer nights when the windows were open you could hear that typewriter clicking away all over Midvale Avenue."

As do many playwrights, I suppose, George Kelly constantly drew upon the people he knew for characters. Charles Kelly always claimed that the lead in *Craig's Wife*, the play that George Kelly was working on that summer of 1924, was Charles' mother. Niece Mary, Charles' sister, recalls an East Falls woman who appeared in several Kelly roles under different names.

"Uncle George was visiting us once. He came into the house one day shaking his head. 'My day's ruined,' he said. 'I wish I hadn't gone to Slim Kelly's house. I stopped for something there and Mrs. Kelly came to the door. She had her sleeveless dress on and her arms were fat.' He couldn't bear this."

Marion, present during this conversation, joined in. "He wanted ladies to be ladies always; it didn't matter if you had to scrub a floor. But when *he* appeared you were Act One, Scene One. And when he came home for dinner and there were children around, they had to be quiet. We had the best of everything for him, but of course we had no maid. He'd be holding forth, reciting his play. You'd have to excuse yourself to run out into the kitchen to get something or stir the gravy.

"He couldn't stand anyone not paying attention to what he was saying or reading and he'd say, *'Will you sit down!'* "

This was at another "Kelly gang taping" and Charles was around, drinking iced tea, eating pretzels, drinking more iced tea.

"In those early days of his successful plays, after *The Show-Off*," Charles said, "he dealt with the people around here and his own experiences. He wanted to create the impression that the Kellys had always lived in *great* wealth. In his interviews he used to say he was privately tutored when he was a young boy."

This amused Marion.

"You know what that 'private tutoring' was? It was a Mrs. Minifor who taught in the Brecht School, where Uncle George went for a couple of years. She took a fancy to him. I met her when she must have been ninety and she remembered George well. She told me he used to come to her home every afternoon and be tutored, poetry, she thought it was. And *that* was all the 'private tutoring' he had. But Mrs. Minifor said he *was* remarkable."

The Judge, also, came to The Falls that summer and spent a week there with his mother, the Cruice family, and George. But neither brother, in correspondence or conversation, seemed to mention the other's presence. Walter, no doubt, spent his spare time with cronies at the Gunboat and George wouldn't go near the place.

When George returned to New York he took with him the completed script for his new show, *Craig's Wife*. He also came back embittered because *The Show-Off* was not awarded the Pulitzer for the year 1924, as he, Rosalie Stewart, and most of

New York's critics had expected. Instead the much coveted prize
went to *They Knew What They Wanted* after acrimonious debate
because the award jury was overruled. More than a half-century
later George Kelly was still resentful.

"*The Show-Off* really won the Pulitzer Prize," he recalled to
Miss Salzburg of the University of California in 1973. "The only
way, under the Pulitzer will, that the jury's verdict could be re-
versed was for propaganda or immorality. These two things were
considered and the jury gave this play the prize.

"Then the head of Columbia University wrote a letter *reversing*
the jury's decision in favor of his former pupil who had just been
placed as chairman of a newly established course. It was a funeral
in New York because the critics had panned the other offering
while *The Show-Off* was a big success. All sorts of protest letters
were written.

"In any event, I won it the following year with *Craig's Wife*."

I promise I will not touch upon the subject of controversy again
except to quote from a leveling opinion expressed some few seasons later by one of New York's most distinguished critics.

"The recent Pulitzer awards raised the storm that inevitably
follows the giving of any prize," said Charles Hanson Towne
of *Smart Set*. "The general public is always dissatisfied. Heaven
help any jury.

"We can all remember how indignant we were when, a few
years ago, the award did not go to 'The Show-Off,' George Kelly's
remarkable play, but to some other of far less obvious merit. Then,
as if to atone for its error, the Pulitzer committee next year set
the seal of its approval upon another play of Mr. Kelly's, 'Craig's
Wife,' which had not half the merit of its predecessor. They
seemed to fear public antagonism; but they only created another
kind of antagonism, and made themselves something of a laugh-
ingstock."

With George Kelly directing, Chrystal Herne in the title role,
supported by Charles Trowbridge as her adoring husband, *Craig's
Wife* was first performed in Buffalo, New York. It took courage,

plus confidence in the new Kelly play, for Rosalie Stewart to choose, as a tryout town, Buffalo, a city with a reputation for the coldness of its audiences.

"From 'The Torch Bearers,' and 'The Show-Off,' with which George Kelly entertained several seasons of theatregoers on Broadway, to 'Craig's Wife,' which opened at the Majestic, is indeed a far cry," reported the *Buffalo Evening News*. "The broad satire, the skillful caricature of the earlier plays, if not missing in this, the latest of his dramatic endeavors, are pushed into the background.

"Mr. Kelly, as he shows in flashes throughout the play, is still master of the lighter touch, but he restrains his gift of humor to impress his point. What counts in 'Craig's Wife,' however, is not the lightning but the thunder and the storm that follows. Which only means that Mr. Kelly has demonstrated he is capable of writing plays intensely interesting in quite another genre."

The play opened on Broadway at the Morosco Theatre, October 12, 1925, for a run of 360 performances. Most critics acclaimed it. I think a short review from *The New Yorker* offers a reasonably accurate consensus.

"George Kelly has achieved a cold, hard gem of playwriting in 'Craig's Wife,'" said this magazine. "Intent on presenting the situation of the woman whose desires for independence become inevitably, with no evil intent on her part, a relentless matter of the exclusion of everything that might in the least jeopardize her own safety, Mr. Kelly has written an extraordinarily fine play.

"Mr. Kelly's female marionette is the woman to whom her home has become the center of her life. It is only incidentally a place for living in; it is primarily a symbol of the triumph of her existence, and it is to be kept spotless, chaste, and inviolate, as befits a shrine. . . .

" 'Craig's Wife' is not the play to bring you cheering to your feet. It is, however, the play to make you marvel for days at the complete mastery of his trade that is Mr. Kelly's. It is the play that, joined to your memories of 'The Torch Bearers' and 'The

Show-Off' makes you wonder how anyone can fail to recognize the identity of America's greatest dramatist."

For its author, *Crag's Wife* made what in those days of tax-deductible innocence was considered a fortune. This, wisely invested, judiciously but generously spent, provided a lifetime of comfort for its owner, sustenance for a widowed sister (Mary A.), temporary succor for a financially hard-pressed brother (P.H.), occasional presents for nephews, party frocks and other expensive gifts for countless nieces, and an unexpectedly pleasurable life for George E. Kelly's valet-cook-companion-consort (William Weagly), a native of Waynesboro, Pennsylvania.

In addition, the playwright, who departed this life at age eighty-seven, left an estate of sufficient size to bequeath one thousand dollars to each of a number of charitable organizations, five thousand dollars to "Tap" Kelly, the bedridden daughter of P.H., a most generous legacy to the aforementioned Weagly, plus a tontine that provided lifetime incomes for nine nieces and for Weagly, as well, and for the longest-lived beneficiary of this agonizing, hate-inducing codicil, what might turn out to be a great deal of cash.

To Nephew Charles V., his most congruous and certainly only intellectually compatible relative, he left nothing. For this fiscal snub, Charles has no explanation and, since he is able to live well enough on his own income, no bitterness.

14

"HATE SEEMS TO BE THE REAL SOURCE OF HIS INSPIRATION"

WHETHER YOU SUBSCRIBE TO CHARLES HANSON TOWNE'S theory that *Craig's Wife* received the Pulitzer only because a mortified jury wanted to make amends or whether you're convinced (as I am) that the Kelly offering was the best in a season of great theater doesn't really matter. It became more than entertainment history. For, just as Victrola, Frigidaire, and Coke are, or were, symbols for a record player, an electric icebox, and a soft drink, so did "Mrs. Craig" become the generic term for a neurotic who was morbidly house-proud.

Perennial revivals by pros and amateurs have not been able to dim the classic qualities of *Craig's Wife*. It reads as well and plays as well as it ever did. Only a few years ago I sat through a nonprofessional staging of this play. I marveled at George Kelly's dramatic skill, his depiction of character, the cleverness of his actor-proof lines. I left the campus theater cheering Mr. Craig's belated declaration of independence, enjoying the subsequent denouement and loathing Mrs. Craig in 1975 as much as I had in 1925.

"Hate," wrote Joseph Wood Krutch, a noted critic, speaking of Kelly in the September 20, 1929, issue of *The Nation*, "seems to be the real source of his inspiration, and one is almost inclined to suspect that behind the harshness of his attitude lies some personal experience which would have to be known before one could entirely understand the vehemence of certain emphases which destroy the proportions of the work for the ordinary spectator. He likes certain persons and despises certain others with an abandon which seems not quite reasonable.

"He has idiosyncratic standards of judgment and he distributes rewards and punishments according to some personal canon of poetic justice which leaves the spectator less satisfied than resentful . . ."

Nephew Charles, the only surviving relative likely to ascribe a reason for his uncle's phobias or even admit George Kelly had any, can give no explanation for this. It's almost unthinkable to place the blame on a lady once described as "one mother in a million," yet I do believe this is where some of the responsibility for son George's behavior must lie.

Admittedly, Mrs. John H. "Grandma" Kelly was courageous, brilliant, generations ahead of her time, devoted to literature, an iconoclast and savage protector of her inner family circle. Yet she scorned her nonintellectual husband and bore his many children grudgingly. You ask why and the answers come fast. The pill had yet to be compounded and "rhythm" was not in vogue.

At meals and other times, and in the presence of growing children, she sent their father to Coventry and kept him there for months at a stretch. She was constitutionally unable to display affection, never kissed the children "good night" or even "goodbye" when two of them went off to war; and she let George know he was a weakling compared to his brother John.

I'm guessing now but I imagine that from puberty George may have suspected he was different from other boys. I wonder if he ever played games with the corner gang, football, baseball, "Red Rover," or anything else where physical contact was involved. He detested sports, but then, so do I; as spectator or participant, they've always bored the hell out of me. I sometimes claim (and with pride) that the last sporting event I saw was the Dempsey-Tunney fight in 1926.

There is no one left who knew George when he was young and who hung around with the kids from St. Bridget's on Midvale Avenue. Consequently, all these recollections I've gathered from

mature men and women—members of the family and friends—
who knew George when he, too, was mature. With the exception
of the discerning Charles Kelly, Jr., no one suspected George's
homosexual tendencies; as a matter of fact nieces were shocked
when I even hinted at such a dreadful possibility.

Gwen and Herb Edwards, Kelly's close friends and next-door
neighbors when the playwright moved to Laguna Beach in the
early 1950's, who entertained George and William Weagly several
times a week for years, tersely said, "Bill swished; George didn't."
Counsel for the defense would tear me apart if I offered this as
evidence in a court of law. But I think it relevant. Besides, there
are stronger clues that explain, if only in part, the odd-couple
relationship between the brilliant George Kelly and the far less
intelligent William Weagly, a relationship that severely restricted
Kelly's social life among his peers. Of these speculations more
later.

It's safe to play the role of psychiatrist if you aren't one; you
can't be thrown out of the AMA. My analyses may be subject to
question; George Kelly's peculiarities may have been genetic or
the result of childhood episodes of emotional accident. I'm not
going to pretend that I've fathomed George E. Kelly's homosexual-
ity, his enjoyment of hate, and his misogyny. But the aberrations
were there.

Even though the family, by then used to prominence, appeared
to take it in stride, Philadelphia was indeed proud of George
Kelly when *Craig's Wife* won the Pulitzer.

" 'One of the Kelly boys' from up the Falls of Schuylkill way
was highly honored yesterday," said the Philadelphia *Inquirer*.

"But the Kellys weren't excited or thrilled about it, nor were
the neighbors of the Kellys. When a Kelly is honored, that's to
be expected.

"A dispatch from New York revealed that George Kelly's play,
'Craig's Wife,' a Broadway success, had been awarded the one-
thousand-dollar prize for the original play, performed in New
York, best representing the educational value and power of the
stage in raising the standard of morals, good taste, and good
manners.

"Thus, the Philadelphian's latest effort becomes the Pulitzer Prize play of the year. When a reporter conveyed the glad tidings to George Kelly, at the home of his mother, 3605 Midvale Avenue, last night, he uttered a noncommittal 'That's nice'—that's all."

Once again, and this would happen for the rest of his life, George was forced to share his glory with others in the family.

"Mrs. Kelly," the *Inquirer* continued, "mother of a rather remarkable trio, was a bit more thrilled, but not much. Why should she be? Hasn't another son of hers, Walter C. Kelly, achieved nation-wide fame on the vaudeville stage? He has!

"Hasn't another son of hers, John B. Kelly or 'Jack' as he is best known, achieved international fame as an oarsman? He has! Jack holds more sculling records than any other man; has won more championships than any other living man. . . ."

A few months after the Pulitzer award George paid a sentimental journey to the tiny County Mayo village where the Kellys came from, a visit Niece Grace would make a half-century later. Both Kellys told the story of that trip to Marion Smith.

"George," said Marion, "went to the village but he couldn't find the right house. He was the new, successful playwright and he wanted to see his father's brother, Patrick, who was a professor at the University of Dublin. He didn't know which of these houses the family lived in; they were all neat, sort of colorful, and quaint.

"So he walked along and looked at different ones until he saw a house which appealed to him. There, he walked up the steps and pulled the bell. A very pretty woman, with white hair and rosy cheeks, came to the door and held it open. Inside, on the wall in back of this woman, was a picture of my grandfather, George's father. So George *knew* he was in the right house.

"The woman who came to the door didn't recognize him. He said, 'I am George, the son of Patrick's brother, John.' And he said, 'There was weeping, hugging, rejoicing, and singing.' "

Marion paused.

" 'You know,' my Uncle George said, 'they *really* wept because my father, John, had left Ireland when he was only seventeen to come to America and that was fifty-eight years before.' "

Charles added a slightly sardonic touch.

"Speaking of that visit," Nephew Charles said, "here's what my Uncle George told me.

" 'This sweet, little white-haired old lady brought in the teapot, made tea for me, and then served cake. "Oh, my God! John's son," she kept saying over and over again to me. At the same time she kept picking up the cake and eating it. I didn't get any.' "

Marion looked at me.

"I guess you saw in the paper that Grace bought her grandfather's place in Ireland."

I said I had.

"Well," Marion went on, "she told me she'd visited the place several years before and when the last member of the family living there died, the house was put up for sale. I suppose she was notified. She was kidding and said Rainier bought a trailer he'd take to the 'estate' in Ireland and he and the children would live in it.

"Grace said it's the original cottage and was in excellent condition except that it hasn't any electricity or running water."

Mary Daly, Charles' sister, laughed. Then she told me about the Princess' first visit to the family's "ancestral" home, a story that we all agreed might bear the same title as the well-known fairytale, "The Princess and the Pea."

"When Grace was there at the house for the first time it was during an awful heavy rainstorm. The place consisted of only two rooms plus an outhouse. Grace had to go. So she said to the old lady, 'May I use your bathroom?' The lady said, 'Well, it's really too rainy out there. Come with me, dear.'

"She took Grace into the bedroom and gave her a potty, which Grace used, covered it over, and said to the woman, 'What shall I do with this?' So the woman told her, 'Don't worry, dear, I'll dispose of it.' "

Mary chuckled.

"And do you know what my brother Charles said? 'Dispose of it, hell! I'll bet the old woman bottled that pee and sold it.' "

15

"HE PLAYED EVERY PART"

AFTER HIS RETURN FROM IRELAND IN JULY OF 1926 GEORGE Kelly would begin the most theatrically active, if not the most successful five years of his life. In that brief period of time he wrote and directed five Broadway shows, two within a ten-month period.

While the first of the quintette, *Daisy Mayme*, was in production, Kelly came back to The Falls, where he saw his mother for the last time. This was on her deathbed, September 21, 1926.

Daisy Mayme, with Josephine Hull starring, had its pre-New York tryout in Rochester on October 26.

A. J. Warner, critic for the *Rochester Times-Union*, had the following to say in part:

"In 'Daisy Mayme,' Mr. Kelly has again, by the keenness of his observation and the high quality of his craftsmanship, set aside the concealing wall of an average house in an average American home and has held up to view, for a little while, the motives and characteristics that govern the lives of its inmates."

Said *The New Yorker* critic, " 'Daisy Mayme' towers above any other comedy of the season, above every other play except 'Broadway.' It is a play I want to see several times, can I say more?"

Brooks Atkinson was not so enthralled. Said this *New York Times* critic, " 'Daisy Mayme' puts another chapter to Mr. Kelly's saga of the middle-class without advancing him as an interpreter of contemporary life."

Stars of the play were Madge Evans and Josephine Hull. The latter, who had played a leading role in *Craig's Wife* the previous season, became a friend of Kelly.

Charles recalled a hate mutually shared by Miss Hull and George Kelly. "Did you ever see Josephine Hull?" he asked.

I answered that I'd enjoyed her performance in *Arsenic and Old Lace*.

"That wasn't what I was going to tell you about," Charles went on. "What my Uncle George and Josephine had in common was a loathing for *Harvey*, which I suppose you saw.

"Well, they used to talk about *Harvey* and how they both detested it but hadn't mentioned their dislike for the play to anyone else, or so they thought. But sometime later he had a play going in Saint Louis, a revival. He ran into Florence Reed, who was playing *Harvey* in the same city. You know Florence had a voice that came from subterranean caverns.

" 'Oh, George,' she said, 'I'm glad to see you; your arrival is *most* opportune. You can join our club.'

"He look puzzled. '*What* club?' And she answered, 'The Hate *Harvey* Club.' "

Another member of the "Hate *Harvey* Club" was Tallulah Bankhead. Elaine Beyer recalled one of Miss Bankhead's visits to the Cruice household in The Falls, although Elaine warned me this had nothing to do with the mythical rabbit.

"Tallu was *crazy* about Uncle George," Elaine said. "She was playing something in Philadelphia—I don't remember what anymore, I was just a little kid at the time—and she came up to our house to spend the night. That was because she found out my Uncle George was there. I suppose he'd seen the show and invited her; I don't know.

"At any rate, you know how he hated profanity; never used it in his plays and never tolerated it wherever he was."

Elaine chuckled.

"And neither would my mother; she might have been even worse about profanity than Uncle George. Well, that night Tallu, Uncle George, and Mother were downstairs in the living room talking. I was at the top of the stairs on my tummy listening. I want to tell you the air was blue with profanity, words Tallu was using you wouldn't find in the dictionary.

"Well, the next morning at breakfast, I'm waiting for Mama to kill Uncle George, and Uncle George to make some sort of apology. But neither of them said a word and naturally, I can't admit I was there to listen."

She smiled.

"It was that way with my Uncle George; if he liked you or if my mother liked you, you couldn't do or say anything wrong, even the most awful swearing."

Marion Smith (oldest of the Cruice daughters) told another story of her Uncle George's tolerance for the actions and deeds of those he liked.

"I have a daughter and three sons, you know. My youngest boy is Peter; he's way over six feet and he dresses like a beatnik. He went to the Academy of Fine Arts for the past three years and before that, for a couple of semesters to the Philadelphia College of Art. He moves in and out of the house, annually, like spring.

"I say to him, '*Don't* come in when your Uncle George is around, because he won't like it; he hates open-toed sandals and all that kind of thing.' But one day, my Uncle George is visiting me—I hear Peter come up the steps. It was too late to stop him; there was nothing I could do.

"So I said, 'Uncle George, I'll have to apologize. You haven't seen Peter since he's grown up; you're really going to see him now.' I said that because Uncle George was always talking against hippies; he *despised* them."

Marion laughed.

"Peter, you know, isn't affected by anybody; he just does his own thing. So Peter walks up the steps, he's got on those damned old sandals and his shirttail is sticking out. He says, 'Hi, Uncle George,' and after a little while he goes up to his room, which I always keep in readiness for his unscheduled returns.

"I must have said something by way of apology or scolded him because—and I couldn't believe my ears—Uncle George said to me in no soft tones, 'Why don't you leave that boy alone? He's different from the others; he's going to look different; he's going to *be* different. So you might as well get used to it."

Elaine shook her head.

"Uncle George wasn't so tolerant with me. I love sunbathing and after I was married and living in Drexel Hill I'd stretch out in the yard, of course wearing very little. He'd be visiting me for a couple of weeks. I'd have to post Paula and Wayne, my two kids, where they could look down the road and tell me quickly if they saw their Uncle George coming. Then, I'd have to dash into the house and get some clothes on before he arrived at the front door. He simply couldn't bear nudity, or even semi-nudity; he would have given me hell!

"My children used to be upset about that ogre who frightened their mother. I'll never forget the first time they met Uncle George, and this became a kind of family joke.

"For months I'd been preparing them for their granduncle's visit. I was particularly concerned about what Wayne would do or say. So I drilled him. I told him, when he was introduced, to shake Uncle George's hand like a little gentleman. Then he was to say politely, 'How do you do, sir?' and go right out into the yard to play because Uncle George doesn't like to have kids around, they're too noisy.

"Well, I was rather proud as Wayne followed instructions. He shook Uncle George's hand and said, 'How do you do, sir?' But he didn't stop there. He kept right on going. 'Sir, they don't want you around, you're too damned noisy. Better come out in the yard and play with me.'"

This led Marion to a further comment.

"That wasn't altogether true about Uncle George not liking kids; he just didn't want them around *all* the time. He preferred the company of adults. At any rate, there is one incident which stays in my mind because it was so outstanding. You know how you just can't get high school kids interested in Shakespeare? It's a pain."

We all agreed.

"We'd have Uncle George up to the house for dinner. When we finished we'd go into the living room and, apropos of absolutely nothing, he'd blast off into one of the lines from his plays. We'd say, 'Oh, keep on, Uncle George, what comes next?' And he would talk and talk, back and forth, giving the whole play, taking different parts.

"Well, one evening, as we left the table, we were discussing Shakespeare. The boys, Bob, George, and Peter, had gone up to their bedrooms to study. They'd been allowed to be down for dinner with Uncle George if they promised to behave, and they had.

"Uncle George was talking about *King Lear*. Somebody made a remark about a woman we know being as faithful as Cordelia. That started him into King Lear's lines and one of the guests— it might have been my sister, Elaine—said to Uncle George, 'I bet you know every line in Shakespeare.' He answered, 'I do; I trained myself.'

"So somebody called his bluff, and that is what made our lives so exciting when Uncle George was around. Whoever it was then said to Uncle George, 'You say you know all the lines? Okay. Now what did Lady Macbeth say in Act Two, Scene One?' And he started off."

Marion said it was as though they'd turned a key.

"One thing led to another. He played every part; he was every voice, he was murderous or gentle, Ophelia, Henry the Eighth, Lear, Hamlet, Desdemona, Iago, hour after hour, after hour! Absolutely thrilling. I looked up the stairway and there was my son, halfway down. And I could spy at the top, Peter, who was then around ten, four years younger than George. They were both watching Uncle George, whose eyes were fiery.

"Well, when he'd finished, it was very late. We were dumb-founded; he really had called our bluff and all of us applauded. That's how Uncle George found out that the kids were there because they applauded louder than any of us. So George came down into the living room and walked over to his granduncle.

"He said, 'You know, Uncle George, Shakespeare never meant

a thing to me, just junk I had to wade through, stuff that was hard to take; but you brought it all to life and I can't wait to read what you just recited.' "

Marion had something else in mind; we waited for her to gather her thoughts.

"Uncle George," she went on, "wasn't always serious. I've told you, I guess all of the family has, how we had to have high tea for him at four o'clock *every* afternoon, that this performance was a must, a ritual which *had* to be observed. After being very formal and proper, sitting at the table, he'd get up and say, 'Ladies and gentlemen, let's betake ourselves to the drawing room and talk.'

"So we'd get up and dutifully walk out. Uncle George would be coming last. And you know what would happen and why all of us, including the children, loved him? This handsome, wonderful, dignified gentleman would pull a vaudeville stunt, suddenly making himself trip, and do an old-fashioned pratfall right into the living room."

16

"HE SAT WEEPING
IN A BACK PEW"

GEORGE KELLY SAVORED THE DREAM OF EVERY PLAYWRIGHT, two successes running simultaneously on Broadway. Different in some respects—the first, *A la Carte*, a musical revue, the second, *Behold the Bridegroom*, a standard three-act play—both bore the Kelly trademark, bitter expeditions into the banal, selfish lives of American families and contempt for women. Each had its own variation: *A La Carte* concerned itself with the middle class; *Behold the Bridegroom* attacked the wealthy.

Kelly's, or rather Rosalie Stewart's revue had its tryout in Boston's Tremont Theatre, August 4, 1927.

"With a show more than three and a half hours long, Rosalie Stewart opened the season . . . and her own career as a producer of revues, at one and the same time with 'A La Carte.' It was a great show while it lasted, and all the while it lasted, which is saying considerable. Talent poured upon the stage with a lavishness that marked Miss Stewart as a very generous woman—which she assuredly is. And, barring a few slight hitches, barely noticeable, the show moved along with commendable serenity for a first-night performance," reported *The Boston Globe*.

Advertisements in local papers featured Rosalie Stewart, George Kelly appearing in considerably smaller type. This would be no slight; public recognition was meaningless to him.

Broadway regarded George Kelly's contribution to *A La Carte* more seriously when it opened at the Cort Theatre, August 18.

"The chief advance interest [for *A La Carte*] of course centered in the three sketches that were Mr. Kelly's," said Richard Watts, Jr., in the *Herald Tribune*. "They are by no means the usual sort of dramatization of last year's snappy anecdotes that are provided by routine revue librettists. Rather has Mr. Kelly provided lengthy cartoons of the middle classes at play that are not so far from the mood of his 'Daisy Mayme.' The first shows guests at an Atlantic City boarding house gabbing idly on the front porch.

"In another, a vaudeville prima donna and her maid talk of the other acts while the prima donna is waiting to go on. The third lampoons the dilatory methods of lady golfers. In none of them has Mr. Kelly attempted to build to a punch line at the conclusion. He has sought his humor, instead, in characterization, in the satire of familiar types, in the general comedy of recognition."

Judith Anderson was the star of Kelly's 1927 production, *Behold the Bridegroom*, which opened at the Cort Theatre, December 26, and as attendance built up, moved to the larger Majestic several months later. The public obviously liked it and so did most critics, although among the latter some expressed reservations. *The New Yorker* didn't like it at all.

"In 'Behold the Bridegroom,' Mr. Kelly has deserted the folksy drama. It is about people endowed with everything the heart can desire except credibility. Instead of making a gorgeous study of the minutiae of middle-class life, Mr. Kelly has splashed an impression of unrequited passion among the very rich."

Not even the star escaped.

"Judith Anderson, who plays Tony, has about four excellent minutes in a speech of ruthless self-analysis. The rest of the time she smouldered and pined conventionally."

Promoters of Philadelphia's Free Library Grace-George Kelly Gala almost a half-century later got in touch with Miss Anderson and had her say telephonically a few kind words about the late George Kelly. I should add that Miss Anderson shared this honor with two more Kelly stars of the past—the Misses Helen Hayes and the late Rosalind Russell.

According to a respectable number of psychiatrists, students of Krafft-Ebing, Kinsey followers, and devotees of Mr. Harold Robbins, the approach to age forty is usually a difficult period in a man's life, be he heterosexual, homosexual, or a combination thereof.

At some point during this dangerous age, George Kelly became involved in an unfortunate incident, an evaluation of which at worst is calumny and at best what current journalism describes as investigative reportage. But before probing this episode I want to review certain George Kelly characteristics that, I admit, offer only collateral evidence to conclusions that seem inevitable.

As for generosity, a quality some, although not all members of the family attribute to George Kelly, I find no supportive evidence. The family and William Weagly did all right, but with the exception of small gifts to charity mentioned in Kelly's will, that was it. The Dramatists Guild of the Actor's League of America, Incorporated, the American Foundation for the Blind, the Women's SPCA, and the Pennsylvania SPCA each received one thousand dollars, not much for a wealthy, generous man who the family claimed was a soft touch.

While George occasionally took in a stray cat or fed a hungry dog, his name didn't appear as a sponsor, donor, or subscriber on the programs of charity affairs. I doubt if he ever yielded to the pitch of door-to-door solicitors working their way through college selling subscriptions to *Pictorial Review.* I would further doubt that he ever invited any of these usually presentable young men to enter his house while he "thought it over." In the first place, Weagly was always around and in the second place (really the first place) I believe that George Kelly had learned his lesson. So much for preamble.

Elaine Beyer was telling me about her Uncle Walter's profligacy, how he never permitted anyone else to lift the tab, how he yielded to sob stories and supported old cronies. This I believed.

"My Uncle George," Niece Elaine went on, "was far more discerning. He would size someone up although he did unbounded charity."

She paused in thought.

"Do you know he supported a crippled elevator boy none of us knew about; sent him all through college, then supported his wife, sent their children to college? That was merely one of many episodes but you never knew it until someone, the person, would mention it in some way."

I asked Elaine if she'd ever met those recipients of George's generosity; she said, "No," adding, however, that her Uncle George couldn't be taken in by phonies.

Gwen Edwards, George's next-door neighbor in California, gave me an expanded version of this philanthropy.

"Years ago Mr. Kelly told me that he came back to his hotel at night and noted that the night clerk, who was lame, seemed very, very pale. Mr. Kelly said he got into conversation with the young man, who told him he was going to college during the day and working at night in the hotel to pay his tuition.

"Mr. Kelly asked the boy how many hours did the job take and when the clerk told him, Mr. Kelly said that the boy wasn't getting enough rest.

" 'Well then,' said Mr. Kelly, 'I've got to do something for you. I'll give you a lump sum of money to go to college. I think you should pay me back the money because it would be good for you. However, if you don't pay me back, I won't mind.'

"Mr. Kelly told Herbert and me that he gave the boy money for college and that every once in a while the boy would send back a payment on the loan until it was all paid off."

I mentioned the story to Nephew Charles, who has few illusions about his Uncle George or anyone else for that matter. Then I asked Charles if he'd heard about this magnanimous action.

Charles nodded and smiled knowingly.

"Yes, I think so," then added, by way of explanation, "Uncle George was a homosexual."

I don't believe one word about the Kelly scholarship award to some unknown weary night clerk. From this alleged act of uncharacteristic generosity, I offer that George E. Kelly was caught with his pants down, literally. He was either the victim of a ruthless "single" performer or the dupe in what used to be called the Margie Game, wherein a "cop" and his lure entrap their mark.

It wouldn't make a whit of difference which way George was taken, but I'm certain he was taken. As far as I can reconstruct George Kelly's life this episode occurred in the mid-1930s, when the playwright was at the top of his career. Someone else in the public eye, even one with as much to lose as Kelly, might have accepted the gamble and told his blackmailer to go to hell, or hired Bill Fallon, the "Great Mouthpiece," who'd handled many such cases, to represent him in court. But to his public, Playwright Kelly was known as a fanatical purist, an author-director who took strong positions on morality. What a field day the press could have had!

George Kelly had learned his lesson. Casual sexual encounters were far too dangerous and could be costly. But he needed someone around permanently to possess, to love (and not necessarily sexually), or only to gossip with. It must be someone he could trust, someone who would respond to kindness, to affection, and to generosity. Of course, this choice could not be a woman although at the snap of a finger he might have had any number of beautiful, talented, sophisticated females scurrying to his bed.

Instead he chose for his lifetime partner as unlikely a candidate as you can imagine, a slightly built, plain-looking, unsophisticated, high school educated (the commercial course), lonely small-town bookkeeper. The man selected to share Kelly's life was William E. Weagly. From this jointure Weagly parlayed a career of his own, enjoyed a life of ease, toured Europe and America first-class, dined in three-star Michelins, was a prince's guest, dwelt in the shadows of the theatrical great and near great (at least those willing to tolerate him for George's sake), and amassed sufficient money to leave his survivors a comfortable inheritance.

A living legend in the small, south central Pennsylvania town where he was born and raised, Weagly, upon his return there for a visit after a seven-month tour of the Continent, was the subject of a series of interviews on page one of the Waynesboro *Daily*. His opinions were sought and freely expressed on such diverse topics as London's fogs and congestion, the madness of Parisian taxi-cab drivers, the beauty of the Italian Alps, the romance of Rainier and Grace Kelly, life in the Palace, and the humor of matchmaking Father Tucker.

Weagly, who was born in 1896, may have been in his mid-thirties when he met George, his senior by nine years. There are several stories of this encounter, any of which might be true. Niece Grace Frommeyer has the simplest version.

"My Uncle George at the time had a suite at the Concord Hotel in New York. He'd had a valet who drank too much beer and he wanted a replacement. He met Weagly, who worked on the same floor as the agents Stewart and French. Weagly appeared to have the qualifications and so Uncle George hired him."

In New York, in California, in Europe, and almost everywhere but Philadelphia and the family's seashore homes, Weagly was recognized as the playwright's associate and good friend. Those who refused to treat him as such were the subjects of George Kelly's ire and would not be reinvited to George Kelly's home. Even though he might have prepared and served the meal, Bill Weagly's place, regardless of who was present, was that of co-host, his seat at one end of the table. Furthermore, Kelly insisted that all invitations to him must include Weagly and wherever the pair went, William was to be accepted as a social equal.

But this equality bit was something The Falls Kellys refused to take. At those rare family gatherings where Bill was present, he came not as a guest but as a servant and was treated as such, ate in the kitchen with the hired help or didn't eat at all. However, when members of the family visited George in California, they had their choice of treating William Weagly decently—and this applied even to Her Serene Highness—or staying away. Some cousins, nieces, and nephews accepted the conditions and spent time with Kelly in California and some stayed away.

I don't know who in the family suspected the relationship between Uncle George and William Weagly. John B. must have; he was far too worldly not to. He understood his brother and knew George was unlikely to live platonically with another man.

Except for the very young generation of Kellys, for someone to be "queer" or "gay" is disgusting and not to be spoken aloud. If you *must* bring up the subject, it's best to describe a homosexual as "effeminate." So there was nothing to be gained by making family members squirm, asking questions for which I would not have received answers.

Once, when Elaine Beyer was talking to me about George's visits to her home, she referred to Bill.

"You see, every year, when Uncle George came to Philadelphia, after we all were married, he would stay elsewhere because he wanted his private home. He had Mr. Weagly with him. Mr. Weagly was my Uncle George's butler, valet, and secretary."

Our conversation in this area dead-ended. Lizanne (Mrs. Donald B. LeVine) John B.'s youngest, has only the vaguest recollections of Weagly.

"I used to visit my sister Grace when she lived in California. Uncle George used to pick us up in his car and take us for drives. William was *never* with us."

This would have been in the early 1950s. *High Noon* had just been released and Grace was on her way to stardom. Lizanne was in her twenties, and by then Weagly and Kelly had been together for at least fifteen years. Peggy (Mrs. Margaret Conlan, Jack's oldest child), remembers Weagly, and her memories of him are pleasant.

"I haven't any idea where Uncle George and Bill met but I remember them being together and the summer they spent with us in Ocean City. Bill was a very charming gentleman in every *possible* way."

I don't think Mrs. Conlan was hinting at any emotional relationship between Kelly and Weagly. She went on.

"My sister Grace and my daughter Mary once visited them out in California for two days; I mean Uncle George and William. When they returned, Mary said, 'Oh, Mummy, William is just so perfect for Uncle George; he did everything exactly the way Uncle George wanted it done.' "

Grace, and Peggy's daughter Mary Davis (offspring of Mrs.

Conlan's first and unsuccessful marriage) must have treated Weagly respectfully.

"George once said to me," recalled Gwen Edwards, " 'I'm not having my sister Mary come out here from Philadelphia. She'd expect Bill to run around waiting on her.' "

Jeanne Cruice Goit Turner, who visited her Uncle George when he lived in Sun City, California, toward the end of his life, regarded Weagly as no more than one of her uncle's domestics.

"The only other servant my uncle had, besides a gardener, I guess, was William," Jeanne said. "William was in and out of the place, sort of there in the background. But he didn't go out to dinner with us."

Except for Gwen and Herb Edwards' opinions, I think the most objective point of view about the family's attitude toward Weagly comes from those two old Falls residents and lifelong Kelly friends, John Cain and Dan McCormick.

"I don't really know where Weagly worked or how he and George met," said Dan. "I've heard he was a bellhop in a New York City hotel where Kelly had a permanent residence. At any rate they got to be friends and lived together, if I'm not mistaken, for fifty-five years." [Maybe it really was that long—nobody actually knows.]

"When he came to Philadelphia," John added, "Weagly was passed off as George's valet; he was *never* treated on any other level; the family would not accept him in any other way. That was in Philadelphia. Elsewhere it was different.

"Weagly was a very quiet fellow; nothing special about him and I don't know what the hell they talked about all those years. Bill was not intelligent; actually he was George Kelly's shadow. I know he never was in show business or anything resembling that."

Dan, John, and I were having a few beers at the bar of my favorite neighborhood saloon, Denny Cavanaugh presiding. Denny filled them again and Dan took up the conversation.

"When George came to Philadelphia and bought a house up in Mount Airy [an area adjacent to The Falls] John and I would go there for dinner. Weagly would cook, come in and say 'hello,' then disappear upstairs. He never participated in our talks.

"I really think George would have been pretty lonely without him. He went all over the world with Kelly."

Dan thought for a few minutes.

"You know, it was a strange friendship; but I suppose George wanted to be with somebody. As for Weagly not being George's intellectual or social equal, I don't think that was important. George Kelly didn't want any competition . . . and he didn't want to live by himself."

John put down his glass.

"You know," he said, "the family really treated Weagly horribly. I don't think, when George died, Weagly was allowed to come to the funeral."

For the record, Weagly did attend George Kelly's funeral but not as an invited guest. He sat weeping in a back pew at St. Bridget's.

17

"WRITING IS A FRUGAL
AND PAINFUL PROCESS"

GEORGE KELLY TOOK THE FIRST REAL THEATRICAL CLOBBERING
when New York critics tore apart his 1929 Broadway offering,
Maggie, the Magnificent, which opened at the Cort Theatre, October 21.

"It was last night, a very bitter and even more confused tragi-
comedy, entitled 'Maggie, the Magnificent,' that brought George
Kelly back to Broadway as a playwright after a silence of two
years.

"It was, in fact, a rudderless little play of sordid family quar-
rels that in spite of the dictaphonic skill of stretches of its dialogue
and its many richly sardonic moments, proved itself as presented
. . . to be the least convincing of Mr. Kelly's contributions to
our theatre," said John Mason Brown in the *New York Evening
Post*.

Robert Littell in the New York *World* liked the play no better.

"If George Kelly's name were not on the program it would
be hard to believe that he wrote 'Maggie, the Magnificent,' which
is not a good play by ordinary standards, much less so by the
standards raised in 'The Show-Off,' 'Daisy Mayme,' and 'Craig's
Wife.' "

Littell's summation may be the reason *Maggie* folded after only
thirty-two performances.

"Have you ever been among strangers who quarreled and talked
about family affairs at great length, affairs in which you could not

be interested? In which the more they yammered and insisted upon them, the less and less interested you became? 'Maggie, the Magnificent' made almost exactly the same impression."

If you're aware of George Kelly's background and *then* read the *Maggie* script, you understand, while not approving the playwright's lifetime problem with his humble beginnings, his fawning respect for the upper classes and his belief that a society run by the Dobsons would be better than one ruled by the Kellys.

For example, the alacrity with which chauffeurs, butlers, maids, and cooks respond to their masters' commands, is to Kelly evidence that the rich know how to run the show. In contrast, the slovenly way Mrs. Reed operates her boarding house in *Maggie* demonstrates limitations of the poor.

According to Foster Hirsch, his biographer, Kelly himself had second thoughts about this play.

"I went wrong," Kelly told Hirsch. "I started to write one thing and wound up with another . . . A playwright must never get off the track."

Two members of *Maggie*'s cast would be heard from for a good many years after Kelly's play folded. One of these was James Cagney, the other, Joan Blondell. For the latter's talents, critics were unanimous in their praise, plus a word or two in favor of the former.

"Except for the tantalizingly brief appearances of Joan Blondell . . . and the perfect gas-house lingo of James Cagney, the acting was, to say the least, hard and graceless," said Robert Littell.

John Mason Brown, too, liked Miss Blondell.

"There is one bright spot in the writing and playing of 'Maggie, the Magnificent,' which deserves special mention and that is Joan Blondell's uproarious travesty of the hard-as-nails wife of Maggie's brother, a part incidentally which Mr. Kelly has written with his old-time vaudeville assurance and gusto."

I should preface any references to this actress with the fact that over the years I have been in love with Miss Blondell (and the Misses Barbara Stanwyck, Joan Crawford, and Eleanor Powell, as well) without revealing my feelings toward her or the other stars.

For the past couple of decades I have had occasion to spend time in Hollywood, most of it fruitlessly. Upon my last visit there, knowing Miss Blondell had been in a Kelly play forty-five years before, I called on the actress. I asked her if by some chance she might remember the late George Kelly of Philadelphia.

Most actresses wouldn't even admit they'd been born in 1931, much less a Broadway performer so long ago. But when I put the question to Miss Blondell, her reaction was instantaneous; a cheerful grin swept across the face of this still attractive grandmother.

"George Kelly," she repeated. "I sure *do* remember him. He was a wonderful, charming, brilliant man and a great director besides."

Miss Blondell poured coffee for each of us; was silent a few moments; then prodding her memory gently, went on.

"I was very, very young, just starting out in the industry, but I knew Mr. Kelly from New York. All of us used to meet regularly at the old Garden of Allah Hotel on Sunset Boulevard. It was a marvelous group of people and I was happy to be accepted as part of it.

"Let me tell you who was in it and you'll understand why I was so flattered. There was Frank Rowan, Albert Hackett and Frances Goodrich, Dorothy Parker, occasionally Scott Fitzgerald and George Kelly. What we had, I guess you might say, was the Algonquin's 'Vicious Circle,' Western division.

"Conversation would be sparkling. Let me tell you, George wasn't the least bit shy with this group of his peers. What was said at any of these lunches was far, far funnier than any dialogue I've ever read. I wish I could remember some of it. But I do recall something, though.

"We used to have all manner of contests, some highbrow and others not so and one day Dorothy Parker had an idea. We'd all do or say something; there'd be a prize for the wittiest and another for the nuttiest; probably a drink or maybe the lunch check, I don't remember. Well, can you guess who got the prizes?"

I couldn't imagine so I shook my head.

"You'd think George would have won first prize for the wittiest and it would be easy to imagine me coming in first as the nuttiest. That's not what happened. Dorothy was the judge. I won the first and George came in second. But, believe it or not, I only *showed* for the nuttiest; George Kelly won that hands down. *He* was the nuttiest."

During this period in the rise and leveling off of George Kelly's career, he maintained a close relationship with his brother Jack and the latter's beautiful wife, Margaret, a cover girl and swimmer of note. There never was an open break between the brothers even though George had little respect for John B.'s athleticism and, later, total disrespect for the sculling heroics of Kell, John B., Jr.

"Uncle George once told me," Marion Smith recalled, "how sad it was to waste a whole lifetime in sports."

While George may not have approved of Jack's athletic dedication or his political views—John B. was then Chairman of Philadelphia's Democratic City Committee—he did respect this brother, and when problems arose pertaining to the family it was John B. whom George consulted. Although he kept in constant touch with his sisters, even Anne, whom he did not like, there was little contact with Charles, Walter, and Patrick.

"Walter and George could be in New York together and I don't believe they saw each other," Charles, Jr., said. "George rarely was in touch with my father or my Uncle Pat. Yet my Uncle George told me that P.H. was a nice person, which, for him, was quite a compliment."

George Kelly fared better with his next Broadway show, *Philip Goes Forth*, than he did with *Maggie*, or than he would do with his last three productions, to follow over the next decade and a half.

In *Philip Goes Forth*, hate once more is the motivating force. The play opened on January 12, 1931, at the Biltmore, with an important cast which included Madge Evans, Dorothy Stickney, Cora Witherspoon, and Harry Ellerbe as Philip, an uninspired would-be playwright.

"George Kelly, our master craftsman when it comes to technique, has, to use a vulgarism, got a load off his chest in 'Philip Goes Forth,' which opened this week, because for some years he has been accumulating a fine lot of grudges against the new generation of arty-arty folks and one can understand how he simply could not resist showing them up . . ." said one critic.

Robert Coleman admits first of all that he is still a Kelly fan. "We consider Kelly to be one of the few really fine playwrights of the modern American Theatre. And while the newest Kelly opus certainly is not one of his best, it is better than ninety percent of his competitors' best . . ."

Following a favorable résumé of the play, Coleman concludes with, " 'Philip Goes Forth' merits the attention of every intelligent playgoer."

After ninety-eight performances, *Philip Goes Forth* folded; five years would elapse before Broadway saw another Kelly production.

Kelly, apparently, had given up his apartment and was back in the Concord at 130 East Fortieth Street. There's an undated letter written on that hotel's stationery sent to the then teen-age Grace Frommeyer, daughter of George's sister Annie. Grace thinks the letter was written shortly after *Philip Goes Forth* closed.

"Dear Grace," wrote her uncle. "You should have let me know that you wanted to see the play. I could have arranged it very easily for you. Anyway I am sending this to tell you that I can't be here next weekend. I had made an appointment to go out to the country and will not be back till Monday afternoon.

"I haven't been well for the past six weeks—was so tired I got bad colds—and the doctor told me I was terribly run down and should get as much rest as possible and get away from the city. So I have been doing that as much as I could. I am going south the latter part of the month on a motor trip.

"Yours 'in the work.' "

Grace said Uncle George usually signed his letters with some joke they shared. What this "Yours 'in the work,' " meant, Miss Frommeyer does not recall. There's no mention of his trip to the

South but further correspondence indicates that Kelly spent a wretched winter, most of the time in bed with heavy colds, and by the spring of 1931 was fed up with New York's climate.

Ever since his first Broadway success, *The Torch Bearers*, Hollywood had been beckoning Kelly. But, like Brother Walter, he was contemptuous of motion pictures and rarely went to see them and on many occasions told Rosalie Stewart he would *never* write a film script. It may have been the lure of Southern California's highly touted sun (smog-concealed these past few decades but most visible in 1931) that persuaded Kelly to sign with MGM for a reputed salary of two thousand dollars a week. Certainly money, even a sum as large as that was in the Depression years, would not have been the bait; George Kelly had been a rich man since 1925.

He had his own office but nobody gave him anything to do. He had his own private secretary but she was of little use. If he had any typing, he preferred to do it himself. He was an official "consultant," but on those few occasions when the movie makers sought his advice, they didn't pay any attention to what he said. He had a generous expense account that he didn't need and didn't use.

I am not suggesting that Kelly's experience was unique. It was not. So many successful writers of that era—F. Scott Fitzgerald, Ben Hecht, Gene Fowler, Charles MacArthur, to name a few— were given the same treatment. That last trio made a joke out of their contracts, entertained lavishly at company expense, lived elegantly, and in general had a ball.

Not Kelly; he was miserable! He clung to the puritan ethic that work was holy, that if you were paid a dollar you had to earn it. However, the California climate was kind to him; his health improved and he wrote that he never felt better in his life. He lived modestly in an apartment that was within walking distance of the studio; lunched almost every day at the Garden of Allah; and except for a nagging conscience, was enjoying life. All the rest of his years George Kelly's feelings about California were ambivalent.

"He would be in Philadelphia," Nephew Charles recalled, "and say to me, 'I don't know what I'm doing on the East Coast; I've always hated the East Coast; I don't like these terrible extremes of weather. I *like* California because the climate is equable. And it's pleasant the whole year round.'

"Then two years later, he'd tell me, 'I don't know what I'm doing out in California. This *eternal* weather drives me insane. I'm an Eastern boy; I was bred in the city; I *like* the changes of climate. I cannot *stand* those desolate wastes of California.'

"As Uncle George tells it, he finally felt he wasn't earning his keep. He left Hollywood and went back to the East Coast. Two years later he returned and stopped into the office. Neatly piled there were all his salary checks."

MGM finally put Kelly to work, writing the script for a film called *Old Hutch,* with Wallace Beery in the title role. Charles Kelly, Jr., remembers what his uncle had to say about that.

"He told me that reading the script for *Old Hutch* was an eerie experience. 'I'd worked on it,' my Uncle George said, 'and brought it into the studio for a conference. I'd just begun to read it when I looked up and there was Wallace Beery in the Land of Nod, snoring loudly, so I got up and walked out. I left the script with them and sometime later they called me back for another "conference." '

" 'They handed me the script for my approval but when I read it I found they'd made changes in the text. So I said what they did was not realistic. I said, 'Look, for example, the letter is being received before it was sent.' So somebody said, 'Don't worry about things like that, Mr. Kelly. Remember, you're writing for an eight-year-old audience; they'll never notice the difference.' "

Old Hutch was shown in 1935 and George Kelly got screen credits. He was totally unimpressed and went to work revising an unpublished play he'd written a long while before. The following year, after a tryout in Pasadena, he brought this production, *Reflected Glory*, to Broadway, where it opened September 21, with Tallulah Bankhead, his friend, in the starring role. Reviews were unfavorable.

The New Yorker reported, ". . . It is the sort of play in which the other characters just sit around, talking in expectant undertones, until it amuses the star to come in and shout at them in her justly celebrated voice. There can be no question that Miss Bankhead is very good at shouting, as she is good at throwing props around and superb at investing the flattest lines with a brusque comedy of her own, but she is not a play all by herself. She is probably as *nearly* a play as anybody could be, but that isn't quite enough, except for her own peculiar public, which, I'm sure, would be enchanted to spend the evening just watching her knit a sock.

"The extent of Mr. Kelly's desperation can be judged more or less by the fact that 'Reflected Glory' is about an actress who has to choose between a home and children and a luminous career on the stage . . . The hoary proposition is . . . robbed of any possible suspense by Miss Bankhead's own performance, which makes it quite evident that she would pull any home in the world down around her ears in ten minutes, and after that, perhaps eat the children."

After eight performances *Reflected Glory* closed. George returned to Hollywood, where he took an apartment at 1360 North Crescent Heights Boulevard. From there he kept up a steady correspondence with the family back in The Falls. He did not go East for two years, not even to attend the funeral of his sister Annie, although he had supported her during her illness.

In a letter dated August 7, 1938, George responded to a note written to him by Brother John in which the latter apparently had enclosed a snapshot of George in the company of another doughboy during Kelly's short hitch in the army.

"Never having had a faculty for remembering incidents, it is not to be wondered at that I haven't the slightest recollection of the lovely picture that you sent me recently. When or where or how that happened to be taken, is and will remain a mystery."

John B. must have asked his brother what he was doing.

"I am working," George went on. "I always said that I would like to reach a point when I could and would take writing very

George E. Kelly at seventy-seven.

leisurely—just do it if I felt like it—on certain rainy days. But that day will never come. For writing is a frugal and painful process—that takes all the mental and nervous vigor of which one is capable. I am working at the moment on a very light, and unserious comedy."

George mentions the Virginia Judge: both were then living in Hollywood. When Walter was injured, it was John, three thousand miles away, who was asked to help.

"Walter," wrote George in that letter of August 7, 1938, "called me on the telephone recently, but I haven't been around to see him yet. I'm in no special hurry, for I know that my appearance doesn't exactly make his day. I'll drop around and see him soon, nevertheless."

The visit between brothers may or may not have taken place, I don't know. In either event, the Judge died five months later.

18

"AVOID VULGARITY. THAT'S NEVER FUNNY"

WHILE HE DID DIRECT A 1938 WEST COAST REVIVAL OF *The Torch Bearers,* his earliest success, Kelly's theatrical career otherwise was quiescent until 1945. Then, in the spring, he returned to New York with *The Deep Mrs. Sykes.* This play, a bitter demonstration of Kelly's misogynism, opened at the Booth Theatre on March 19, 1945, and ran for seventy-two performances.

Catherine Willard, supported by Neil Hamilton, played the title role. Reviews were mixed.

" 'The Deep Mrs. Sykes,' " said *Time,* "is the first play in nearly a decade by the man who left his imprint on the Twenties with 'The Torch Bearers,' 'The Show-Off,' and 'Craig's Wife.' 'The Deep Mrs. Sykes' is not their equal. It is a little too talky, too thin, too pat. But it asserts its theatrical independence at every turn, it makes grown-up assumptions, and the best of it seems written with a rapier rather than a pen.

"Playwright Kelly is no punch-puller—and no knight of chivalry. He brings down the whip, with a kind of cold fury, on the whole 'female' nature. Yet he carefully digs beneath behavior for motive, explains Mrs. Sykes as well as excoriates her . . . The result is more like a solved cryptogram than a thing of flesh and blood. But, if not a satisfying experience, 'The Deep Mrs. Sykes,' with its verbal claws and vivid theatre is very often a stimulating one."

After his 1945 show closed, Kelly went back to Los Angeles

with William Weagly. In a modest apartment near Fairfax Avenue and Sunset Boulevard, Kelly completed *The Fatal Weakness*, begun earlier. Except for a 1947 revival of *Craig's Wife*, which he directed, this would be Kelly's farewell to Broadway, even though he wrote a half-dozen more plays in the remaining twenty-eight years of his life. Fortunately for the living George E. Kelly, and for his memory, none of these was produced, at least professionally.

One of the latter, *When All Else Fails*, written in 1950, was presented in 1976 by a group of untalented amateurs. Though augmented by imported professionals, an actress and a director, it was a complete failure.

Even with the knowledge that Her Serene Highness might be hovering about Philadelphia with scores of family paying court, freedom of the press was upheld in the Quaker City. William B. Collins, the *Inquirer*'s theater critic, was on hand for the premiere, presented by Temple University, February 10, 1976.

" 'When All Else Fails,' " reported Collins, "is a funereal failure in its exhumation. Living playwrights have the right to bore us now and then. Dead ones do not—not even if they were from Philadelphia." It is only fair for me to add that between Mr. Collins and a colleague, Miss Ruth Seltzer, Society Editor, there was no consensus. Miss Seltzer saw the play a month later. She *loved* it.

The Fatal Weakness, with Ina Claire in the lead, opened at New York's Royale Theatre, November 26, 1946. The fact that it was a Theatre Guild offering kept it alive longer than the reviews indicated it merited.

"Ina Claire," said Howard Barnes in the *Herald Tribune,* "employs all her comic wiles to keep up a front of gaiety in 'The Fatal Weakness.' George Kelly has made her work in his new comedy at the Royale Theatre . . . Fortunately for this production, the star is never daunted by a non-stop assignment. She spins through dull passages of exposition as though they were worthy of her grace and subtlety."

In a "Where Are They Now?" piece, published in the February

2, 1970, issue of *Newsweek,* there's a brief description of the life Kelly led then.

"For twenty-four years now, Kelly has been absent from Broadway. But the eighty-two-year-old veteran of the theatre is an alert, avuncular presence. Wintering far from the glare, the tall, spare, lifelong bachelor lives with an ageing private secretary named William in the antiseptic retirement town of Sun City, California (pop. 6,000) where property owners must be over fifty and the lone bar shuts down nightly at ten.

". . . Tempered now with age, Kelly's life and art remain as smooth and even as the tablelands of Sun City. 'Avoid vulgarity,' he advises aspiring playwrights. 'That's never funny to me. Avoid the obvious. Do not say the thing they expect you to say . . . Don't go too far. A laugh is good for so many beats—and no more.' "

Kelly was with Niece Marion Cruice Smith during the last few months of his life.

"After Smitty, my husband, died, Uncle George invited my cousin, Milly, and me out to his California home. Milly is P.H.'s daughter. We spent that January with Uncle George. When we were getting ready to leave he looked so sad, and it never entered my head . . . you know—me with my grandchildren and the family and all. . . .

"He said, 'I hate to see you go. I would like to come East to live.' This was the afternoon we were leaving. He had business interests out there; he had furniture; he had everything, and he was eighty-seven. I figured, 'Oh, well, my Uncle George is just being sentimental for the moment because we were leaving.'

"So we kissed him good-bye and had fun teasing him. I went by train because I won't fly. So it took us four days to get home. I was back on a Sunday and soon after that the phone rang at midnight. It was Uncle George calling from California. He said, 'I'm coming East.' He had flown only once before in his life."

Marion smiled.

"I could understand that. I'll never forget when that plane landed. A redcap was pushing him: he was seated in a wheelchair.

I'm such a damned sentimental nut, I'll show you the hat he was wearing."

Marion went into another room and brought back a kind of sombrero.

"Uncle George was wearing this; he called it his 'planter's hat,' and he had a cane, made of a yucca branch. And he was there looking like a lost child. He was just beginning to get senile. He wasn't when we were out there. But he'd had a fall and the doctor said this was a contributing factor.

"He was carrying this yucca cane in one hand and a little black bag with all his important things in the other. And as the chair rolled down I ran out to hug him and to love him. We were so glad, after all these years. Then he said, 'I came home to die.'

"That was about the fifth of May; he died June seventeenth. The last week he lived with me. What was frightening about his senility was that five minutes after he'd have a spell when he seemed to forget who he was or what he was doing, he'd recover and talk intelligently. His mind would be keen.

"I remember during this time he got a cable from Hempstead, England, asking him about putting on *The Show-Off* there. They wanted some information. I said that he'd better have them get in touch with Samuel French in New York. He said, 'No, I'll talk to them,' and he did."

Mrs. Smith remembered another incident.

"Just a few days before he had his stroke a newspaperwoman called him on the telephone for an interview. He said he didn't care to be interviewed. Whoever it was, was trying hard and said, 'I've heard so much about you, Mr. Kelly. You sound very British.' He answered, 'Madam, I am merely speaking English the way it should be spoken.'

"Uncle George and I were sitting at the dinner table and suddenly he said, 'Marion, I'm very dizzy.' No one else was there with me and Uncle George was a big man. He put his hands on both sides of the table and said, 'Something is happening.' He started to tremble so I got my arm around his waist and under his arm and walked him over to the chair where he sort of kerplunked. It was a massive stroke."

George was rushed to Bryn Mawr Hospital, where he lived for a week, conscious and coherent most of the time. Nephew Charles was the last member of the family to see him.

"I came to say good-bye," Charles said. "He held my hand and tried to whisper something but he was too weak and I couldn't understand what he said."

Obituaries in the press of Philadelphia and New York were long, detailed, and glowing. Most of the newspapers throughout the hinterlands were satisfied to run a one-paragraph dispatch:

"George Kelly, of Philadelphia, uncle of Princess Grace of Monaco, died last night. Mr. Kelly was a former playwright. A brother, John B. Kelly, Sr., father of Her Serene Highness, held the World's Championship for the Senior singles sculls in the 1920 Olympics and with his partner, won the pairs World's Championship that same afternoon."

19

"ONE OF THE MOST GLORIOUS MEN I EVER MET"

WHEN I WAS OUT IN LOS ANGELES DIGGING UP INFORMATION on George Kelly I needed the telephone number of an old actress friend of the playwright. So I stopped in to see Joe Rivkin, vice president of the William Morris Agency, which once represented the lady. Joe gave me what I wanted and I asked him if he'd known George. Joe shook his head.

"Only by reputation."

Then Joe Rivkin smiled. His eyes lit up.

"But I knew his brother John B. He was one of the most glorious men I ever met."

I pursued the subject briefly with this unanticipated source.

"Well," Joe recalled, "many years ago Toots Shor was a very dear friend of Jack's and mine. We followed ball games together. Jack lived and breathed every pitch, every play. I never met a more enthusiastic fan. There was a man who was *alive*. He was 'with it.'"

Talk about Jack Kelly to almost anybody who's been around Philadelphia for a while, particularly past and present members of the working press, and you'll get a fond smile and an anecdote. Si Shaltz and I were at the Pen and Pencil Club late one evening. Si used to be my opposition when we both covered South Philadelphia beats, he for the *Record* and I for the *Inquirer*. I raised the question; Si grinned.

"Get out your pencil and pad, son," he said, "and listen. Remember Dave Zinkoff who used to cover City Hall for the *Evening Ledger?*"

I urged Si to get to the point.

"Okay, then. This must have been in the mid-Thirties. One night Jack Kelly took a priest friend of his, Dave and me to the Arena for the fights. In one of the prelims an Irish kid was getting a terrible lacing. Each time, between rounds, the boy kept crossing himself. Dave looked at the priest.

" 'Father,' Dave asked, 'do you think that'll help?' The priest didn't answer; Jack did.

" 'Tell you, Dave, it won't hurt. But if the kid knew how to box it would help a hell of a lot more.' "

Si and I were drinking boilermakers; the second loosened Si's tongue.

"After the *Record* folded in 1946 and I needed a job, Jack gave me one raising funds for the Olympics. Then later I did the same thing for the Hero Scholarship Fund, which Jack founded. As you *should* know, the Fund provides scholarships for kids whose fathers were cops or firemen who died in line of duty. We worked together closely on that and Jack and I got very friendly.

"The day after Grace won the Academy Award, Betty [Si's wife] and I ran into Kelly at some social function. I said, 'Jack, you must be proud of your daughter.' He grinned and said, 'I'm proud of *all* my daughters.'

"I'll tell you something else. I've heard, and I guess you've heard too, that Jack was not only a tightwad but anti-Semitic besides. And that just *ain't* so. At one crack, when the Jews really needed cash on the line, Jack plunked out fifty thousand dollars for Israeli bonds."

"One thing about Jack Kelly," said Bill Reiter, the Pennsylvania Railroad's lobbyist, "he was no four-flusher. We were going to the Derby and filet mignon was served. An extra dining car was reserved for the politicians and everything was on the house. So the Catholics aboard protested that they weren't going to eat meat because it was Friday. Jack turned to them. 'Why, you damned hypocrites, you won't eat meat tonight but tomorrow you'll go out and lay somebody else's wife.' "

I hate to redact Bill's punch line but I do know of one wife John B. was "laying." So I keep wondering if there weren't more than a measure of hypocrisy involved in Jack's pretense of a satisfactory marriage, during which he carried on clandestine affairs. And I do feel this covert modus operandi of Kelly *père* is at least partly responsible for the rebelliously overt modus operandi in which Kelly *fils* conducts *his* romances and publicly admits that *his* marriage is a failure.

Over our coffee Bill went on.

"Jack and I went to the Derby for thirty-two years, which is the length of time I knew him. Naturally on our way down everybody discussed who he thought would win. Usually someone in the crowd would mention the winning horse in 1950 or if he was old enough, in 1920, maybe even 1910. Old Harve Taylor could go even further, to 1890.

"Then we'd say that the favorite the year when we were going might have been an offspring of a winner years back. That would bring on more attempts to charge our memories. We knew some past winners but Jack Kelly knew them all, every single one! For one hundred years!

"I knew what Jack could do, Harve knew, and some others did. But not everybody. So one of Jack's tricks was to get a doubter who'd put his money where his mouth was to the extent of five hundred bucks. As soon as he did and Jack matched it, Kelly would rattle off the names and collect.

"I want to say something else about my friend Jack Kelly," Reiter added as we said good-bye. "In this game of politics a man's word should be his bond even though often it isn't. Jack's word *was* his bond; he never broke a promise."

Jack Kelly's early life was no different from that of his siblings. He shared their poverty; he quit school at nine or ten, and he worked for the Dobsons. What distinguished Jack from his brothers was his tremendous love of sports, his magnificent physique, and his ability to weld these into a perfect athletic machine. John B. Kelly's international reputation was won in sculling, which, above all sports, was his favorite. But, had he wanted to badly enough, he might have achieved similar success in golf, football, baseball, basketball, swimming, and boxing.

At some time during his life he participated, if only briefly, in every one of those activities and a few more, like water polo. Kelly wrote about this violent game in a series of newspaper stories for the long-vanished *North American* shortly after he won the 1920 Olympic sculling races. In the same piece he admitted that baseball for him was no major sport.

"I can play our national game well enough to bat fourth on a grocer's picnic and not be compelled to play right field."

Those who played with or against him remember that Jack was a dependable ally or a formidable opponent. Pugilism came closer to Jack's heart than anything except sculling. He fought at one hundred and eighty-five pounds but never became a professional. He was quite vain about his physiognomy and had no desire to wind up a career with cauliflower ears or a flattened nose. This is not to say Kelly ran away from physical combat; on the contrary, when he had to, he fought gamely.

Actually, it was John's ability to box that got Brother George out of the army and I suppose now is the time to say how. This is what he told the late John N. "Cap" Cummings, an *Inquirer* columnist.

"My C.O.," said Kelly, "was a fight fan. When I was over in France during World War One, I'd heard that he and a couple of officers from the Division were looking for somebody to put up against a two-hundred-and-fifty-pound Frenchman at a show. Apparently this big Frog had been working out, where he could be seen, and he looked so damned good he scared off all possible contenders. They couldn't seem to find anybody willing to get into the ring with him."

Jack told Cap he got the chance to see the Frenchman in action. "I said to the Colonel I can take this guy, and he said, 'Go ahead.'

"We were the feature bout. I don't remember the Frog's name but we'll call him Louie. He was powerful and built like a Mack truck and looked as though he had plenty of staying power. I knew I'd have to take him fast. He came at me in the first round swinging like Matt Adgie, 'The Fighting Iceman,' if you remember him. If he connected it would be all over but his footwork was bad. To make a long story short I knocked Louie out in the second round.

"Man, I really was in solid with the Colonel. I got in solider three weeks later when they sent me into the ring with a big Basque who must have tipped the scales at three hundred and fifty. But this guy had a punch like Primo Carnera's and I knew, five seconds after we were in the ring, that he couldn't hit me and I could hit him anytime I wanted to.

"My big worry was that he'd fall on me when he landed. I took him in the third round and felt like calling 'timber' when he tumbled down. By this time the Colonel would have given me anything I wanted."

Although he didn't tell Cummings (and I doubt if he mentioned "Maggie" either) what the Colonel presumably "gave" Kelly was Brother George's release. Before Jack was discharged from the army in 1918 he'd risen from private to sergeant to lieutenant and fought ten more heavyweights, winning every match. Arthur Daley, of *The New York Times*, talked about what could have been Jack's thirteenth bout.

". . . Kelly entered the AEF boxing tournament, which was to serve as a springboard for Gene Tunney's winning of the heavyweight championship. The brawny Jack was a terror. He knocked out twelve opponents in succession but broke an ankle before he was to face the younger and less experienced Tunney. And after Gene won the world professional championship Jack kidded him constantly.

" 'Aren't you lucky I broke my ankle?' "

Daley has a couple more Kelly stories—in fact every sports writer I know has a favorite one about Jack. I realize I'd intended to go straight on into John B.'s biographical data, but since I've just mentioned Daley (even *I* can read him and, as I mentioned before, I *hate* sports) I don't want to pass these by. The *New York Times* writer was talking about the 1920 Olympics at Amsterdam, where The Falls sculler beat Jack Beresford, winner of the Diamond Sculls at Henley. That was the race from which Kelly was barred because he was not a "gentleman," having once earned a living as a bricklayer.

"Among the other bets he placed on himself, the handsome giant from Philadelphia wagered a champagne dinner for nine that he'd be first off the starting mark. And there wasn't a cagier starter than Kelly," wrote Daley.

"The official at the getaway was a Belgian. He would order the contestants into position with the command, *'S'il vous plaît.'* The go signal was *'Départez!'* at which time he'd fire the gun. He repeated the words. Did everybody understand? No one understood better than Jack, who had noticed that the Belgian's Adam's apple bobbed just before he gave with the *'Départez!'*

"At the first bob, Jack was winging and at the first stroke he shouted to the losing bettors on the embankment, 'The dinner's on you, boys.' He won, by a length, of course."

The other Daley story concerns a championship race, this one in the U.S.

". . . the starter was Elliott Saltonstall of the Harvard Saltonstalls. He approached his assignment warily and cast a suspicious eye in the direction of the green-hatted Kelly.

" 'Mr. Kelly,' said Saltonstall, 'I understand you're a tricky starter. But there will be no beating the gun on me.'

" 'Yes, sir,' said Jack, giving him a broad grin.

"Five of the six finalists paddled slowly to the line. Jack let his shell drift. Saltonstall wondered what trick he was up to and withheld the starting shot until he dared wait no longer. At the crack of the gun, five boats leaped downstream in a shower of spume and spray. Kelly never moved. The starter stared at him pop-eyed. Jack poured on the charm with his warming smile.

" 'May I go now, Mr. Saltonstall?'

" 'Of course,' screamed the starter.

"Jack won anyway. The margin? One length, natch."

Dan, a Kelly, but not a member of the family, told me a couple of other stories about John B.

"In 1953 I went to work for Kelly Brick on the outside and became a journeyman bricklayer. I think I was making about one hundred and seventy or one hundred eighty dollars a week. Mr. Jess Otley, who was John B.'s partner, offered me a job inside. But all he'd pay me was one hundred dollars a week and I couldn't live on that.

"I took the job anyhow because it was a sure way to learn the business. About two or three months went by and I happened to bump into John B. in the hallway. He said, 'How are you doing, Dan?' I said, 'Okay, Mr. Kelly, I'm learning the business.' And then he asked me if I was making enough money and I answered, 'Not really.' Do you know what he said then?"

I shook my head.

"He said, 'All right, Dan, I'm going to give you a raise.' What I expected was another five dollars because in those days, if you got a five-buck raise you were happy. But Mr. Kelly gave me a twenty-five-dollar-a-week raise; he didn't *have* to give me that. He was a generous man.

"Every time we would go out to lunch—if you were around in the hallway or where he'd see you, he'd take you along and pay the check. Once a year he used to take the girls to the track, treat them for a whole day, and every time he went out on a trip, he always brought every girl a present, a watch maybe, or some other expensive gift."

I was having lunch with Elaine Beyer and I mentioned Daley's story about her Uncle Jack's pleasure in picking up meal checks.

"I've got one for you on *that* subject." She laughed. "Richard and I had just been married and of course we had no money. I was dying to go to lunch at the Bellevue but naturally I hadn't the means to spend on anything so glamorous. At one time I used to go there every week.

"Well, this day I'm talking about, my sister Connie and I managed to scrape up enough for a modest lunch and we went to the Bellevue to have it. John B. chanced to be there. He saw us, walked over, and handed Connie and me each a fifty-dollar bill and said, 'Now go out and buy yourselves nice hats.' And he paid for our lunch besides.

"That was all we needed. We checked and found out what time and what day Uncle Jack would be at the Bellevue; Connie and I would be sure to be there then. Not for months did we miss. In the beginning we were letting him off easy and didn't order much but gradually, you know . . ."

Elaine laughed.

"We increased our lunch each time until finally the biggest day and the biggest meal we ever ordered, Uncle Jack didn't show. We kept looking and looking but he wasn't in sight and we were frantic because we couldn't, between us, scrape up enough money to pay the check. Suddenly we saw Uncle Jack coming in the door, a big grin on his face. He'd known all along. Of course, he took care of the bill but we didn't try to pull anything like that on him again."

20

"HE CAME UP
TO GRACE'S CHIN"
OR "HE WAS TITTY HIGH"

JACK QUIT DOBSON'S MILL ABOUT 1902 WHEN HE WAS TWELVE years old and went to work for Brother Patrick. Brother Charlie, who showed no favoritism, was in charge of the outside workers, which meant John B. did his job as well as anybody else or suffered the consequences. The hours were long, 6 A.M. to 6 P.M., Saturday, half-day. Whatever spare time Jack had he spent along the Schuylkill watching the oarsmen and finally became one himself.

That was in 1908 and a year later, as a member of the Schuylkill Navy's junior four-oared gig, he won the first of one hundred and twenty-four subsequent victories until he retired eighteen years later. When there was ice on the river Kelly boxed as a light heavyweight in local and area gyms or played basketball and sometimes swam in indoor pools. He was good enough to get offers from professional promoters but he never wanted to lose his amateur standing.

As soon as winter ended, Kelly was back on the river. In 1910 he won his first singles race and by the end of that year he was the victor in eight events including one in which he was a member of the four-oared shell that led the way in the Schulykill's National Regatta.

Those carefully nurtured so-called amateurs who worry about

getting their proper rest and insist on star treatment would shudder at Jack Kelly's schedule during those years on the river. Even then he was putting in a sixty-six-hour week for the P. H. Kelly Construction Company, first as a water boy, then as a full-fledged journeyman mechanic.

"One of my first jobs," Kelly recalled when he entered politics in later years, "was carrying water for thirsty construction workers putting up the John Wanamaker Store. But on March 16, 1907, I was indentured as a bricklayer's apprentice and on May 1, 1910, I got my union card as a member of Local Number One, BM and PIU [Bricklayers, Masons, and Plasterers International Union] of America."

A big sculling year for Kelly was 1913, when he won nine races including senior doubles, senior four-oared shells, senior paired, and senior singles. His first victory of that season was in Boston, where he won the American Henley singles. One of Jack's favorite stories is about that race.

"On the way up to Boston," Kelly wrote in the Philadelphia *North American* a few years later, " a well-known sporting writer from one of the New York dailies happened to have the seat next to me. I knew him but he didn't know me, and the usual traveler's conversation ensued with the inevitable question, 'Where are you bound for?'

"He told me he was going up to cover the races, and I said I was also on my way to see them. When he learned I was from Philadelphia he said, 'That fellow Kelly is breaking all records down there, isn't he?' And when I said, 'I believe he's a bit overrated,' he immediately took up the cudgel for Kelly.

"He said, 'How do you figure that way?' and I replied, 'Because I row with him every night and he never beats me.' He didn't want to ask me who I was, so he just gave me a look of pity, you know, one of those 'You hate yourself' looks, and dismissed the subject."

The day following, after he'd won the race, Kelly was sitting in his business suit, unrecognized, on the steps of the Union Boat Club. The same reporter came by.

"He asked me where Kelly was, as he wanted to interview him. I said he would be going for a spin in five minutes and told him I would bring him out. I went in to change my clothes and when I came out, there was a battery of cameramen there to snap me and he came over and said, 'One on me, Jack.' "

Between his job and sports Kelly had little time for girls. This is not to say he stayed away from them. He was handsome, virile, eligible, and an early celebrity in The Falls and elsewhere. So while I have no proof, I would imagine he was pursued by women from the time he reached puberty. I also would imagine that St. Bridget mothers tried hard to ensnare Jack for unwed daughters. But Kelly, like so many Irishmen, had no desire for early wedlock. He was twenty-four years old when he met the young girl he finally married, but he was past thirty before he married her.

Her name was Margaret Majer, and she lived at 2115 North 32nd Street, in the Strawberry Mansion section of Philadelphia, a mile or two south of The Falls. When Margaret was born in 1899, the area was a respectable, tree-lined neighborhood for working or lower middle-class families who occupied two- and three-story brick houses and took Sunday walks around the nearby reservoir, just off Fairmount Park. Now, following three decades of Jewish "infiltration," Strawberry Mansion is nearly 100 percent black.

Margaret was neither Irish nor Roman Catholic, two definite handicaps in her mother-in-law's eyes. The fact that the future Mrs. John B. Kelly, Sr., abandoned her own Protestant faith to become a Catholic convert and joined St. Bridget's lessened, rather than raised Grandma Kelly's opinion of her daughter-in-law. Fortunately for family amity, such as it was, Grandma Kelly survived her son John's marriage for only two years.

Jack and Margaret met in 1913 or thereabouts at the swimming pool of the Philadelphia Turngemeinde, a German club then located at 17th Street and Columbia Avenue. There've been so many romantic stories of this fateful encounter that a biographer has his choice of believing all, some, or none of them. I prefer to believe none; Margaret was then fourteen, Jack, twenty-four.

They did see each other occasionally before Jack went into the service. When he returned, was discharged, and later won the Olympics at Amsterdam in 1920, she wrote him a congratulatory note. A year later they began to date more frequently and in December of 1923, both appeared at City Hall to make application for a marriage license. The wedding took place at St. Bridget's January 30, 1924. All the family with the exception of the P. H. Kellys attended the ceremony. Paul Costello, Jack's rowing partner in the Olympic double victory, was best man.

John B. started business for himself in 1919 with a five-thousand-dollar loan from Brother Walter and with Brother Patrick's blessing. By the time of his marriage Jack was well on his way to financial success and could easily manage The Falls home he, himself, built on Midvale Avenue. What sort of marriage did Jack and Margaret have for their thirty-six years of "togetherness"? I'm afraid the answer is not a good one and this report comes from members of the family, although there is by no means complete agreement. Since I have already formed my opinion of John B. Kelly, Sr., I think the best way to reach an objective point of view is to find out what kind of woman Margaret Majer is, or at least was, until a stroke felled her in 1974.

First of all she was stunning, a blonde and the 1920 cover girl for a national magazine. She was sports-minded and a fine swimmer herself, not of championship caliber but good enough to win local events and to coach the University of Pennsylvania Women's Swimming Team. She was intelligent, highly moral, believed in the sanctity of marriage, shy about making new friends but once accepted, she was intensely loyal to them. She was an excellent hostess and knew how to keep a secret, no minor assets for the wife of a public figure. She gave generously of money and time to worthy causes and, almost until her stroke, was one of the principal fund raisers and supporters of the Women's Hospital and Medical College adjacent to The Falls.

As far as rearing the four children is concerned, she was a

The COUNTRY
GENTLEMAN
The OLDEST, ... L JOURNAL *in the* WORLD

*Cover girl—the future
Mrs. John B. Kelly, Sr.*

strong disciplinarian. However, if results count, this was only a half-asset. One daughter, Peggy, her father's favorite, is twice divorced and did not remarry; Ma Kelly's son, John B., Jr., left his wife and six children to become Philadelphia's best known philanderer. On the plus side one daughter, the Princess, did well for herself before, during, and after marriage and the Kelly, Sr.s' youngest daughter, Lizanne, is still wed to the man she married, and with two attractive children to show for it.

To Ma, marriage de jure, if not de facto, was sacred; for years she struggled against tremendous odds to preserve her own. I don't know if this should be placed on the debit or credit side of the ledger. I'm sure most people thought she and John B. lived "happily ever after," but from what I've gathered, such was not the case.

What people thought of her as a successful mother was so important to Mrs. John B. Kelly, Sr., that even when she knew her son's marriage was on the rocks, she urged him to "keep up appearances" and stay together. At least that's the opinion of

Kathy McKenna, Kell's Councilmanic Administrative Assistant, a woman who understands her boss and his familial relationships better than anyone.

"When things in their marriage went from worse to worse, it was suggested to Kell, 'Do what you have to do but stay home. Do what your father did; keep up appearances. We have, look at us!' "

Kathy paused to catch her breath. Conversation involving Ma Kelly causes Kathy to pant and pulsate so rapidly you can see her heart throb. This might all be upsetting to watch if Mrs. McKenna weren't so pretty.

"Well, Kell's attitude was, 'Go ahead, *look* at you! I'm not built that way and I'm not going to do it. I can't be a hypocrite. I don't intend to live with this.'

"Ma Kelly was a very strong matriarchal force and still is. The worst thing any of these children [Ma Kelly's] who are parents themselves can say to *their* children is, 'I'm going to tell Ma Kelly!' Oh, ho! the end of the world."

I asked Kathy if Kell was aware of unhappiness in his parents' marriage. Kathy paused for a few moments before answering.

"I really don't know. I *do* know that he was very much aware of the fact that everybody believed you had to put a good face on everything. And certainly you don't wash your dirty linen in public. But you also made yourself suffer."

Was Kathy reflecting Ma Kelly's attitude, I asked.

"You did, whatever it was that you were preserving. What we all have done. I don't know if Kell was actually aware of his father's other interests or infidelities. I think that he undoubtedly felt it; he may very well have known. He never *said* anything to me about it.

"I understand that John B. had girls, and there was a special lady, a very 'heavy' lady in there. I mean a 'big attraction.' Kell has said other things to me, having to do with his own effort to run for mayor. He cited an example having to do with his mother's stopping Pop Kelly which I couldn't understand. She threatened to leave him if he did."

Kathy was referring to John B.'s near acceptance of the Democratic nomination for United States Senate in 1936.

"This tiny little woman and this enormous man. How could she stop him? But she did! She did!"

Kell himself suggested the real reason why his mother was disturbed when he and Mary separated and Kell decided to live his own life.

"My Dad was not a very great religious person," Kell told me. "He attended church generally more for the children, my sisters, and myself, rather than for great sincerity in his beliefs. My mother, of course, was not a Catholic until she married my father. She went through the routine and did the basic minimum but she is not an active Catholic today. People who don't know her are inclined to think she is. And she is not upset over my separation from the Catholic religious point of view."

He was silent for a few moments.

"I'll tell you why she was distressed. It's because the separation makes her look like less than a perfect mother."

While Ma Kelly never showed her daughters-in-law much affection she did sympathize with Mary. Charles Fish (remember, he's the real estate man who used to date Grace and vouches for her premarital chastity) recalled a conversation he had with John B., Jr.

"When Kell and Mary were married they started to have babies like every eight months, you know. Ma Kelly, the old Dutchman, got hold of him, Kell told me. She said 'Listen, Kell, you've got to stop this. You're going to *kill* this poor girl.' He said, 'Well, Mother, what can I do? After all, my religion!'

"And Ma said, 'Listen, boy. God gave you brains before He gave you religion.' "

My odds-on favorite of all the Kelly women (and, as I noted before, they're all easy to love) is Kell's oldest child, Anne, a green-eyed blonde. Later, I'll have much more to say about this understanding young lady of twenty-one, who's even more stunning than her Aunt Grace. But for the moment, I'll confine *my* remarks to *her* remarks about Ma Kelly. It was a warm afternoon in April; Anne and I were drinking ice-cold tomato juice in the living room-bedroom-kitchen of her tiny West Philadelphia apartment.

"I really identify with my Grandmother Kelly," Anne said. "I think she's a terrific lady. I just admire her, and I know her very well. She's a very practical, down-to-earth woman and she knew what she wanted and went out and got it. She's a bastion of strength; she doesn't waste time.

"I remember when my cousin ran off and had twins. That's my Aunt Peggy's daughter, and she was fifteen years old at the time. Everybody was bemoaning the horrible immorality. But Grandma Kelly realized the one thing that would keep them together would be money. You know, helping them out financially, putting them on their feet. And that's what Grandma did.

"That's what made their marriage last as long as it has, at least so far. And it turned out okay largely due to Grandma's willingness to accept the situation. It's her basic strength. She's very opinionated and I think she's done things that are wrong.

"She's a matriarch. As long as she lives, what *she* says for this family, is what goes!"

One of Ma Kelly's friends, perhaps her best and certainly her oldest, is Dorothea Sitley. Until her retirement recently Mrs. Sitley was Director of Publicity for all the Gimbel department stores and whenever a celebrity came to town to plug a movie, a book, a show, or anything else, Dorothea was on hand to help him. She also ran the locally important "Gimbel Award" given to Philadelphians who have performed some outstanding service to the city during the preceding year. As a result Mrs. Sitley knows a great many of the country's and the Quaker City's VIP's, publicity-conscious phonies, important writers, actors, actresses, and quite a few politicians, one of whom was the late John B. Kelly, Sr. Dorothea lives in Philadelphia; we sat talking in her living room.

"I knew Jack Kelly prior to meeting the family," Mrs. Sitley said. "But this was before he was married; his friends were friends of mine. Then, soon after Jack's marriage, I met Margaret.

My husband was alive then and we became friends with Jack and Margaret as couples. Their children and ours grew up together; each of their children were my godchildren, and ours were theirs.

"Margaret Kelly was always the pilot of the whole family; she kept them together; she kept them going and happy. Jack would come in late; he would have been out doing all the things he shouldn't have been doing and with no excuses. Margaret kept the wheels turning just the same. She was very strict; she brought up the children very well."

I was tempted to say this was a matter of opinion but I restrained myself.

Mrs. Sitley continued. "Jack was liked by everybody; he had a very sweet disposition. Margaret has one too, underneath, but she's like Grace. She just stands back and doesn't make friends. But when she does, it's for life.

"Margaret was not only physically strong; she was very athletic. Down at the seashore, Ocean City, she used to go swimming four and five times a day; she'd swim way out. And she was a great one for exercise. Every time I've gone with her—I went to Florida with her until last year—Margaret would have me down on the floor early in the morning doing calisthenics."

I mentioned Jack's supposed infidelities.

My hostess sighed, hesitated for a few moments, raised her eyebrows contemplatively, made up her mind. "I had a friend who worked at Elizabeth Arden's and I used to go over there to see her. This particular Christmas she said, 'Come on over here. I want to show you something. Jack Kelly ordered twenty-seven compact handbags some with cosmetics in them.' They cost like one hundred and fifty dollars apiece. And he had ordered twenty-seven of them for different girlfriends. He was so lavish with *everything*.

"When I saw this my heart dropped. I said, 'Oh, my God! I bet he didn't give one to Margaret.' So the next time I saw Jack—it was at a Christmas party and he came over and kissed me. Well, he hadn't given Margaret one of those bags.

"He was moral from the standpoint that these were light flirtations; they were even with my *own* friends that I knew about. And he knew that I knew that a couple of women had told me. I would see Jack hanging over some friend; everything was in a light vein. He teased people and he made fun of himself.

"Of the four children, Peggy was Jack's favorite; she was the oldest. She had the sense of humor he had and they were always playing tricks on one another. She was just as wild as her father was. Crazy ideas. And this is where the difference came in because Grace was the introvert in the family and she felt left out. Because it was Peggy and her father together. Lizanne was the baby and her mother was always with her.

"Grace had her bedroom on the third floor and she'd sit up there and read. But Peggy and her father—they were so much alike. They had charisma you'd recognize immediately. But Grace was the quiet, serene one. Grace was so very shy. She was nearsighted. People would say to me so many times, 'That Grace Kelly is a real snob, isn't she? She never speaks to you.' But that isn't so. It's because she can't see."

As I recalled from a conversation I had with one of John B.'s old friends, this refusal to wear glasses was the kind of vanity Grace shared with her father.

"Jack took pride in not wearing glasses; he was as nearsighted as he could be," said Tommy La Brum, a retired press agent who was closely allied to Kelly's political career. "He'd walk down Walnut Street, and a guy would say, 'Hello, Jack.' I'd say to Jack, 'That was so-and-so. Why didn't you speak to him?' And Jack would answer, 'I didn't see him.'"

Tommy chuckled.

"Jack was beautifully built but he never carried anything in his pockets. Didn't want to spoil the contours."

When Mrs. Sitley told me sadly that she thought her friend Margaret wouldn't be any better I mentioned that I'd talked to Mrs. Kelly at the Library Gala less than a year after she'd had her stroke. I added that Mrs. Kelly appeared to understand my questions and answered them intelligently.

"That may be so," Mrs. Sitley commented, "but she did that because she knew what she would be asked. She can say two or three words without any problem, but if you ask her something where she has to think, then she's lost."

For almost the first time since we began our conversation Mrs. Sitley smiled. She said she was recalling an episode involving Margaret, John B., Grace, and Oleg Cassini.

"Oleg had a crush on Grace and she had a crush on him. When I was still with Gimbel's, Margaret called me one night. 'Dot,' she said, 'I just received a letter from Grace and she said she wants to bring Oleg Cassini down to Ocean City to stay there at the place. Jack says he'll kill him if he walks in the door.' Margaret knew that I'd had Oleg at the store. So she asked me what I could do. She said, 'You know Oleg. I don't dare let Jack know I even called you. But I can tell him if what you say about Oleg is all right. Then Jack will let him come.'

"I said, 'Now wait a minute. Oleg is *not* for Grace. Definitely he is not for her. He's charming, but he's careless, just like a child wandering around.' "

My hostess laughed.

"We don't have any liquor at the store and so we go over to the Ben Franklin for a drink. He forgets his wallet and doesn't even bother to get it from the hotel and he has this Alex Obolensky with him. So I had to pay for the drink. Then he put his arms around me right on Chestnut Street and hugged and kissed me. 'Don't know whatever I'd have done without you.' "

It occurred to me what Oleg Cassini should have done was pay the check.

"Well," Mrs. Sitley went on, "I told Margaret about Oleg and she said she'd tell Grace that her father wouldn't like it and she'd consulted other people. So, of course, Grace came without him."

Jeanne Cruice Turner, daughter of John B.'s sister Mary, recalled conversations she had about Grace Kelly's aborted romance with Cassini and a few other words about her famous cousin's attitude toward matrimony.

Grace Kelly with Oleg Cassini, 1954.

"Father Tucker was looking for the proper bride for Rainier and the blood lines [on both sides, apparently] were just right. He had Italian and French ancestry and she had German, Irish, and a little more or less Spanish."

A very proper stand to take, I thought, for a man with such royal blood as Rainier's.

Jeanne went on. "Father Tucker wanted to arrange the thing. When Grace first came to New York she'd spend weekends with me. This was when she was modeling there and doing a little bit of theater. She'd come up to Westport and I would arrange dates for her with our local doctor, and various eligible men. We'd sit up—I remember when I was going to California and had to catch an early plane. We still sat up half the night, even after coming from a show.

"She'd be talking about her prospects. I remember saying, 'Whom will you marry? You'll have to find someone who is important, certainly as important as you.' And she said, 'Where do we find such a man who hasn't been married and divorced and who's acceptable? I suppose he has to be a Catholic.'

"Oleg Cassini would come to pick up Gene Tierney to go to a marvelous home for the retarded. He and Gene had a child there. Several times Oleg came up with Grace. He'd have dinner with us and then go off to see his child. I could tell that he was very enamored of Grace. But she was not serious about Oleg. He was non-Catholic and he'd been married, you see."

Jeanne laughed.

"Of course, knowing that her father would have a stroke if she'd married Oleg, I really think that the most important thing for Grace was that her husband be a Catholic. So we decided that we should look for a lawyer, not somebody in the theater. And I got such a kick when I heard it was the Prince she was engaged to."

Before her Prince came along, and despite parental objections, Grace continued to see Oleg.

"The compromise on the Cassini affair was that Grace would not see Oleg for a year," said Kate Shea, who used to work for John B., works for Kell now, and is privy to most family secrets.

"Grace was the dutiful daughter," Kate went on, "and she had so much respect for her father that she agreed to this. But she really kind of slipped every once in a while. She had to make sure that the photographers didn't take pictures of Oleg with her. It always appeared that Grace was arriving at these affairs by herself."

I asked Kate if Oleg and John B. had ever met. She laughed.

"They met but the encounter was very cool. Later Oleg told Gabby Davis [Peggy Kelly's first husband] that having dinner with Mr. Kelly 'was like eating a chocolate eclair filled with razor blades.' "

Dom Legado, a Philadelphia *Bulletin* photographer, remembers John B. Kelly's reaction to Rainier's appearance when the engagement was announced.

"I've been with the *Bulletin* for forty-four years and I've covered every possible assignment you can think of—name it and I've done it. Well, about twenty-two years ago we get word that

Grace Kelly's coming to Philadelphia to announce her engagement to a Prince.

"Of course, we didn't know who the Prince was. However, I was assigned to go out to take pictures. When I arrived, I was greeted by Mr. and Mrs. Jack Kelly, who informed me and other photographers there would be no pictures. That was at Grace's request."

For a newspaper photographer, member of a breed entirely apart from the rest of humanity, this kind of rejection was a serious challenge.

"I told Jack, whom I knew for years, how important it was, that here was a Philadelphia girl marrying a Prince. He looked at me and the rest of us.

" 'I never heard of this guy,' he said. 'Do any of you fellows know who the hell he is?'

"Well, Jack was trying to help and told us he'd go back, talk with Mrs. Kelly, and see what could be arranged. He came out and said that his wife had agreed to have one photographer; it would have to be a pool deal. I said fine and all the photographers gathered together and elected me."

Dom smiled modestly.

"So, sure enough, it wasn't long after that this limousine comes up and there was Grace and the Prince. The first one out of the car was Morgan Hudgins, who was a former picture editor at the *Bulletin*. After he quit, he did a lot of p.r. for various movie stars, and he was representing Grace at that time.

"First thing Morgan says is, 'There'll be no pictures.' And I said, 'Horseshit! You once were my boss and you've got to remember I'm still with the *Bulletin*.' This was at the Philadelphia Country Club. At that time we used our Speed Graflex, which required two sides, two films on a holder. So Jack let me make two pictures, Grace and her fiancé and, of course, Jack and Mrs. Kelly. I thanked them and was ushered out of the place.

"When I got back to the office they were surprised to find out we had pictures, and no story. I'll never forget Bill Dickinson,

Prince Rainier III and Princess Grace. Two views of Monaco's royal couple, 1956: above, at an official city luncheon, Bellevue-Stratford Hotel, Philadelphia; below, watching the United Nations Handicap race at Atlantic City.

who was an editor. He said, 'Goddammit! We got two pictures and no story.' Bill asked me if I could fill in with some of the stuff. I said I could name some of the people who were there, like Mayor Dilworth and Mat McCloskey, and Jim Tate, who was President of City Council.

"Bill said what did the Prince look like and I told him he was a fat little guy who came up to Grace's chin ["titty high," the

Inquirer's Ted MacFarland phrased it], and that Grace was wearing some kind of dress that was eggshell color. Damned if I wasn't right, and God knows I'm no connoisseur in *that* line."

Shortly after the engagement party ended at the Philadelphia Country Club, John B. invited the press to his Falls home.

"There were dozens and dozens of reporters and photographers from all over the country," recalled Legado. "I'll never forget Jack saying, 'We'll put all the TV men down in the basement and leave the still men on the second floor.' So we worked in shifts. Jack said to me, 'Dom, it's a good thing I built this house myself or we'd *all* be in the basement by now.'

"So, of course, there were lots of pictures made and you know when a group of cameramen get together it was, 'Look over here, Grace,' and so on. We forgot all about that Prince business and we'd say to Rainier, 'Over here, Joe,' or 'Give us a smile, Joe,' or 'Move your ass, Joe.' "

There is no record of Rainier's reaction to this lack of respect nor is there a record of H.S.H.'s response, if any. As a matter of fact, if it weren't for Grace, there'd be damned little record of Rainier.

The last person Dorothea Sitley and I talked about was Lucy DuVal. I'd almost forgotten this once legendary figure. But back in the 1930's and 1940's, when Jack Kelly's political star was high, his influence felt from City Hall to the White House, Lucy DuVal was then a name to inspire respect, fear, and even hatred in Democratic circles. Reporters who covered that beat in those days claimed that Mrs. DuVal was in a large measure responsible for both John B.'s party successes and his failures. There also were rumors that Lucy was Jack Kelly's mistress. This Mrs. Sitley denied vehemently.

"Lucy," said Dorothea, "was *not* intimate in that way with Jack."

Mrs. Sitley advised me not to see Mrs. DuVal. This was on March 26.

"She's in a nursing home and they say she's mental, that she knows nothing."

I'd every intention of disregarding Mrs. Sitley's advice. I found out shortly afterward that the effort would have been futile.

"Lucy Burlington DuVal, the most powerful woman in the history of Philadelphia politics, died in oblivion Saturday, March 27," wrote Joseph F. Lowry in the *Evening Bulletin*, Wednesday, March 31, 1976.

"She passed away far from the focus of the Democratic City Committee, where she served as executive assistant to the late John B. Kelly when he was party chairman from 1936 until 1940.

"Most of the many friends and enemies she made while 'running,' as some charged, the party in those years when it was struggling against a strong Republican tide, did not note the death of the five foot three, thin Duchess of Windsor-type fashion stylist."

Lowry spoke of Mrs. DuVal's illness.

"First she suffered a stroke and then a broken hip . . . and finally died after a heart attack. She had been in and out of four hospitals and nursing homes. Most of that time, she had private nurses around the clock. This care, a confidante said, left her 'almost broke.' "

" 'Lucy was self-effacing,' said Mrs. Curtis Bok, widow of the Pennsylvania Supreme Court Justice and a close friend of Mrs. DuVal. 'She lived for her friends. She had no close relatives. She was a lady, and in her presence, every man was a gentleman. She was a very sweet woman.' "

Others, according to the *Bulletin,* did not agree with Mrs. Bok's appraisal.

"Many infantrymen in the Democratic army who knew Mrs. DuVal said:

"Kelly was a prisoner of his secretary.

"—Mrs. DuVal was not only Kelly's right hand, but 'both his hands.'

"—She made ward leaders and committee persons stand in line to wait for Kelly and she would not even let them sit down.

"—She caused more rifts in the wards than 'Bricklayer Kelly' was able to patch."

Joseph Sharfsin, a distinguished member of the Philadelphia bar and former colleague and friend of Jack Kelly, remembers Lucy quite well.

"She was made for Jack," said Sharfsin, a former City Solicitor and quondam mayor of Philadelphia. "The reason was simple. Jack—I don't mean to say he hated work but he didn't break his neck to do it—in his business or in the Democratic City Committee. And that's when Mrs. DuVal came into the picture.

"She was a very imperious woman; you were almost frightened by her presence. She created a certain psychological feeling which let you understand that any recognition you received in that office had to be by her grace. The result was that she protected Jack from the importunities of some thirty-five hundred committeemen who were free to walk in. She served an ideal purpose as far as Kelly was concerned.

"Because he backed her up completely this notion arose that there was something between them. But I've another reason not to believe that kind of relationship existed. She was a severe person, nothing alluring about her. If anything, she would be very uninviting to a man; Jack was debonair, witty, and fun-loving. And if he were going to depart from the straight and narrow, he had many opportunities."

I was aware that Sharfsin and Kelly were intimates over the years and so I asked him if he knew of any supposed "great love" in Jack's life. The name "Ellen Frazer" had been given to me and I wondered if she were "*the* woman."

"Of course." Joe smiled. "She was Jay Cooke's sister-in-law. She was divorced from someone whose name I don't remember. For example, if you went to a baseball game, if you went to a football game, you'd see them together, Mrs. Frazer and Jack. They found ways of being together.

"Maybe everybody didn't notice but I did especially because I was struck with its incongruity. Because these two guys, Jack and Jay, hated each other. It was worse than a political feud. And here was his sister-in-law obviously very fond of Jack.

"Mrs. Frazer's father was J. Robert Glendenning, a very handsome, important man with two daughters, one the wife of Jay Cooke and this girl of Jack's, her sister. Mrs. Frazer was good-looking but not the kind of severely stylish woman, more the outdoor type. But you could tell she was always very happy with Jack. The fact that she was a socialite didn't mean much to Kelly; he really was attracted to her."

The Kelly-Frazer romance was recalled by my friend, Francis Gowen, with whom I have two things in common. Francis and I are fellow Sherlockians, and I once wrote a book in which his granduncle was the villain.

"Ellen Glendenning," Francis began, "was born in Chestnut Hill. Her father, Colonel Robert Glendenning, gave the beautiful Glendenning Rock Garden out on the East River Drive, just before you get to the Frederic Remington statue. I don't know if he was a financier; he had a great deal of money. He was also, interestingly enough, a very early balloon devotee, before Connie Wolf.

"Ellen married in the Twenties, a very charming man by the name of Percival Frazer, and they had three children. And about the late Thirties or very early Forties, they were divorced. He went off to the navy during the war.

"Somewhere during those years Ellen met John B. Kelly, who, I guess at that point, was the defeated Democratic candidate for mayor; a man of great charm. It was always known to us who were her friends, that she and John B. Kelly were very, very fond of one another. When I used to visit her son I was still in school. And before I went off to the service myself, invariably Jack Kelly would be at Mrs. Frazer's home every afternoon."

Francis paused to gather his thoughts.

"From another person, I've been told that Jack wanted very much to marry Ellen Frazer but Mrs. John B. Kelly forbade it. Mrs. Frazer was a marvelous, charming woman, very vivacious, lively, and amusing. She was a pretty woman, I think—I'm talking now from the eyes of a sixteen-year-old. And I think that she, and the kind of man I imagine Jack Kelly would be, fitted well together because they were both very dynamic.

"I remember he always drove up in a shiny black limousine, which impressed me enormously. Because, if you remember during the war, we had gas-rationing cards, and he never seemed to lack for gas. Ellen, subsequently, when they could not get married, left Philadelphia and moved to Palm Beach. There she married a delightful man by the name of Lucius Ordway, whose family owned a great deal of the Minnesota Milling and Mining Company, known today as Three M. She was very happy with him; that marriage lasted until he died about five or six years ago.

"Ellen died recently in Florida. She was a lovely person, a child of the Twenties. I think it common knowledge that if he'd been able to get a divorce, she and Jack certainly would have gotten married."

Again I ran into Dom Legado, the *Bulletin* photographer; he had another story about Ma Kelly and her familial protectiveness.

"I was covering a match race on the Schuylkill between Kell and an Australian. I guess this was when I was starting in the business and we were all young. Grace, too; she was there. The race was nip and tuck, but the Australian just about beat Kell. At the finish line Kell was so exhausted that he fell back and when he did, went overboard.

"Naturally, we kept on taking pictures. Below the finish line was a raft. I jumped down on it to get closer. A Park Guard motorboat moved in to do the rescuing. And although Kell is a great swimmer, when you're exhausted like he was, what could he do?

"They got Kell, but he was all excited when they brought him to the raft, even though everything was fine. I turned around and right above me was Mrs. Kelly and the girls; tears were being shed."

It was then that Ma approached Dom.

" 'You're a newspaper photographer, aren't you?' Mrs. Kelly asked. When I said I was she said she'd rather I didn't use the picture and she'd be grateful. I said I understood her feelings that she didn't want people to think she, Grace, and the other girls were crying because Kelly lost.

" 'I'd appreciate it, Mr. Legado,' Mrs. Kelly said."

I asked Dom what he did with the picture of Ma Kelly and her daughters weeping as Kell was pulled onto the raft.

Dom shrugged his shoulders and raised his eyebrows at the absurdity of my question. "We used it, of course."

Charles Kelly, Jr., has a few words to add about Ma Kelly. "My Aunt Margaret," he said, "was a beautiful woman, one of the most beautiful I ever saw. In Grace's picture, *The Country Girl,* which she did with Bing Crosby, well, when the son dies it has a traumatic effect. She's leaving the studio and has the boy with her. Bing whistles at her; she turns back and looks at him. And I was looking at my Aunt Margaret. I saw her in that flashing scene.

"Aunt Margaret was a very strong person. Her children call her 'My Prussian General Mother.' "

I asked Charles if he felt that Ma was correct in stopping Kell from accepting the Democratic nomination for mayor.

"Oh, I don't think she had the right to interfere," Charles commented. "But then that's typical. Of course the thing she was concerned about—I've never discussed it with her but I *know* what it was. She didn't want Kell subjected to the kind of vilification that had occurred in the case of her husband. I remember when people would call on the telephone and say, 'Is it true that Cardinal Dougherty is going to have an office in City Hall if John B. Kelly is elected mayor?'

"They tell one story to the Protestants and another to the Catholics. 'Is it true that Mr. Kelly sends his children to Protestant schools to be educated?' And my Aunt Margaret didn't want her son to be a target for that kind of thing. And then, the second thing that she was much concerned about was that his playboy career would come to light."

21

"SHE LOOKED LIKE SHE HAD WHAT A REGULAR WOMAN HAS"

MA KELLY STRODE BOLDLY INTO THE SPOTLIGHT EARLY IN February, 1975.

"If Jack Kelly never becomes mayor he will probably have his mother to blame," wrote Ralph Frattura in the *Bulletin* February 2 of that year.

"Kelly—socialite, bon vivant, City Councilman—wanted to be mayor. He wanted the Democratic Policy Committee's endorsement Friday.

"And he might have gotten it.

"But his mother stood in the way.

"She made two telephone calls to at least two influential party members late last week asking that her son not receive the endorsement.

"She explained that politics is disruptive of family life.

"Her husband, the late John B. Kelly, Sr., the original 'Kelly for Brickwork' magnate, was a politician. He was a Philadelphia Democratic Chairman and, in 1935, ran for mayor.

"Mrs. Kelly, now in her seventies, remembers the problems, the phone calls at all hours, the meetings . . ."

It had been forty years since her husband lost the mayoralty after one of the city's dirtiest in Philadelphia's long history of dirty campaigns, and Ma never forgot.

"The Kellys," said Jack when the votes were in, "can take it." Ma neither could nor wanted to ever again.

Harlow.

"Grandma Kelly humiliated my father," said Kell's daughter Annie. "She did it! You know that little old lady! She called Pete Camiel; she must have had something over his head."

Anne opened the palms of her hands expressively as though she was unable to deny her admiration for the old lady.

"She's literally an amazing person. I hope she recovers."

Jules Lavin, Ma's escort these past half-dozen years and upon occasion a Palace guest, upholds Ma's decision to intervene.

"Margaret's story to me," said Jules, "is a mother's story. Number one, politics is a dirty business. Kell, being separated from his wife and family, is a target for a man like Rizzo, or it would seem to any opponent. In fact, Margaret had it on good advice that one of the posters being prepared, should Kell be selected as the primary candidate, reads, 'Will the First Lady Be Harlow?' "

And Mrs. Kelly did not want to expose her family, particularly Grace, to this.

Jules' reference to "Harlow" calls for an explanation to those unfamiliar with Philadelphia's life-after-dark. For the Quaker City's Beautiful People I offer a light refresher course. My personal feelings are that Kell's association with Harlow, an absolutely breathtaking transsexual, was the final prick that spurred Ma to action.

My direct knowledge of Rachel Harlow is admittedly slight. I met her a few times at parties given by friends but I get sleepy about 10 P.M., which is just about the time Rachel and other guests are only arriving. I'm afraid that, despite Miss Harlow's magnificent physique, her alluring décolletage and her long blond hair, I couldn't quite make up my mind. I think it was her rich contralto voice, speaking the patois of Philadelphia's Ninth Street fruit merchants, that confused me.

Since force of circumstance, or whatever it was, caused Harlow's (the nightclub) to close, I will not be able to see the lady in action. Consequently I must rely on the opinions expressed by my friend, Sandy Grady. In quoting Mr. Grady (who falls asleep as early as I do) I am by no means implying that this distinguished former sports writer turned political sage is either a member of our city's jet set or a nightclub habitué.

"The orange ceiling lights barely cut through the smoke," wrote Sandy in the *Bulletin* of October, 1972. "In their hot mists, the bodies twist and writhe as if on an invisible griddle. And the music—the Rolling Stones blasting their 'Symphony for the Devil' —crashes into your ears at one hundred and ten decibels. That's the level of a pneumatic jackhammer or an artillery barrage. Old Gustave Doré must have pictured hell like this when he did those lithographs of The Inferno.

"But it's only Harlow's on a Saturday night, and to the four hundred people pulsating in this three-story former warehouse, it's heaven—if heaven had a tape deck and a four-dollar cover charge.

"And there's no doubt who's the High Priestess of the orgiastic, bell-bottom cult. Harlow: A head like Queen Nefertiti, ashen mane tossing in the lights, long body in the blue pants suit, half-mannequin and half-deer. Everyone watches when Harlow dances. It's like Billie Jean King on the center court of Wimbledon. Some nights you could hold a City Council meeting in the joint. Jack Kelly and Tom Foglietta are regulars . . ."

The son of poor South Philadelphia parents, Richard Finocchio at twenty-five submitted to a transsexual operation in a New York hospital on June 8, 1972. In eight days he ("she," I suppose now) emerged as a magnificent female who, as Kell and other well-informed sources claim, is a complete woman.

Stanley Green, restaurateur, man-about-town, husband of Agnes, a dazzling redhead (his fifth wife but as far as I know, the only lady with that color hair) is one of these well-informed sources.

"I did a fashion show with Harlow," Stanley said. "It was for charity and Harlow was one of the models who helped out. You know, when models get together, because they're in a little room, nobody even looks at each other. Rachel said, 'Help me on with my pantyhose.' So I did."

Unabashedly Stanley admits that he stole a peek.

"Harlow looked like she had what a regular woman has."

Richard Finocchio became Rachel Harlow legally and within two years, before fading into sudden obscurity, took the jet set by storm. She was seen everywhere, in her own popular club, as a performer in other night spots, much-sought-after guest at society parties, and on the arms of well-known bon vivants, one of whom was Kell.

As for Kell's relationship with Harlow, Stanley puts it on the platonic side.

"Any time Kell was with Harlow, Edelstein [another Kell associate], Agnes, and I were present. There were always four or five people around. My honest-to-God opinion was that Kell's ego, maybe, you know, he likes publicity and things like that. It was a fun thing. Actually, nothing ever happened. And Kell didn't realize the adverse publicity he would get."

Local gossip columnists were quick to seize on "L'Affaire Kelly-Harlow" and John B. Kelly, Jr., may have gotten more publicity than even he wanted. It was one of these columns that reportedly reached Ma Kelly's eyes. As Stanley phrased it, "This broke the straw."

"Rizzo headquarters," reported *Daily News* columnist Larry Fields, "say they are going to put up a sign at Fifteenth and Chestnut Streets, 'Rachel Harlow for our First Lady.'"

This, in the opinion of another close Kell friend, another man-about-town, Harry Jay Katz, is "when the shit hit the fan."

Kell, the pawn, still speaks to his mother or at least greets her politely when they meet. He's resigned to the fact that John B. Kelly, Jr., is not likely to be mayor of Philadelphia in the foreseeable future. Kathy McKenna, who shared Councilman Kell's dreams with him, is bitter. Mrs. McKenna blames it all on Ma.

"When the Democratic Policy Committee convened to select its candidate for mayor," Kathy said, "Jack agreed to appear. I was beside myself. I was absolutely jubilant. I managed to tell everybody on Cherry Street [the Kelly for Brickwork Company office]. I decided that Jack Kelly was going to be mayor. It was high time. I don't think that I can be without emotional bias. I'm very fond of Kell; he has never been anything but good to me.

"I think what interested Kell so much was that an aura of invincibility had been built up around the incumbent, Mayor Rizzo; that 'you can't beat Frank Rizzo!'"

Kathy obviously didn't believe Rizzo was unconquerable, and neither did Councilman Kelly.

Mrs. McKenna continued. "Well, Kell rises to a challenge of this nature; he is a natural competitor. For him, that's what it's all about. It's what Kelly knows best, the art of competition. He *wanted* to run; he could bring back the days of Clark and Dilworth and he had support from many grass-roots Democrats, old-time Democrats who still believe the election of 1935 was stolen from Pop Kelly. He was going to make up for something he really felt belonged to the Kellys for a long time.

"When he delivered the speech that night, which Councilman Izzie Bellis and I wrote, and Kell edited, he was almost Aristotelian. He was brilliant, powerful, strong. He was positive, he was prepared. I certainly remember the closing remark which I wrote and which brought them to their feet. And that was something to see!"

Kathy shook her head as she recalled the tag lines of Councilman Kelly's dramatic appeal.

" 'If you know the Kelly family, you know that we're winners and always have been. I say this to you, and I can win! I will win! I want to win! And I can hardly wait.' "

Kathy smiled sadly as she recalled the scene.

"And they *leaped* to their feet; they burst into applause. Kell stood there and laughed; just threw his head back and laughed. He received many, many queries and he answered all of them with great ease. He *should* have had that nomination.

"The following Friday the Committee's announcement was made. Kell had had the nomination wrapped up all week but on Friday morning he had not. That was when Ma Kelly picked up the telephone and called Councilman Schwartz [George X. Schwartz, President of City Council] and State Senator Camiel [Peter J. Camiel, then Chairman of the Democratic Committee]. I certainly don't know the details, but I do know, and I was told, a little of that which, to me, is hair-raising.

"It went something along the lines of 'If you endorse my son as the Democratic party's candidate for mayor of this city I will go on television and I will tell the city that it should not have my son for mayor and I will tell the city why. And I have better access to that than do you. And I will financially support his opponent!'

"Obviously the party decided that it wasn't going to run a family feud. This was a political campaign and they didn't need any subdivisions. Councilman Schwartz's words were, to someone quite close to me, 'Ma Kelly surfaced.' "

Kathy trembled with anger.

"I'll say she surfaced! She destroyed her son, she destroyed this forty-eight-year-old man; she treated him like an erring little boy. He defied her once and she was going to fix him and *she did*!

"Ma did it single-handedly with no help from anybody. If she didn't think he should have run, she had a right to say that but I think she had the duty to keep it in the family. I don't believe any parent has the right to destroy a child as she did publicly so that forever he would be known as a forty-eight-year-old mamma's boy.

"Kell was totally devastated. When the news came he disappeared; no one knew where he was. Eventually, he called me from his apartment. He'd gone home to get himself together because he was thoroughly embarrassed—humiliated that his mother would do this to him. His voice sounded like ashes, there's no other simile."

Kathy is of the opinion that a Higher Power entered the scene although I don't think she was prepared to say exactly Who.

"Shortly after that, Ma Kelly had her first stroke. It may be that all has worked out for the best."

It's not easy to understand why anyone would want to be mayor of Philadelphia. If ever there was a dead-end, thankless job, this is it. However, as the French say, *"Chacun à son goût"* or as we Americans phrase it less elegantly, "That's what the old lady said when she kissed the pig."

22

"THE BIG THING WAS LISTENING TO THE LONE RANGER"

I DO NOT WANT TO CREATE THE IMPRESSION THAT THE JOHN B. Kelly, Sr., home was a dour one and that their four children were raised in an atmosphere of hatred, fear, and bickering. Such was not the case. There are clear indications that husband and wife were incompatible; that "The Prussian General," as Kell calls his mother, ruled the family with a heavy hand. It's also a fact that John B.'s outside activities—politics, business, sports, women—kept him away more than most fathers.

But there also was great warmth in the household. John B. and his wife loved their children deeply and this affection was returned. Peggy, Grace, Kell, and Lizanne have happy memories of growing up in their big, comfortable Henry Avenue place. Jack was wealthy; there was always a Packard or a Cadillac and a small car in the garage; there was "Fordie," the black chauffeur-houseman, who was almost a member of the family, and there were other servants besides. There were private schools, there were frequent pleasure trips, there were wonderful summers at the Kelly vacation home in Ocean City.

There were visits from famous Uncle Walter and Uncle George and the excitement of watching the Virginia Judge perform at Keith's or the Earle in downtown Philadelphia and the nearby Orpheum in Germantown, or sitting in the orchestra at Kelly play openings in New York.

There would be important dinner guests like Governor Earle

and United States Senator Guffey, and telephone calls from FDR in the White House. There'd be a flow of newspaper reporters coming up to The Falls for interviews with Olympic star Pop Kelly, and magazine writers doing pieces on him. It was a wonderful house to grow up in. Ma was beautiful, Pa, devastatingly handsome. What a thrill it was to sit in the back of their long, black open Packard and ride along Chestnut Street with pedestrians constantly shouting, "Hi, Jack," to their father, the most popular man in Philadelphia.

People were proud to shake Jack's hand; he was a champion. One of his favorite pictures, a group composite, shows him in the company of what the caption labels, "The World's Greatest Athletes." The photograph, syndicated in the early 1920's, shows the faces of famed athletes whose names are familiar even to nonfans. Included are Jack Dempsey, Gertrude Ederle, Johnny Weissmuller, Paavo Nurmi, William T. Tilden II, Helen Wills, Walter Johnson, Bobby Jones, Willie Hoppe and, in the center-fold, John B. Kelly and his doubles partner, Paul V. Costello.

At almost every big sporting event in the city Jack and his family were guests of honor, had the best seats, and met the contestants. This was one of a champion's perquisites.

Then there was that *really* big night of October 12, 1940, when the four Kelly kids, ranging from fifteen-year-old Peggy down to nine-year-old Lizanne, sat in a box at Convention Hall. There they watched their father step to the microphone, raise his arm to silence the crowd, and say, "Ladies and gentlemen, the President of the United States."

The Cruice girls, Charles Kelly, Jr., and his sister, Mary, had a large share in the excitement that always permeated the John B. Kelly home.

"I had a terrific childhood," recalled Elaine Cruice. "We could walk to Uncle Jack's; it was only three blocks from our house. We were there all the time, playing tennis and everything. Our little house on Midvale Avenue didn't have any ground around it so we spent our time at Uncle Jack's. Most of our young romances were made right there.

"Uncle Jack had a doll's house so big you could stand up and walk around in it, built in back of the tennis court. Peggy and I were very close even though there was a four-year difference in our ages. She was a little devil."

Elaine chuckled.

"Peggy and I used to smoke cigarettes in the playhouse. Once Fordie caught us and were we scared! He said he was going to tell. He didn't but he frightened us to death and we were waiting for our mother to mention it.

"Fordie was the houseman; he did everything and he knew *how* to do everything. He kept the cars polished; he could serve, put on a big party, supervise bartenders and buffets, and keep the garden in beautiful condition. He was such a dear! A tiny, little fellow. And we loved him as youngsters. He was a big part in our growing up.

"Fordie was a servant but I think that originally he worked in Uncle Jack's contracting business. I forget the name of the other colored man who was Uncle Jack's houseman."

Elaine sighed.

"Fordie was a dear, he was a fixture. When Uncle Jack died, Peggy ran to Fordie and cried to him more than she would to her mother. Fordie must have died soon after Uncle Jack."

Kell, his sisters, and most of the Kelly cousins remembered Fordie as an important part of their childhood and adolescence. John B.'s affection for "Fordie" was expressed more concretely.

"Godfrey Ford," stated John B. in a codicil of his will, "has been with me for forty-five years, and has been a faithful and loyal servant. Therefore, I want him to be kept in employment as long as he behaves himself well, making due allowances for minor errors of the flesh, if being slightly on the Casanova side is an error. I want my survivors to feel an obligation regarding his comfort and employment. In addition, I give him one thousand dollars outright. I have already turned over to him the bonds I bought for him at Christmas each year."

Whatever the reason for later deviations from the norm, Lizanne is certain that during her growing-up period and that of the other children, feelings of peace and security blanketed the Kelly household.

"None of us had any major problems, psychological ones, or hangups, I mean," recalled Lizanne, who is as pretty as Grace and seems to be considerably more lively.

"I was the youngest, the brat sister, and Grace, as she's told me, resented me terribly when I was born. And I *was* a terrible brat to Grace. When she had boyfriends I'd come in and hang around. She'd say, 'Get out of here, Liz,' and then afterward she used to say, 'I'll get back at you when you start dating.' But, of course, by then she was too old for revenge."

Lizanne's education, like that of her brother and sisters, was in parochial schools.

"I started Raven Hill Academy when I was two years old," Liz said. "I was the Baby Jesus in the Crib at the Christmas plays. My sisters left in eighth grade but I graduated from Raven Hill. The nuns were strict but it was a marvelous school, small. There were only about fifty students from nursery to twelfth grade.

"I played a lot of sports there and later when I went to Penn, I played hockey and tennis and I was captain of the basketball team. I made All-College, All-American Hockey. I happened to be the first 'Pat on the Back' in *Sports Illustrated.* I think this was my senior year at Penn in 1955. My family advocates physical education—it's a must."

Lizanne, like Sister Grace and Uncles Walter and George, had her fling at theater.

"Another Kelly name is up on the theater billboards," wrote Jack Brady in the Sunday *Bulletin,* April 21, 1955. "This time it's that pretty, blond, wide-eyed Lizanne, the youngest of the John B. Kelly family. She is starring in 'The Moon is Blue,' a little-theater production of the Old Academy Players at their tiny theater in East Falls.

"This is the place where her famous sister began her theatrical career at the age of eleven, when she played a small role in a one-acter called 'Don't Feed the Animals.'

" 'I'm no Grace,' Lizanne laughed backstage. 'I have no ambitions to go on the professional stage. No, not even to go into the movies.' "

Kate Shea, like Mrs. Sitley, says that Peggy was John B.'s favorite.

"Kell came into the office one day to announce to his father that his first born was a girl.

" 'Don't feel bad, Kell,' Jack told him. 'My greatest joy in life is Peggy.' "

Kate, who is very fond of Kell, shook her head despairingly.

"Jack was telling this to his *son*."

The Kelly girls were popular; Charles Fish said that there were so many boyfriends calling at the Midvale Avenue house for Peggy, Grace, and later for Lizanne that John B. made no effort to identify his daughters' dates individually.

"He was an overwhelming man," said Fish, "but he'd call all of us 'Son'; he just couldn't remember our names."

Charles smiled when he recalled one of Jack's hobbies.

"The big thing in John B.'s life was listening to 'The Lone Ranger,' which went on between seven-thirty and eight every night. Everybody had to shut the hell up. I remember the sponsor was Silvercup Bread. I recall, quite vividly, when I came to pick up Grace and she was giggling.

"She motioned to me with her fingers on her lips to be quiet. 'Dad's in the closet under the stairway there,' she said. Silvercup Bread gave away some kind of device which glowed in the dark. 'You have to send a label and thirty cents to get it.'

" 'Well, Daddy's in there playing with it, flashing it off and on by himself.' "

Sports figures abounded at the Kelly dining table; athletes from the United States, Canada, and England were frequent visitors. For Margaret, Peggy, Lizanne, and Kell this must have been fascinating. For Grace, it must have been exquisitely boring.

Jack had an enormous fund of anecdotes that he told and retold well. One of his favorites he called "Dibble's Good-bye." Don Donaghey of the *Bulletin* related this in the January 24,

1960, issue of his newspaper, some six months before John B.'s death.

"In 1920, in the Schuylkill Navy People's Regatta, Kelly owed Canadian star Bob Dibble the whack of an oar. Dibble, a World War One hero, had beaten old Kelly, then age thirty, three times. He could not abide Dibble's dig in one of the defeats. Coming under the trolley bridge Bob hissed as he took the lead, 'Good-bye, John.'

"Being a Kelly, Jack was going to get Dibble someday. He was patient because he wanted to beat a man who was up to full war strength. Lieutenant Dibble had been hurt in France. On July 5, in the championship single at a mile and a quarter, it was Kelly over Dibble at last—a matter of seconds.

"When Dibble pulled over to shake the hand of Kelly and make amends for the 'Good-bye, John' crack, he went weak and pale and fell into the stream. Kelly went after him. It was no easy matter; Jack bumped his belly against the oar rig and was in almost as bad shape as Dibble when the Park Guard rescue mission reached him.

"When Jack said Dibble looked 'terrible' when he fell out of the boat, he left himself wide open to the question—how did you look? Said Kelly, 'Terrible.'

"Kelly gave the shell in which he won the race to the Franklin Institute, where it is on display. It had been paid for by Brother Walter Kelly, the Virginia Judge.

"At the time," concluded Donaghey, "Kelly, now a millionaire, said, 'I was low on funds and high on hope.'"

23

"IF IT HADN'T BEEN
FOR MR. KELLY . . ."

WHILE THERE WERE MANY WHO DENOUNCED JOHN B. KELLY'S politics, his endorsement of Senator Joe McCarthy, and his own belief that Communists were hiding under millions of American beds, I don't know of anybody who ever questioned Jack's good sportsmanship whether Kelly was a participant or a promoter.

Although Jack himself didn't ride, he loved horses and horse racing. One of his great joys was the Atlantic City Race Course he founded and of which he was President. He was a moderate bettor and when the season at the A.C. track was on, he could be seen in his box almost daily with family and friends.

John Webster, who covered horse racing for the Philadelphia *Inquirer*, wrote of one incident that cost Kelly's track a considerable amount of money and at the same time displayed the expected John B. Kelly spirit of fair play.

"Kelly," said Webster, "loved to stand erect and jaunty in his box after a race and, holding up his tickets, chuckle, 'I had that one.' On bad days, with all losers, he'd dismiss it with a rueful, Celtic grin. Once a friend marked him as a good loser.

" 'But I don't want to be a good loser,' snorted Jack Kelly. 'Man, I want to be a good winner!'

"There was that day in 1948 when the meeting came to a close. A big gray horse called Even Break was backed down to six to five in spite of his record of bad post manners.

"Sure enough when the gate's doors flew open, Even Break,

Ma Kelly and four of her and John B.'s children in 1935—left to right: Grace, Kell, Peggy, and Lizanne.

tight in his stall, planted his feet firmly and chose not to run. Off went the field winging, and a quick fellow called Vanslam, freed of favorite's contention, won at something like four to one."

Johnny Webster said that after a review, the stewards ruled the race official; that Even Break's stall door had opened properly, and that there'd be no refunds from wagering pools.

"But the crowd was noisy and growing ugly," Johnny continued. "Jack Kelly explained the ruling to the fans . . . the response came in catcalls, imprecations . . . and abusive personal cracks, many of them directed at him.

"That was too much for Jack Kelly, a sportsman first, last, and all the way around the track. Conferring with his directors, he found them solidly behind him. He decided the racing association would refund all wagers on Even Break, though it was contrary to racing rules.

"Said Jack Kelly: 'I've always conducted myself as a sportsman and I can't stand to have anybody say that I'm not. If they think they lost their money unfairly, they get it back.' That cost the track a fast $72,000."

For this piece of good reporting, I forgive Webster his tag pun. "Jack Kelly was a gentleman and a sculler."

Philadelphians had many good and probably more important reasons to respect Jack Kelly and be grateful to him as well. For one of these, we return to Joe Sharfsin, former City Comptroller and short-time mayor. The incident that Joe related to me occurred when the Republican party was in power locally and the Democratic, nationally.

The year was 1939, the Great Depression wasn't over, and the city was in even worse shape than it usually is, or at least no different. John B. was still smarting over his 1935 defeat for the mayoralty, while working with the National Democratic Committee to reelect FDR and smash the Quaker City's Republican regime if he could. The time seemed right; Philadelphia was forty-one million dollars in debt, an election was coming up so taxes couldn't be raised, and the city was issuing scrip instead of cash to jobholders.

"I went down to Washington to see if I could raise some dough, fifty million dollars' worth. I talked to Jesse Jones, head of the Reconstruction Finance Corporation and the man to approach," Joe said. "When I came home that evening I got a call from Jack Kelly, who told me he'd heard I was in D.C. that day. Then I realized I'd goofed. Jack was Chairman of the Democratic City Committee and I should have consulted him first but I didn't.

"Kelly had every right to be sore and could have killed chances for that fifty-million dollar loan. He didn't. Politically it would have been better for him to let the city go broke. But he was too decent for that so he didn't block it. He did insist, however, that a million bucks go to clean up the Schuylkill. I don't have to tell you it needed a cleanup."

(Governor Duff later labeled the river's sticky fluid, "shilt," and spent another thirty-five million trying, in vain, to continue where Jack Kelly left off.)

Kelly had developed a strong personal following and, had he

*Democratic City Committee Chairman
John B. Kelly and Mrs. Kelly.*

felt the game was worth bucking Ma, he might have made a political comeback. Many, even including Republicans who had been running Philadelphia for three-quarters of a century, believed John B. should be given another chance. One such supporter was a member of a Falls Lutheran church.

"I can't recall his first name," said Charles Kelly, Jr., "but his last one was Borland and he was The Falls' shoemaker. One Sunday his pastor was tearing Jack apart. Mr. Borland arose from his pew and publicly denounced the minister, then walked out of the church in protest."

Taylor Grant, a radio and TV commentator whose program, "Something To Say," was blasted from the air because it offended members of the Establishment, recalled his friend and Falls neighbor, John B. Kelly.

"After my return to Philadelphia I was doing all the news of Channel Three, which is NBC, with my own crew. So they asked me to handle the world's premiere of *To Catch a Thief*, starring

Grace, at some Chestnut Street theater. It was a big deal with floodlights and everything else for promotion—the works.

"It was an exclusive and I was asked to talk only to Grace. I was all set. Grace walked up, said, 'Hello, Taylor,' and I started to ask her questions. She said, 'So sorry,' but her contract prohibited her from doing interviews of this sort."

Taylor Grant was furious; he'd agreed quite reluctantly to do the favor for Columbia Pictures and now they were double-crossing him.

"When I told Columbia what Grace had said to me they weren't going to reverse her. But I thought to myself that her father must be with her so I sent someone in to talk to him and let him know what they did to me and what Grace said."

Taylor laughed.

"A few minutes later Grace came out all by herself and we had a delightful, long conversation on tape. And then I sent the tape to the lab for processing, a rush job because I had to have it back for the eleven o'clock news. They protested but got it to me on time and I started to roll it."

Grant shook his head.

"After all this, *no sound at all.* So you know what I did? While the silent film ran behind me, I'm bowing and chattering. And that's what will always come to my mind when I think of Grace."

Taylor smiled.

"That's not quite true. I do think of something else, another interview that Jack set up for me with Grace. Rainier was there, too. This was Grace's first visit back to The Falls after she married Rainier. She's pregnant and everybody knows it. It's hard news, the fact that she's pregnant and with all the publicity. It was also the beginning of the rock-and-roll era and you'll see that's not a non sequitur.

"During the course of our interview I mentioned her pregnancy and I asked her if she'd decided yet on a name for the child. She said no and as she did I saw her cast a slightly worried look at the Prince. Just enough to let me know I hadn't been

John B. Kelly—the famous oarsman in 1931, doing his daily one hundred strokes on the rowing machine.

letting him in on enough of this interview. Also that there was something here that was distressing or disturbing her, or maybe only amusing her.

"So I turned to Rainier and asked him. He just couldn't wait to answer. He laughed and said, 'We've only decided what *not* to name it.' Naturally I played along and said, 'What's that?' He chuckled. 'I will never name the child Elvis.' "

Taylor went on. "I'll tell you this, Jack Kelly was a happy man. And he was as handsome as they come. There wasn't too much he and I could talk about, yet we had a fairly enjoyable association. We didn't discuss sports and, as for politics . . . well . . . But I liked his intensity about a lot of things and we both had the competitive spirit."

Jack Kelly was vitally concerned with the health of his fellow citizens. He wrote a piece titled "Are We Becoming a Nation of Weaklings," which appeared in the March 1956 issue of *Ameri-*

can Magazine, the same publication that some thirty years before published a story about John B.'s mother.

Jack's article, later reprinted in *The Reader's Digest*, complained that "American youngsters today are weaker and flabbier than those in many other countries, and they are growing softer every year. Their physical fitness—or lack of it—constitutes one of our gravest problems. If parents and teachers fail to wake up to the alarming trend, we shall become a nation of weaklings . . ."

I should have liked to have heard Brother George's comment if he read John B.'s literary effort. It's interesting to observe that George, who positively loathed all forms of physical effort, was three years older than Jack and outlasted him by another seventeen.

There wasn't any question about John B.'s interest in the personal welfare of youth. Freddie Meyer, a Pulitzer Prize-winning *Bulletin* photographer, told me this.

"Mr. Kelly [Freddie never referred to John B. by any other title] had a total interest in young people. Everything they did or wanted to do meant something to him. He wasn't stuffy and kids could approach him. And he had a dignity about him. Of course, Mr. Kelly's main interest was in sports, sculling in particular. But did I ever tell you how he was responsible for keeping the Davis Cup in America?"

I looked puzzled; Freddie grinned.

"No, Mr. Kelly didn't play tennis as far as I know. Australia had the Davis Cup; they defended it and the U.S. won it at Germantown Cricket Club, which wasn't far from Mr. Kelly's home in East Falls. I was covering the story of the Cup's return.

"Well, we're ready to roll and there's no Cup. We waited and waited on the veranda of the old club, which was so famous for tennis because Bill Tilden had been a member. We were ready to quit when suddenly this express truck shows up and the driver says, 'I've a package to deliver. Who's going to pay?'

"Well, there was nobody around with any dough, just a bunch of reporters and photographers. The package was crated and when none of us was able to pay the charges, the REA guy says, 'Okay, I'll have to take it back,' when Mr. Kelly walks up."

Jack, recalled Freddie, asked what was going on and someone told him.

"Mr. Kelly ran to the truck, paid the charges, and opened the package. It was the Davis Cup!"

Freddie laughed.

"I guess not many people know it, but in a manner of speaking, if it hadn't been for Mr. Kelly, America would have lost the Davis Cup."

Dennis, our bartender, gave us a refill of Yuengling's lager and Freddie continued.

"There isn't a reporter or photographer, including me, who hasn't something good to say about Mr. Kelly. He's done so many of us favors and it just wasn't to get his name in the paper, I assure you. Let me tell you one when I was just breaking into the business, young and eager, and I was sent out to cover a thirty-six-mile cross-country in Fairmount Park.

"Mr. Kelly was the starter and he also was judge at the finish line. I wanted to get something different from the usual presentation, you know, with the winner standing there getting his award. So I said to Mr. Kelly, 'Would you do me a favor?' He says, 'Sure, kid, what is it?' So I asked him if he'd come to the twenty-four-mile post where the runners would be rounding Memorial Hall.

"He looked at me and said, 'What do you want me to do there?' I said, 'Well, it would be a lot better picture if you'd run alongside of the leader and tell him what his time was.' Mr. Kelly grinned and said, 'Okay, kid.' Then up we went to Memorial Hall and when the first man came round, Mr. Kelly, with his peaked cap and wide lapeled jacket, ran right along with the guy until I got my pictures. That's the kind of man *he* was."

Charles Kelly, Jr., had another story involving Grace, her father, and Rainier.

"One day shortly after Grace and Rainier had been in Philadelphia I ran into my Uncle Jack. He was fuming.

" 'You've eaten at the Barclay, haven't you?'

"I said, 'Yes, when I can afford it, which isn't often.'

" 'Damned right it's expensive! I just got a bill today from them. Ninety-five bucks! Lunch for four people.' "

Charles reminded me that this was nearly twenty years ago when lunch in excellent Philadelphia restaurants could be had for no more than five or six dollars. "And if you tossed in a few bottles of vintage wine it might run the tab to double that. Obviously my Uncle Jack wasn't a party to that lunch so I asked him who was."

" 'Jeanne and Charles took Grace and Rainier there,' my Uncle Jack said. 'My son-in-law must have ordered every damned expensive dish on the menu and *he* had no money, so what they did was sign my name to the check.' "

Charles, Jr., explained that after all, Rainier was Jack Kelly's son-in-law.

" 'But what in God's name could four people have eaten for lunch that cost ninety-five dollars,' my Uncle Jack asked me and I said, 'Well, maybe Rainier had his sandwich toasted.'

"My Uncle Jack paid the bill, of course. But if there was anything in the world he loathed, it was pretentiousness. He hated Monaco, where you'd have servants all over you. He'd say to them, 'Go away! I'll call you when I need you.' Whereas, my Uncle George adored the Palace and the life that went with it. But Uncle Jack couldn't bear the protocol in Monaco."

Syndicated columnist Earl Wilson, who covered the Kelly-Grimaldi event, spoke of John B.'s uneasy presence at Monaco.

"Spoofing the idea that Grace is a prisoner in the Palace, her father joined gin rummy pal, Ike B. Levy, a Philadelphia TV tycoon, for a session and announced, 'I got out on a twelve-hour pass but I want to be back on time so I won't get jugged for going AWOL . . .'

" 'What a laundry service you get at the Palace!' he exclaimed. 'I took out a clean shirt and decided not to wear it. I put it down somewhere and when I looked for it again, it had been sent to the Palace laundry and came back with the sleeves pleated.' Taking off his coat, he exhibited the royal pleats and told his chums, 'I expect more respect from you commoners.' "

Mostly everyone who knew Jack Kelly says he was a generous man. There are some who differ. One dissenter is Phil Klein, who used to be a newspaper reporter but decided that was no way to get rich. So he went into the advertising business and made a million or so before he was forty years old. He does live well, no doubt, but gives all the rest to charity. Phil and I were discussing John B. Kelly. The subject of Kell came up first.

"Kell," said Phil, "is a sweet, wonderful fellow, no doubt about that. Why he ever decided to separate from his wife I don't understand. He's known as a playboy but he's not really one. You see him at every dinner and he *buys* his tickets for all events. He has far more charity in him than John B., who liked freebees. Kell sends in his checks for one hundred and fifty dollars or one hundred dollars, and then he goes! The old man didn't."

Phil paused.

"I'll say this, though, about Big Jack, which is what I called him. He never let a friend down. He stuck to them right to the end."

For the best example of John B. Kelly's loyalty I return to Kate Shea. Kate, you may remember, worked for Jack and currently is in the employ of Kell. Miss Shea, who'd broken several ribs and a leg in a fall, was my captive at Pennsylvania Hospital, where she was in traction. Kate and I had been talking about John B.'s dedication to his friends, one of whom, Dr. Lehman, called upon Kelly to make what most felt was very close to the supreme sacrifice.

One of Philadelphia's most famous trials in recent years was that of Dr. James A. Lehman and his wife, Adelaide. Both, residents of Chestnut Hill, were indicted and tried on charges of defrauding the U.S. government of nearly three hundred thousand dollars in income taxes for the years 1953 through 1957. Dr. Lehman, one of the city's most prominent surgeons, was on the staff of five Philadelphia hospitals and a consultant to two others. He'd been John B.'s friend for many years, and when

196 / THOSE PHILADELPHIA KELLYS

Grace was stricken with appendicitis in 1959 Dr. Lehman flew to Monaco to perform an emergency operation on Her Serene Highness.

At the Lehman's trial before U.S. Judge Harold K. Wood in June of 1960, defense counsel assembled a long parade of character witnesses to testify in his clients' behalf. One of those marchers was John B.

"It was shortly after Mr. Kelly's first operation," Kate recalled. "Jim Lehman was on trial and they needed character witnesses to testify. And so Mr. Kelly got out of his sickbed. I don't think he realized at this point he was close to death but he did know he was a *very, very* sick man."

A nurse accompanied Kelly from Women's Medical College Hospital to the courtroom, where he was barely able to climb to the witness box. Shortly after the trial, which resulted in a hung jury (and the Lehmans' subsequent acquittal in a new trial), I sat next to the U.S. prosecuting attorney, Walter E. Alessandroni on the train from Philadelphia to Harrisburg. We talked about the case, and Walter, who knew John B. well, mentioned Kelly's appearance on the stand.

"My God! What guts it took for him to come to court that morning," Walter said. "He looked absolutely awful, bent over like an old man. And when you think how rugged and handsome he was. He *must* have known he was dying, but that wasn't going to stop him from testifying for an old friend. He managed to put on the old Jack Kelly smile and even waved his hand at me when the nurse led him out."

John B. didn't return to the hospital directly.

"He stopped in to Cherry Street to take a look at a new office we had there in the back," said Kate. "He hadn't seen it before. This was the last time. I went out to the hospital before that first operation. His sister Grace had had a colostomy and she had died from it. Mr. Kelly had a premonition and said to me, 'All I can think of is, do I have it, too?' So then I went out to see him after surgery.

" 'When I came out of the anesthetic and they said, "No bag," I felt I had it licked,' Mr. Kelly told me."

But John B. didn't have it licked. There was a second exploratory, and this time Dr. Lehman closed up his patient without operating.

"I'd go to the hospital every day," Kate said. The second time I went there the nurse said, 'He's going to tell you he's not going to make it.' But I went in and what was I going to tell him? He said, 'Kate, you know, Margaret came in with Dr. Lehman and told me I have about four weeks. What do you think of that?'

"I said, 'Mr. Kelly, that's in the hands of God.' He smiled and told me, 'Yes. But I'll tell you what, Kate, if I go up or down, I'll put in a good word for you.' "

After a few more days at the hospital, they brought Jack Kelly back home to die.

"I kept going to see him on Henry Avenue," Kate recalled. "This particular day I had a cold and couldn't stop coughing. 'Do you have a cold, Kate?' he asked, and when I said, 'Yes, Mr. Kelly,' he smiled. 'I can't afford to get sick, you know, so you'd better leave.'

"Well, I closed the door and never saw him again. Mrs. Kelly was sitting at her desk outside the room and I told her I'd been chased out. She asked why and I told her that it was because I coughed and he didn't want to get sick. The next day Mr. Kelly died."

That was June 20, 1960, only ten days after John B. Kelly stepped down from the Federal Court witness box where he'd made his last public appearance. Obituaries were glowing; city flags were flown at half-mast. For all of us who'd known Jack Kelly it was as though we'd lost a close friend and a good neighbor to call on if you ever needed help. And you knew he wouldn't turn you down.

I recollected only vaguely Taylor Grant's comments about Kelly's death on Grant's six o'clock newscast. But I did remember it had moved me deeply. So I called Grant and asked if he'd dig up his copy for the evening of June 20. He did, and this is it in part:

"From the age of ten, right on through the painful adolescent years, we lived within short walking distance of that nice, big, red brick house on Henry Avenue. Kelly bricks, of course. We all knew that the head of the household there was the man making news all the time, gaining fame in such a variety of ways.

"Recently, more than a quarter of a century later, a series of circumstances brought me back to live in the old neighborhood and I find myself once again, of a summer evening, passing the familiar brick home.

"I recalled the night when John B. and I shared the speaker's platform; how nervous I was and how he put me at ease by deliberately feigning a nervousness of his own. Old pro that he was, he fooled nobody, not even me. Just made me feel better, that's all.

"I was once hospitalized suddenly and placed in the hands of some doctors completely unknown to me. The first letter I received there—offering me not just the good old speedy recovery wishes, but a confidence-inspiring endorsement of the doctors— was signed John B. Kelly. How could John B. Kelly have known that the best medicine indicated at that moment would be the words he wrote to bolster my faith in those strangers, those doctors?

"These thoughts were very much with me today, as I drove down the East River Drive. A sports fan once said that this particular stretch of the Schuylkill ought to be called 'Kelly's River.' At that moment I noticed the water, which had been clear and beautiful yesterday, was now muddy and disturbed. I hadn't seen it as it was now for a couple of weeks. Not since the day I'd heard the rumor that the man whose colorful life had been so long linked with this scenic nicety was much more ill than most folks thought.

"I turned on the radio in my car. A voice was reporting the death of John B. Kelly. To many Philadelphians the river may never seem the same again."

24

"JUST SHED
A RESPECTFUL TEAR"

"FOR YEARS I HAVE BEEN READING LAST WILLS AND TESTAMENTS, and I have never been able to clearly understand any of them at one reading," admitted John B. Kelly in the preamble to *his* last will and testament.

"Therefore, I will attempt to write my own with the hope that it will be understandable and legal. Kids will be called 'kids' (and not 'issue') and it will not be cluttered up with 'parties of the first part,' 'per stirpes,' 'perpetuities,' 'quasi judicial,' 'to wit,' and a lot of other terms that I am sure are only used to confuse those for whose benefit it is written.

"This is my Last Will and Testament and I believe I am of sound mind. (Some lawyers will question this when they read my Will; however, I have my opinion of some of them so that makes it even . . .)"

This was the airy touch Kelly set in the twelve-page document he wrote on April 14, shortly after his first operation. It was filed for probate June 28, less than a week after a solemn high requiem Mass was celebrated at St. Bridget's, burial following in Holy Sepulchre Cemetery. There was no public viewing.

Kelly grew more serious in disposing of personal items, books, jewelry, automobiles, the Kelly homes in The Falls and Ocean City, household goods, and his insurance, all of which he left to his widow.

"I would like my wife, Margaret, to give my son, John Brendan Kelly, to be known hereinafter by his rowing title of 'Kell,' all my personal belongings, such as trophies, rings, jewelry, watches, clothing, and athletic equipment, except the ties, shirts, sweaters, and socks, as it seems unnecessary to give him something of which he has already taken possession," the Will continued.

In more formal terms Kelly set up a trust for his wife that was one-third of the residue of the entire estate. The balance was left in equal shares to Kell, Baba (Peggy), Grace, and Liz.

John B. had a few words for the husbands, past, present, or future, of daughters Baba, Grace, and Liz.

"In the case of my daughters' husbands, they do not share and if any of my daughters die, her share goes to her children, or if there are no children, then that share goes back into my own children's fund. I don't want to give the impression that I am against sons-in-law—if they are the right type, they will provide for themselves and their families and what I am able to give my daughters will help pay the dress shop bills which, if they continue as they have started out, under the able tutelage of their mother, will be quite considerable."

There were directions for retaining or disposing of stock in the Kelly brickworks companies in Philadelphia and New York upon the discretion of his executors and trustees.

Kelly had this to say about the conduct of his beneficiaries:

"I can think of nothing more ghastly than heirs sitting around listening to some representative reading the Will. They always remind me of buzzards and vultures awaiting the last breath of the stricken. Therefore, I will try to spare you that ordeal and let you read the Will before I go to my reward—whatever it will be. I do hope that it will never be necessary to go into court over spoils, for to me the all-time low in family affairs is a court fight . . ."

For his son, John B. offered special advice.

"To Kell, I want to say that if there is anything to this Mendelian theory, you will probably like to bet on a horse or indulge in other forms of gambling—so, if you do, never bet what you cannot afford to lose and if you are a loser, don't plunge to try to recoup. That is wherein the danger lies. 'There will be another deal, my son, and after that, another one.' Just be moderate in all things and don't deal in excesses. (The girls can also take that advice.)

"I am not going to try to regulate your lives, as nothing is quite as boring as too many 'don'ts.' I am merely setting down the benefits of my experience, which most people will admit was rather broad . . .

"I hereby nominate . . . and appoint my son, John Brendan Kelly, and Provident Tradesman's Bank and Trust Company, as my co-executors of this my Last Will and Testament. I appoint my friend, John Morgan Davis [former Lieutenant Governor of Pennsylvania], my wife and my son, to be trustees under this my Will. I direct that John Edward Sheridan, Esquire, be retained as counsel for my estate. . .

"I have written this Will in a lighter vein because I have always felt that Wills were so dreary that they might have been written by the author of 'Inner Sanctum' and I can see no reason for it, particularly in my case. My family is raised and I am leaving enough so they can face life with a better than average start, financially.

"As for me, just shed a respectful tear if you think I merit it, but I am sure you are all intelligent enough not to weep all over the place. I have watched a few emotional acts at graves, such as trying to jump into it, fainting, etc., but the thoroughbred grieves in the heart.

"Not that my passing should occasion any 'scenes' for the simple reason that life owes me nothing. I have ranged far and wide, have really run the gamut. I have known great sorrow and great joy. I had more than my share of success . . . my wife and children have not given me any heartaches, but . . . have given me much happiness and a pardonable pride, and I want them to know I appreciate that.

"In this document I can only give you things, but if I had the choice to give you worldly goods or character, I would give you character. The reason I say that, is with character you will get worldly goods because character is loyalty, honesty, ability, sportsmanship, and, I hope, a sense of humor.

"If I don't stop soon, this will be as long as *Gone With the Wind*, so just remember, when I shove off for greener pastures or whatever it is on the other side of the curtain, that I do it unafraid and, if you must know, a little curious."

It was a great will and brought laughter as well as lumpy throats to thousands, including me. Even though it cost seven dollars a copy, buyers from London, England, to San Diego, California, made it a "best seller" within a month of its publication in the world's press. However, as one Philadelphian remarked, "When John B. Kelly died, he was worth a million. But he didn't leave one goddamned cent to charity."

Among those irked by this omission, according to Kell, was Bishop Fulton J. Sheen.

"The Bishop said something about a prominent Catholic layman from Philadelphia who died recently and didn't give a donation to the Church," recalled Kell. "There's no doubt the Bishop was referring to my father."

It was revealed that the actual amount of John B.'s estate was $1,193,062.99 in an inventory filed October 10, 1963, by John E. Sheridan.

Obviously annoyed by an editorial that appeared in the Philadelphia *Bulletin*, Counselor Sheridan took that newspaper to task.

"Reference is made to your editorial, 'A Best Seller Will.'

"Your conclusion, relating to the absence of legal guidance, requires a slight amendment. Mr. Kelly and the undersigned worked in close collaboration. The steel structure of legal precedent was 'joined' by the undersigned, to which the testator, John B. Kelly, affixed his philosophical 'bricks,' using a mortar of experience, kindliness, paternal affection—and a sense of humor.

"JOHN EDWARD SHERIDAN
"*Counsel, Estate of John B. Kelly*"

Orphans Court Judge Mark E. Lefever took up the cudgels for members of the bar who might lose a slice of business if citizens wrote their own wills. And, while he didn't express it in the words

JOHN B. KELLY
HAMPION · SINGLES 1920 DOUBLES 1924

Mrs. John B. Kelly with Son Kell at the unveiling of her husband's statue at the finish line of the Schuylkill River rowing course, 1963.

of that old saw—"A man who is his own lawyer has a fool for a client"—the judge strongly urged the use of professionals for those who might have something left for heirs. At the same time His Honor took a posthumous slap at Jack Kelly for assuming authorship of his will which, in the learned judge's opinion, Kelly didn't write, at least in toto as the public was led to believe.

"The will received wide newspaper publicity, editorial comment, and public interest," said His Honor according to *Bulletin* reporter Ms. Dorothy Byrd in the November 17, 1964, issue of her newspaper.

"Because of Kelly's prominence and his statement that he was writing his own will, the ordinary layman might be induced to believe that it is safe for him to draw his own will without professional legal advice and assistance.

"This would be most unfortunate, because home-written wills constitute the commonest source of dispute and litigation in this court. Frequently the jolly testator who writes his own will either (1) creates the seeds of long and costly litigation, or (2) by inadvertent use of words of legal art, which he does not understand, or by omission of important clauses or provisions, he raises doubts as to his intention and meaning . . ."

His Honor admitted that, while Kelly's contribution to the testament might be minor in the legal sense ("art" the judge so labeled it; I can't imagine why), it was at least Kelly's own.

"There seems to be little doubt," His Honor went on, "that Kelly wrote portions of his will, especially those containing his personal philosophy and his advice to his family in his own kindly, homespun, witty style.

"However, the crucial provision of his will, viz., the dispositive provisions, the appointment of executors and trustees, the enumeration of their powers . . . the provisions . . . were written in classic and commonly accepted legal phraseology. It would appear that these clauses were drafted by a lawyer, or at least suggested or checked by a professional scrivener.

"It follows that this will should not be accepted by the unwary and unsophisticated as precedent for them to attempt the highly technical task of writing their own wills without obtaining professional assistance and advice."

A layman myself (a lawyer did draw my will), I should hate to cavil with the pontificalities of Mark Lefever, a classmate at Franklin and Marshall College. But I really do not think John B. Kelly deserved to be damned by such faint praise for creating a will that read more like Benchley than Blackstone. How Jack would have writhed had he heard his style labeled "homespun."

25

"HE'S DOING WHAT HE SHOULD HAVE DONE WITH THE HIGH SCHOOL CROWD"

ON THE EAST BANK OF THE SCHUYLKILL RIVER HE LOVED, NEAR the finish line of the many races he won there, is a six-foot-high statue of John B. Kelly. I think he would have joined the dedication crowd's laughter on June 27, 1963, when Widow Margaret pulled the unveiling cord and there was Jack with a white athletic shirt, "Kelly for Brickwork," carelessly draped over his expansive bronze torso.

To the rescue came Kell and a half-dozen fellow scullers from the Vesper Club. Kelly, suppressing his own laughter, was first to jump up and rip the shirt from Daddy's chest. The leap to rescue his father from humiliation was automatic; like Pavlov's dogs, he'd been trained to respond to a signal.

You can't pinpoint the hour, day, or month Kell's conditioning began but you can, almost with certainty, spot the year. That would have been 1936, when John B. Kelly, Jr., was nine. And if you look back to 1920, the motive sticks out like the proverbial sore thumb. This was the year the Henley stewards rejected John B. Kelly, Sr.'s entry into the Diamond Sculls. In their official opinion Jack Kelly was not a gentleman. Their reasoning was the logic of Kieswetter: John B. Kelly, Sr., laid bricks, gentlemen don't lay bricks, ergo, John B. Kelly, Sr., is not a gentleman. The basis for this decision was simple. Men who work with their hands have an unfair muscular advantage over those who don't.

I don't believe the still unmarried thirty-year-old Kelly raised

John B. Kelly, Jr. (Kell), being congratulated by a defeated competitor after winning the Diamond Skulls at the Royal Henley Regatta.

his hands heavenward and vowed, as has been reported by sentimental gentlemen of the press, "Someday I'll have a son who will erase this humiliation." But it's not hard to imagine Jack saying to himself, or to anyone else within earshot, "Those dirty English bastards. Someday I'll get them."

Over the years, so deeply had John B. instilled in his own son's mind the obligation to win the Diamond Sculls that when Kell failed on his first try, he was frozen to the oars, physically unable to climb out of the scull and face his father.

"The race was over, oarsmen were leaping out of their boats, dropping their oars and jumping back to solid ground," said Kathy McKenna, who's heard this story a hundred times. "They had to go down to the river to peel Kell's hands off the oars and carry him out of the scull. He could not deal with the fact that he'd disappointed his father. He had *lost* the race."

Kathy grinned.

"But a year later, the second time Kell competed in the Henley, he won by *eight* boat lengths."

You might start Kell's story with a telegram John B. sent to Brother Walter at the Friars Club, 110 West Forty-eighth Street, New York, at 6:17 P.M., on May 24, 1927.

"BABY BOY BORN TODAY MOTHER AND BABY DOING WELL STOP JACK."

Family members, at least those older than Kell, remember him as a sweet, stocky little boy.

"My sister, Mary," said Charles Kelly, Jr., "is still carrying the banner for Kell. She's particularly fond of him because she remembers him as a little kid. He was always a very friendly child. When I spun a top for him or he showed you his top, his nose was right on it; he never did anything from a distance. It was always a top he played with."

However, the top was relegated to the attic when Kell passed his ninth birthday and the serious business of developing the boy's muscles began.

"I remember when I called on Grace to take her out," said Charles Fish. "Kell was always lying on the couch exercising his wrists to strengthen them."

Elaine Kelly Cruice Beyer recalls Kell as a "sweet lovable young thing."

"I think it's sad that Kell devoted so much of his childhood to a very regimented life, when other kids were having fun. Up early, doing the rowing, going to school, I think he missed out on a lot. But he did have a wonderful nature."

Marion Smith (oldest of the four Cruice sisters), although fond of her Uncle Jack, feels the same thing.

"John B. had Kell practicing rowing before he was ten years old. Now that's the truth because I remember the little round fat face of Kell down on the wet front of the boathouse. He wasn't out with the kids having fun and getting bubble gum and drinking Coke. He was always in training; meeting his father every day after school, going out on the boathouse slip."

Marion, who still loves Kell despite everything, sighs.

Kell in his debut as coxswain in
Penn Athletic Club gig, June 3, 1937.

"What he's doing now he should have done with the high school kids. Suddenly his father's gone; he's got money; he's a good-looking man. It's delayed adolescence."

Sister Lizanne agrees.

"Kell was *always* in training, very strict training during his high school years. He didn't stay out late; he did date but not much because he had to go to bed early. And he seemed not to mind it then but apparently he missed a fling in his life. When I was a child—Kell is six years older than I am—we got along very well.

"And when I was a teen-ager, he used to drive my hockey team for me and watch me play. He was just a great guy and Mary [Kell's wife] and I are sorority sisters, Kappa Kappa Gamma. They got along very well. I thought it was a sort of perfect match. What went wrong I really don't know."

Joe Regan, who knew Kell at the beginning of his athletic career, has mixed emotions about his former friend and rowing partner. Joe is an alumnus of Kelly for Brickwork. He worked for John B. Kelly, Sr., for many years until, with his boss's encouragement, he went into business for himself. He and I were seated in the Student Union cafeteria at Cheyney State College, where Joe is doing the brickwork on a large construction job.

"I first met Kell when I was a lifeguard in Ocean City. He had been on the beach a few years before I was there and won the Ocean City boat championship. I always wanted to be a rower; I was very impressed with Kell and figured I could row with somebody and be as good as he was.

"Kell asked my brother to be his partner and my brother, Bobby, said 'fine' but he didn't show up to have Kelly look him over and I did. Kell looked at me and said, 'You're a pretty husky guy,' and I answered that I'd love to have the opportunity to row.

"We rowed a mile and then continued. The captain of the beach patrol came over and said, 'I'll put you two together.' Kell said, 'I want you to meet my Dad. He's an Olympic champion.' His father came down, a big, tall man. He got in the boat and we went out. Mr. Kelly didn't say much, just kept staring at the whirlpools in the water. He said, 'Very, very good.'

"After our first session with John B. ended, Kell told me, 'Dad says you're all right. But he doesn't like the idea that you're a weight lifter; he thinks you'll get musclebound and it will slow you up.' I said, 'Okay,' just to get in the race.

"We had what they called the Lifeguard Championships. You needed to win that particular event to qualify for the others. The day of the race Mr. Kelly came down and said, 'You know Kell's blind; he can't see a damned thing so it's up to you to keep your eye on that buoy out there. Go straight and make the right return because you can lose the race otherwise. It's your eyes we're depending on.'

"We won the race by a good margin; it was the *first* thing I ever won. We qualified for the South Jersey championships of all the Beach Patrols and we trained hard. Naturally, John B. had the event publicized. Pictures in the papers. No one had ever heard of these races before."

*Kell as member of the Ocean
City Beach Patrol, 1944.*

Joe walked to the lunch counter, refilled our coffee cups, brought them to the table.

"Again, Mr. Kelly said to me before the start, 'Joe, don't forget that you're the eyes. It's up to you, Joe, to pull us through.' Well, the seas were *rough,* and did I foul it up! We hit the wrong buoy when we got out. I said to myself, 'Oh, God, Mr. Kelly will go crazy. Mr. Kelly with the binoculars on us.' I think we had to row an extra fifty yards to go all around the buoy.

"It was touch and go, but finally we pulled away and we won that South Jersey championship. Kell once said to me, this was after he was married, 'Nothing thrilled me more than winning that South Jersey championship and I've since been rowing all over the country, in fact all over the world.'

"At the beach, you know, down in Ocean City, when we were there for the summer working, Kell had to go home and be in bed by ten or eleven at the latest. His father told him that to be a champion, this was the pattern to be followed. I followed it, too.

It was like my Dad telling me; I wanted to go out nights but I went home to bed instead."

Joe shook his head.

"Kell impressed me so much because his father told him how to eat properly, go to bed early, and train. I smoked and his father said to Kell, 'What! Joe smokes? *No* way will you row with him! You better talk to him.' Within an hour after Kell told me I stopped and haven't lit up a cigarette since.

"Mr. Kelly had a lot of influence on me and there was love between Kell and his father. Mr. Kelly did drive him to be an oarsman. In fact, once I asked him what happened between him and Mary. 'Why in the world would you leave a family like this?' He said, 'There's two sides and well, the old man pushed the hell out of me.' "

I asked Joe if he knew other members of the family.

"Sure, I dated his sisters and was very close to all the girls. I took out Grace with Kell, double dates. I met Lizanne and dated her, too. I think Kell's mother is a charming woman and really the backbone of the family. She, not Mr. Kelly, was the leader. Jack used to say, 'Mom's mad.' Mom was discipline; Mom was everything.

"Mr. Kelly walked in only occasionally. Kell was a great athlete but he had to work at it; nothing came easy for him. He always squinted but he wasn't too proud to wear glasses. His father was a conceited man and wouldn't wear them.

"Grace is a nice person and she was beautiful. Beautiful skin! And a very warm girl. She matured early; I think she was just fourteen when I took her out."

I asked Joe if he knew Mary, Kell's wife.

"Sure. When Kell came back from the Olympics he invited me to a party at his home to meet her. He said 'Atlas,' which is what he sometimes called me because I was a weight lifter, and I called him 'Cyclops.' Well, he said to me, 'I really got myself an athlete, a real sharp girl.' And then I met Mary and I thought to myself, 'Oh, Jeez, Kell, you can do better than that.'

"Of all the girls Kell dated, he was sure this was the greatest.

Mr. and Mrs. John B. Kelly, Jr., cheering their team on to victory (Penn vs. Dartmouth rowing).

Good stock, you know, but I never thought he'd marry her. Well, when he became engaged to Mary he said to me, 'Joe, we made a pact.'

Joe told me the "pact" he referred to was an agreement that each would be the other's best man.

"We were kids; we sealed it with a handshake. At any rate, when Kell was to be married he told me he wouldn't be able to keep his end of the agreement. Because he had so many friends, he'd decided that Mr. Kelly would be the best man. I was invited to the wedding but that's another story.

"You know, Art, if you're in the wedding party, you're usually provided with a tux or tails supplied by the groom. I had to get my own. Then when I met the wedding party at North Phila-

delphia Station I expected Kell would have train tickets for me.
I met Mrs. Kelly, Peggy, and Lizanne there. Mr. Kelly and I go
to get on the train; there's a special car reserved for the wedding
party.

"I go to get on and somebody asks, 'Joe, do you have your
ticket?' and I answered, 'No, of course not, doesn't Kell have it?'
They said, 'No,' so I ran and bought a ticket and had to sit in the
coach, which looked like a cattle car. I *was* annoyed. Peggy could
see it when we arrived at the hotel in Washington where they
were getting married and she said, 'You know Kell, he's so absent-
minded.' "

Joe said he had more problems when he tried to check in.

"We're in line getting assigned to rooms and I discover there's
no reservation for me. Finally, Mr. Kelly said to the clerk, 'Get
something here for Joe. Kell forgot.' The wedding was the following day and there'd be an evening service. Kell came into my
room, didn't make any apologies and said, 'The afternoon service
will be at one o'clock. You better check out.'

"I said, 'Kell, I can't because I have to change into my formal
and be at your wedding at seven o'clock in the evening.' So he
said, 'Well, then, they'll charge *you* for an extra day.' I thought,
'Charge *me!*' But I still never said a word to Kell. How cheap can
you be? He was *always* cheap with the dollar; he still has his
recess money. That's Kell. I told Peggy and she said, 'Joe, there's
no excuse.'

The subject reverted to Mrs. John B. Kelly, Jr., and I asked
Joe if he had any idea why they separated.

"Well, I think when Mary found out that Kell was cheating,
she got ready to change her whole way of life because she didn't
think that could happen to her, ever. And it did.

"I think she's a nice girl. She was very domineering but Kell
trained her that way. He got her involved with the Vesper Swim
Club and she was busy. They were never alone; they each had
separate lives to live. Then Kell got a little touch of what he used
to have before he was married. Got to sow his wild oats and it
went on and on."

26

"HE AUCTIONED
HIS LITTLE BLACK BOOK"

KELL HAS SO MANY PEOPLE IN HIS LIFE THAT I HARDLY KNEW
where to begin. For a starter I chose Leslie Bennetts. One of the
most attractive and articulate of the lot, she's a feature writer for
the *Bulletin*. It required several sessions with Ms. Bennetts to ex-
tract only a small portion of the information this beautiful, blond
reporter compiled about both Kell and his sister Grace.

Of course, I could have settled for Ms. Bennetts' penetrating
profile on John Brendan Kelly, Jr., which she did on assignment.
However, the *Bulletin* prides itself on being a "family" newspaper
ever on the alert for material it considers unsuitable for young
readers. I thought there might be areas withheld by Ms. Bennetts.
I asked this lovely journalist if for once she would be willing to
reverse her role and become an interviewee.

So, with only the tape recorder between Ms. Bennetts and me,
there we were at a corner table in the Philadelphia Art Alliance
one evening when Leslie reviewed her brief but interesting exposure to John B. Kelly, Jr.

"I was amazed how much he told me about himself," said Ms.
Bennetts. "He never tried to find out anything about me. All he
wants is someone attractive on his arm. I don't really think that he
cares or even knows whether the carcass he's parading around has
the brains of a squirrel, so long as she's presentable."

The martinis arrived; Leslie took a sip.

"Other people may find Kell attractive physically. I don't; he's not my type of man. For me, whether a man is attractive depends on both his personality and his mind, his sensitivities and other things which are not present in Kell."

Leslie shook her head.

"He's trying to make up for the incredibly straight life he lived to a certain point. He never touched alcohol until he was well into his twenties. He married a good Catholic girl and had six children.

"So, when he finally did break out of it, he went bananas. A lot of men do that at forty. He hasn't shown any signs of maturing beyond that.

"His relationship with his wife sounded very strange to me. He said he hadn't seen or talked to her in five years. He'd pick up the kids, and she'd stay out of his way. They're still not divorced. I think he likes this."

Leslie smiled.

"Insurance, you know."

My second martini arrived. Leslie had refused a refill. She went on.

"Of course, he's a figure in Philadelphia because of his father's name and the family prominence and his cosmetic attributes. I think he's a fundamentally decent person; I don't know of anything venal Kell has ever done. On the other hand I think you can do a lot of damage by being insensitive, which Kell certainly is."

I asked Leslie, who certainly doesn't lack for men in her life, why, feeling as she did, she continued to see Kell.

"I think I did it because—and this is the reason a lot of women go out with him—he's nice and he's a presentable escort. And I'm curious and want to find out about everyone's world."

Dinner arrived; our conversation was restricted to the usual civilities. I had an after-dinner brandy; Leslie refused one and continued.

"Apparently Kell's life is due to his upbringing. He's had an incredibly repressive Catholic indoctrination combined with all the other implants he received from his father's fanaticism over sports.

"I never met his mother but I think that one of the most in-

Kell in a bevy (four finalists in the Miss North America competition, 1963).

credible stories is that single-handedly she prevented her son from running for mayor.

"I do think Grace [whom Ms. Bennetts interviewed at length] is much brighter than he. When you talk to Kell, he has a set piece for any given subject—he's programmed. When you push a button you get that response.

"Sometimes he'll get his wires crossed and when you push *this* button you'll get *that* response. It's unbelievable because it's so consistent; that's what makes you realize it's mechanical."

Kell was a poor listener, Leslie averred.

"He's not interested in what you do. I *never* talked about myself; I was an audience or nothing. And he talks about Grace constantly. He uses her name all the time."

(In fairness to Kell I must say that during the many hours he and I spent together, the only time he mentioned his sister was when I asked him a question about her.)

Another blond member of the working press who interviewed Kell and knows him socially is free-lancer Patsy Sims. Ms. Sims' literary version of John B. Kelly, Jr., appeared in the January 19, 1975, issue of the Philadelphia *Inquirer*. Patsy told me her unofficial view of the subject a few months later when she had dinner at our center-city house. First, let's look at excerpts of what Patsy wrote for the newspaper:

"It is 7:45 A.M. and there he is, hairy legs pumping up and down, jogging along Fairmount Parkway, right on schedule.

John B. Kelly, Jr., and Princess Grace at the Philadelphia Travel and Vacation Show. Kell was President. The Princess sips some Old Original Bookbinder's Snapper Soup.

"Motorists honk. Some wave. And most of them stare. He waves to a couple, grins, and keeps on jogging until he reaches the multicolored street in front of the Art Museum where he begins a conglomeration of bends and what he calls 'Charles Atlas dynamic-tension exercises.'

" 'Maybe,' he grunts, touching his toes, 'I've been more serious and regular the last five years or so . . . as I get older.'

"Grrrroan.

" 'Let's say I'm weight-conscious and . . . I'm vain about looking in shape . . . or fairly decent shape.'

"Puff.

" 'So I work out, and maybe I'm a little masochistic . . .' "

I now bring you to our back patio, where Patsy, my wife Juliet, and I are having predinner cocktails. Patsy is telling us about her early morning session with John B. Kelly.

"I'd told Kell I wanted to do everything; that I wanted to see him in every conceivable situation and that I understood he went jogging every morning, whether it's winter, summer, or whatever. He said, 'So you really want to do this?' and I said I did. Well, the alarm went off; I said to myself, 'Why in the name of God am I doing this?' "

Patsy sighed at the recollection, swallowed the olive (it was pitted), and went on.

"I go and ring his bell at seven A.M. on the nose. And I could hear this groan behind the door." (Here Patsy, a light, albeit well-proportioned five feet two, imitated as best she could an enormous, unhappy growl.) "Anyway, Kell opened the door; he really looked wilted. He was in his shorts, his cap, and his sweatshirt, then he put on a jumpsuit. Anyway, we're going. And I wanted a real participation thing. I wanted to jog along with Kell.

"Kell kept saying—he really kept looking me up and down— 'I don't think you're in shape to keep up with me.' I had figured that jogging, I could just walk along with him even if I couldn't run as fast as he could. And he kept wanting me to take his car.

"I'm insisting, 'Kell, I don't want to drive your car because I'll run it into a tree.' When we got downstairs he takes me to where he parks and the attendant there is laughing. I'm not in shorts, I was in slacks; it really has its funny side. It was like October or November of the year.

"As it turned out, I did drive his car. The attendant comes out with this huge Monte Carlo. I look at it. It's black and long; I was petrified and I didn't even have my driver's license with me. He said that it wouldn't matter, that the Park Police knew him.

"So he sort of runs off as he says, 'I'll see you down at the Art Museum at the painted street.' I am creeping along, driving Grace Kelly's brother's car and I'm *really* going to wreck it. Well, anyway, I drive down the Parkway, I go about a block and a half, and I haven't passed him. I keep saying, 'Where the hell is he?' and I keep looking behind me. There's no Jack Kelly in sight.

"Suddenly there he is, *way* down at the Art Museum. I was *driving* but he beat me to the museum and by the time I got there he was already doing all his bends and stretches, exercises and everything. When he got through we headed back. When I pulled the car into his garage and went up the elevator, he was already back in his apartment. That's the true story of my jogging with Kell."

And now back to Patsy's published record of the event.

"It is 7:45 and, still sweating, he leans against his kitchen counter and drinks low-fat milk from the carton. Except for the faded blue tennis shorts, the striped pullover and the sweat, he looks and even smells ('Royal Copenhagen' or 'Bill Blass' are his two favorite after-shaves) like the meticulously manicured Jack Kelly who—since he left his wife and six children and moved into the penthouse—has popped up, night after night at *political* dinners and *charity* balls and *sporting* events and Harry's American Bar, and the Saloon, and Fast Eddie's and Villa di Roma with an assortment of blondes and brunettes and redheads."

We are once more on the Jessup Street patio. Juliet is preparing dinner; Patsy and I are polishing off second martinis as our guest discusses a sporting event Kelly attended. One of those blondes who went with him is Ms. Sims.

"Kell had a date with Sharon, a girl who works in Dave Berger's office. Initially I was supposed to go with someone else but didn't. So Kell took us both. What I thought was interesting was that we got there late because Kell doesn't like crowds. At each quarter, or whatever it is called in a hockey game, we left our seats five minutes before the end, so we could get down to the Blue Line Club before the crowd.

"I don't know what the other hockey team was, but our team was the Flyers.

"The Flyers made two goals that night and won the game. They were the *only* scores and we missed both of them because they occurred during the time we were going to or coming from the Blue Line Club.

"Anyway, Kell just has this thing where he likes to avoid crowds and misses half the game by coming late and leaving early. The Blue Line is a private club where they have a cocktail lounge and restaurant. Kell was well known; the waitresses loved him and they loved letting people know they knew Kell."

Patsy laughed.

"I thought how funny it was—this big deal with everybody clamoring to get tickets. And here was Kell spending half the time going back and forth to the Blue Line Club. What's important to him is being seen."

In her journalistic version of the John B. Kelly, Jr., profile Ms. Sims spoke of Kell's friends, first quoting Kathy McKenna.

" 'Kell could fill a telephone book with numbers,' " says Kell's administrative assistant. 'He's had several little black books. Last year he auctioned one off for the Israel Emergency Fund and it brought in a great deal of money.' "

I reported to Patsy that after speaking with scores of Philadelphians I didn't find one man, woman, or child who didn't claim to be a friend of Kelly's.

Patsy's unofficial response: "I didn't find any enemies either because Kell doesn't have a strong enough personality to make them."

And now we return to the *Inquirer*.

"John B. Kelly, Jr., is the rich kid from the Main Line. Tommy Foglietta [Kell's former fellow Councilman] is from South Philadelphia. Their fathers were friends and politicians, introducing their sons to the art of running for public office and winning. It is maybe thirty-five years later. The second-generation Kelly and Foglietta sit in council chambers, smirking across the aisle. Sometimes they verbally tackle one another on the floor, more often for laughs than anything.

"Someday, when they grow up, maybe they'll run for mayor . . . against one another . . . Wouldn't that be funny? Foglietta thinks so. They could have a good time competing and still be friends . . . It could, however, break up the inseparable fraternity that includes Edelstein and restaurateur Stanley Green. It is a fraternity whose long-standing members pull pranks from here to Monaco, meet daily and talk on the phone incessantly, even if it's long distance."

And here's the unofficial version.

"Kell has a little crowd that follows him around and is very much in awe of him. Anything for Jack Kelly; he is their hero.

"They call each other every day at least once to see what the other's doing and keep tabs, even if one of them is in Florida or Monaco. Everything is very artificial, all that Beautiful People type of thing."

Patsy smiled a bit sadly.

"You know, that business where he likes to play up that he is having such a good time, going out every night with a different blonde, being a man about town? Well, I think that Kell is a lonely, unhappy person."

Via the journalistic route Patsy reached a similar conclusion.

"Sitting in the Peale Club dining room, Kell quietly insists he really doesn't like to think of himself competing with his father. Then an elderly man stops at the table. 'He's great,' the old man says, patting Kell on the back. 'But his father was greater. His father was the *greatest.*'

"After the man leaves Kelly admits the comparisons *do* bother him, but quickly adds that he isn't angry. 'That's human nature,' Kell says. 'Everybody was greater in the old days. And you recognize the man's age and his background. But obviously I don't love to hear that "your father was greater than you were." In some respects he was; in others, I think I have a little edge on him.'

"A few nights later, when friends insist Jack Kelly wear an overcoat to a formal party, he reluctantly takes a heavy, black coat from the hall closet and puts it on.

" 'It's just too big for me,' he complained. 'It was my father's.' "

Here I want to say a word on behalf of John B. Kelly, Jr. I think that in many respects he's a better man than his father was—more honest, more open, and, perhaps what's most astonishing of all, a better man at the oars. Kell admits that, generally speaking, "My time for singles is about ten to fifteen seconds better than my father's in comparable races." Then he adds deprecatingly, with the candor that makes him so likable, "But you got to remember that today good scullers are fifteen seconds better than *I* ever was."

27

HAIL THE CONQUERING HERO!

WITH ALL THE FLAK OF RECENT YEARS HITTING JOHN B. KELLY, Jr., and the reams of adverse publicity (if, in his mind, such a phrase is not self-contradictory) oozing from the press, it's easy to forget we're talking about a great athlete. I add that in no way am I referring to his alleged sexual mastery.

In demand as a speaker all over the United States, he represents the ideal athlete in a nation that puts athletic achievements above success in any of the arts. If you're the best double bassoonist in the world, you've got to bring your bassoon and a hundred-piece symphony orchestra with maybe Ormandy conducting. But all that handsome, tall, poised Kell has to do is stand on the podium and his audience is willing to believe what they've read about him in the sports pages of their newspapers.

Just a few clippings from his voluminous scrapbooks give substance to my preamble:

"John B. (Jack) Kelly, Jr., four times a member of the U.S. Olympic team and now head of the Olympic Fund in Pennsylvania, will be the speaker at the Ninth Reading-Berks Chamber of Commerce Sports Program Wednesday night, March 24, at the Abraham Lincoln Hotel," said the Reading *Eagle,* Sunday, February 28, 1965.

"Kelly, who represented this country in single sculls in the 1948, 1952, and 1956 Olympics and in double sculls in the 1960 games, traces his sculling career back to 1944 when he first won the U.S. schoolboy singles crown . . .

"In 1947, Kelly won the A.A.U.'s Sullivan Award as the outstanding amateur athlete in the United States and eight times was the U.S. singles sculling champion beginning in 1946 and ending in 1956."

The *Eagle* spoke of Kell's greatest triumphs.

"Kell twice (1947 and 1949) won the coveted Diamond Sculls Singles at Henley, an event which nearly forty years earlier [actually twenty] had been closed to his father. These wins, doubtless, represent the high spot of his brilliant career.

"He captured the Philadelphia singles championship ten times, was Canadian champion six times, won the Europe singles title in 1949 and the same year became the Swiss and Belgian champ. In 1953 he won the Mexican singles championship and took the Pan American singles title in 1955 and the games double crown in 1959 . . ."

In Cincinnati, Ohio, on August 23, 1973, they labeled John B. Kelly, Jr., as "the most widely known amateur sports figure in the world today." In Seattle, Washington, Kell was tagged as "the best example of amateur athletics anywhere," and in Des Moines, "an inspiration to youth in all fifty states for his sportsmanship, his tremendous athletic abilities and his willingness to share his knowledge, his philosophy, and techniques with the youth of America."

I hope that these foregoing paragraphs, chosen from thousands, prove that there is a noticeable difference between the athletic achievement of John B. Kelly, Jr., and the substitute right fielder of the Mahoopany, Pa., Bluebirds. In fairness, I confess I've never seen the Bluebirds in action or, for that matter, John B. Kelly, Jr.

As far as the préss is concerned, Kell's first known entry into the sports pages came as early as 1937.

"Inheriting some of the watermanship of his illustrious dad, John B. Kelly, Jr., ten-year-old son of Jack Kelly, former national and Olympic single sculls champion, makes his competitive bow this weekend in the opening match rowing races on the Schuylkill," wrote Ross E. Kauffman in the *Evening Bulletin*, June 3, 1937.

Kell, the very spirit of Kelly for Brickwork, with Benedict Gimbel, Jr.

"Young Kelly, fourth-grade student at Penn Charter, will coxswain the Penn A. C. junior four-oared gig against Undine Barge.

"The role is something new to the youngster but he has been steering several of the Penn A. C. boats in recent workouts and is anxious to pilot the gig to victory. He weighs a trifle more than ninety pounds and may have to carry some extra ballast."

I realize this is a blot on my reportorial escutcheon but I simply could not discover how Kell made out. The newspapers apparently ignored the event; the scrapbooks drew a blank, and the coxswain himself must be forgiven if after nearly four decades and hundreds of races in between he's not quite sure how his crew came in. He thinks, though, they placed second.

However, there is no lack of specific information about Kell's conquests in later years. In addition to the dozen or more scrapbooks over which Mrs. McKenna exercises curatory power, newspaper morgues throughout the world are filled with literally millions of John B. Kelly, Jr., clippings. I sought from this mass of memorabilia one single item that would show, without benefit of a scoreboard, John B. Kelly, Jr., at the zenith of his career. I ignored a ticker-tape welcome with cheering crowds lining Broad Street, confetti and unwrapped rolls of toilet paper hurled from skyscrapers at the conquering hero as he stood in an open sports car waving acknowledgments to his wildly enthusiastic admirers.

And I am happy to say I found the object of my search in a dinner menu program that satisfied me for two reasons, one sentimental, the other sociological. On August 6, 1947, a week after a nation cheered his win at the Royal English Henley Regatta, John B. Kelly, Jr., came home to be honored in The Falls.

On the outside of a carefully preserved pamphlet there's a picture of a grinning Kell, wearing his father's ancient green cap as he sits on the shoulders of old neighbors and friends. Page two displays a posed photograph of Kell at the sweeps. His weight, "192," his age, "20." A list of his sculling achievements follows.

The choice of Charlie McIlvaine as toastmaster was a natural and surprised me no more than did the names of those others who shared the podium with him—Mr. and Mrs. John B. Kelly, Sr., Mayor Bernard Samuel, various members of Council, judges, and other city officials. What did throw me was—*mirabile visu!*—the name of Mrs. Bessie *Dobson* Altemus.

I think, had Grandma Kelly been present, she would have tossed a penny into Mrs. Altemus' soup.

28

"THE PILL
WASN'T AVAILABLE"

WHEN INCUMBENT JOHN B. KELLY, JR., RAN FOR COUNCILMAN-
at-Large in 1971, he was then only forty-four years old, scru-
pulously honest, rich, handsome, personable, bearer of a proud
Celtic surname in a city with a huge Irish population, and a hero
where citizens, given the choice of a sports stadium or a school,
invariably vote for the former. He had three more plusses going
for him; he was a member of the leading political party, he was
acceptable to the hacks who ran it, and lastly, he was the only
candidate in sight who had real charisma.

On Friday, October 29, 1971, four days before Philadelphia
voters went to the polls in a general election, the *Inquirer*'s editorial page carried its own carefully measured recommendations
to voters. There was scant praise for many candidates but despite
minor criticism, Kell fared well.

"John B. Kelly, Jr., an incumbent Democrat," said the *Inquirer*,
"has not been as effective as he is capable of being because of
absenteeism and the limitations the present Council system places
on its new members. But he brings to the Council a healthy streak
of independence, an ability to work with Republicans as well as
Democrats and—as national president of the Amateur Athletic
Union—a breadth of view which is a refreshing contrast to the
parochialism too often seen in the Council."

When the votes were in, Kelly led the ticket. . . .

Kell and I are seated in his Cherry Street Kelly for Brickwork office. It's comfortable but not luxurious. His large desk is clean because he's finished his work or there wasn't any work to finish. At any rate, my host looks every bit the president of a company that does more than fifteen million dollars a year.

Kell is completely at ease and when I struggle awkwardly to insert my tape recorder plug into a corner outlet, Kell smilingly takes over.

I asked what he'd like to talk about. He shrugged his broad shoulders, opened his hands outward and raised his palms in a noncommittal gesture.

"Whatever you say, Art," he answered in benign fashion. And what I said was "girls."

Kell smiled, showing a perfect set of teeth.

"Where shall we begin?"

I thought for a moment, then for an opener asked my host how he accounted for his popularity with women and why they seemed to "flock to him."

Kell laughed modestly.

"I don't really know that they do; I question whether that's the case. But the point is I think a lot of it is the family name and reputation, and the sports background probably helps. I'm head of a business that's fairly well known and I have other interests like the Athletic Club. To some girls these are attractions. And also some girls can be turned off.

"I guess a little of the fact that I sort of chase around is that I was always in training before I was married. I never really let loose in the 'old days.' I was a serious international athlete for seven years of my marriage. So, in those days, first things were sports, and second, the business. Sports were my most important priority. *Everything* was sacrificed to that end.

"I was a relatively clean-cut innocent boy; in fact I was on the bashful side. I didn't drink and I didn't smoke."

Kell smiled broadly.

"I probably was considered a big square. But things weren't so permissive then as they are today. The 'pill' wasn't available and today girls are more forward or 'liberated,' or whatever you want to call it. Not like they were ten years ago."

Kell frowned as though the passing of the old days depressed him.

"I try to take girls to nice places—the Royal Ballet tonight, and I think it's a nice place. Oh, once in a while with a down-to-earth kind of gal I'll go to the Milano with the guys and so forth, and hack it up with them there. But it depends on whom you're with. You know, you try to treat 'em accordingly, and I do think I have good taste in ladies."

I mentioned that all those I'd seen with Kell were beauties. He shook his head.

"No, that's not so. But I do think every girl I've ever been out with has something to be said for her. Whether she has brains or beauty or talent, whatever it might be, or that she's just a nice person. I like variety."

I asked Kell if there was anything in particular he sought in his ladies, and I was not using a double entendre either.

"Well," he answered thoughtfully, "I like to see that whatever interest I have in them is reciprocated. I like to think there's something coming back. You know, some 'vibes' or feeling that they are as interested in me as I am in them. I don't like to have a one-sided thing. If I get that message the relationship ceases; I just don't bother coming back.

"I like to see a girl with a good figure who keeps herself in some kind of shape. I like gals who are athletically oriented. If I'm going out with a girl with any degree of regularity, she's going to have to be interested in, like riding a bike, playing a little tennis or swimming or something like that."

Kell chuckled.

"Not just the sedentary type of dame that's afraid she'll muss her hair. I don't like prima donnas."

As I listened to the expert I had a fleeting temptation to turn these informative revelations into a "how to" book until I realized that few potential male buyers have the necessary ingredients for success, like perfect health, stamina, a million dollars, and a body to match. So all I did was listen, somewhat enviously, I admit.

"Well, what do I have a reputation for, blondes or brunettes?" Kell asked a bit proudly. The question was rhetorical but I answered anyway.

"Blondes."

My host gave his reply considerable thought.

"Not necessarily at all. This Irish lady that I was with this weekend, from the old country, County Mayo. She's got sort of reddish-brown hair. And the one I see a lot, Pat Shinn, is a brunette. Saturday [this was Tuesday and it would seem Kell was getting lined up for the balance of the week] there's a girl from Washington going to be in town. Runs a big model agency there. About the number one girl is herself.

"She's a German girl but she's a real dark brunette. Now let's look down the list."

Kell opened his top desk drawer, from which he extracted his contemporary "little black book." This was similar to the one auctioned several years ago, providing a fair amount of war materiel for the embattled Israelis. Kell opened it fondly.

"Here, I'm just looking at the overall picture. Well, I would say that more of them are blondes, a lot not naturally." Kell laughs. "They help it along a little. So, I don't even think about whether they're blonde or not."

I got the feeling that Kell was equivocating, in a gentlemanly manner, of course, rather than ruffle the feathers of nonblondes found on the pages of his directory. Instead of pursuing the distinctions I mentioned the name of a young lady whom I'd been informed was Kell's "one and only." I was not referring to Mary Freeman Kelly.

"Sigrid, you mean," Kelly responded. "She probably *was* the longest lasting and most serious situation I was involved in since I was married. That's perhaps because she followed in right after I separated [from his wife] and I hadn't built up any record at that time."

Kell laughed.

"So Sigrid had an open field with me, so to speak, and she

became *very* possessive and had a *very* lively temper. She used to give me a bit of a hard time. I talk to her on the phone about once a month. Drop her a card now and then, or she sends me a little birthday or Christmas present. And she visited here a year ago. Stayed with the Alan Halperns [Alan is Editor of the *Philadelphia Magazine*]. Alan and his wife, Bummie, are very friendly with Sigrid.

"And then I was in California two months ago at the National Championship, and she came down for a couple of days at Long Beach to visit me there. But we're just . . ."

Kell shrugged his shoulders.

"Well, we get along a lot better when we're not together all the time. If we were together steadily, we'd probably—it would get a little tempestuous again.

"One thing, Art, I'm happy to say, is that of all the gals I've ever dated, that I see at all now, or even that I don't see, I don't know of any that I'm mad at or who are really mad at me. Always, when I broke up, it's never been a *nasty* breakup. Maybe my wife's a little bit upset with me. That could be."

At this point I kept silent although I might have mentioned to Kell that his wife, Mary, with whom I'd had dinner the preceding evening, was more than a little upset. Kell went on to talk about another big romance in his life, this one in the past.

"There was maybe one other gal in France that I was a little heavy with in the early Fifties. I met her in the navy and on international rowing trips and so on. I didn't understand the attitude of French girls and their traditions, from the good families of France. You know that if you take a gal out without a chaperone, you're like engaged, you know. I get a little nervous here and there and you know, they were leaning on me, the family was.

"I had to make a quick escape. I did like her very much. But I chickened out and haven't seen her. And when I left there was a lot of crying and gnashing of teeth and so forth. And I don't know how she views me today."

Is there any one gal in particular at the moment? Kell shook his head.

"Not at the moment. I mean there are several others, a half dozen that I . . . In Philadelphia, there's four or five and I think they're all very nice but I mean they're not particularly right. And then I have two or three in New York and one or two in Washington, three or four in California, a couple in Miami. I got this . . ."

For me, the logistics were startling. I asked Kell how he possibly kept track of all these women. He grinned.

"It's easy." He opened up the little black book and thumbed through it.

"Here we go—Los Angeles, New York, San Diego, New Orleans, Washington, Baltimore, Tennessee—'cause there's two or three cities in Tennessee—Atlanta, Detroit, Cincinnati, Hawaii, Fort Lauderdale, Harrisburg, Mexico City, Kansas City, Dallas, Pittsburgh, Wilmington, Seattle, Denver, a little island in Colombia, Guatemala . . ."

The list seemed endless and the geography exhausting.

"When I was president of the AAU, I was traveling all over. You get in these places and you meet a lot of sports guys and gals here and there and you take her to dinner. And when you come back that way, if you ever do, you take them out again. Send them a postcard here and there and that's how I keep track of them.

"When I go on a trip . . . it's always nice to have friends that you can call upon when you happen to be there. And I have some special ones come visit me here occasionally."

I wondered aloud if Kell had *any* idea what went wrong with his marriage. He was thoughtful for half a minute, then answered with the complete candor and honesty Kathy told me to expect.

"Well, a lot of things, a lot of contributing factors. One is that my wife was more intellectual than I am. She was an 'A' student. I was never that. She has very high ideals, moral standards, and she has other things that I think are . . . well . . . I happen to be compulsively neat. Now, you might say everything is in order in my desk."

That was certainly true.

"My apartment," he went on, "you walk in and out and everything is in place."

I did just that later and again Kell was not stretching the truth.

"For whatever reason, being in the service or military school, the fact that my father was very strict that way, had me rake the beach and make it look perfect *every* Saturday or Sunday morning when I was a young fellow down at the shore. Whatever it was he beat into me, and whatever reason, I am that way."

Kell raised his hands despairingly.

"Little irritating things, the toothpaste squeezings, the fact that the desk at home, Mary and I shared. I had all *my* stuff in one little corner of the desk and the rest of the desk was piled high with *her* stuff. It used to drive me nuts, worrying about bills that hadn't been paid. I worry about things like that, which would get lost in the mess.

"And when she'd go away for a day or so or for a weekend, for a swimming meet with her team, I'd spend a couple of hours putting everything in order, the 'musts' that had to be done immediately, the things that could wait. Then she would scream and holler at me that she *knew* where everything was . . . and . . . well. She couldn't have because sometimes I'd be very embarrassed by unpaid bills and other things, invitations that weren't answered. I guess every couple has some kind of those problems. But I mean that was just *one* of hers.

"Mary has a *great*, misplaced inferiority complex. Pretty gal [I think she's beautiful], looks like the Julie Andrews type. She was a brainy dame. Honors at Penn and that's not an easy school. She's an excellent athlete, you know, a national swimming champion. And an Olympic team member."

I asked Kell where he'd first met her.

"At Helsinki; we dated then in Washington, where she lived, when I was stationed at the Naval Academy. I'd have her come to Philadelphia weekends and of course, *my* mother had to call *her* mother, which was, in those days, the way it went, and arrange for things. But she had this, as I say, this great inferiority complex which was not noticeable until we were married. And *very* nervous and high-strung when she would be competing in anything.

"She had a complex about my sisters and my mother. But to her credit she did not follow the normal family routine by going to work on the Women's Medical College Auxiliary. She became active with the YWCA and today is still active with them. She became like the head person on their board, their head civilian. She also became active with the Children's Hospital, *plus* having a lot of children, *plus* running a terrific swimming program."

Kell sighed deeply.

"We had our best years when we were both immensely busy. And we'd sort of pass each other and say 'Hi,' you know how you . . . Most marriage counselors said, 'You two got to spend more time together.' But when we ever spent time together things got worse. Everything was better, it seems to me, when we were both busy and didn't have too much contact.

"In those days I was busy training; I wasn't going out every night. I think our marriage was a very solid one through the time I was still competing. It deteriorated a little after I stopped serious training and had more outside interests. I was getting more and more involved in civic, charitable, and political things. And sports, too, but more on the organizational level."

Kell and I went on to reasons for the marital disaster.

"My wife is a 'white knuckler.' That's nervous tension. She's nervous as the devil. We got to a point where we would be going on a vacation someplace; Mary was nervous for a week before we went and nervous about coming back. We got so we couldn't go practically anyplace. So this was a handicap. She has a fair complexion so she didn't like to lie around the pools and the beach like I do. She didn't like Ocean City and didn't want to go down there. She got me out of the habit of the shore which I truly loved for a good many years, all my life, as a matter of fact."

I suggested that perhaps Kell's association with Harlow may have upset Mary and members of the family. My host laughed heartily, dismissing the incident as a lark.

"I went with her just a few times. And it was only . . . well, she was leaning on me a little when we used to hang out at her club down on Bank Street. She used to needle me with, 'When are you going to take me out?' and I'd answer, 'Oh, well, I'm busy here and there . . . meetings, business, you know.' She'd say, 'I don't work Tuesdays and Sundays.'

"Well, one night I was having dinner with a couple of other couples who were 'Young Presidents.' So we were in a restaurant on Front Street and they all met Harlow and were fascinated with her. A week or two later one of the gals called me up and said, 'We're having a little party on Sunday night, why don't you come over and bring Harlow?' I think she wanted to liven the party.

"And well, Harlow'd been needling me, and this might be the appropriate time. What the heck? Who's going to know? Everybody'd be quiet."

Kell grinned.

"I sort of—well, there's a little devilment in me and I like to put people on, do something dizzy once in a while. And so I called Harlow; she was delighted to go. She called me back several times about what to wear and this and that."

As the president of Kelly for Brickwork expressed it, this might well be Rachel Finocchio's initial venture into Society and she wanted to be prepared.

"Apparently it was Harlow's first really good dinner date. Of course she is a gorgeous person. Good-looking! And so we went and the people were fascinated; she was the center of attraction the whole night. I thought, what the heck, it's all done now.

"But some smart-ass at the party—maybe one of the columnists . . . And of course I got a good ribbing about it. And then at the Young Presidents party—it was on women's lib, and I thought it would be a good put-on to bring Harlow. So that's the kind of thing I did about three times. That is all I ever took her out. I met her at a couple of parties. Once I had a party where everybody came stag and she came and since the party was at my apartment, somebody might have assumed she was with me.

"At a modeling show where she was, and a bunch of us went out to dinner afterward, people might have assumed she was my date. But it never really was. The extent of it was *grossly* blown out of proportion. I guess people wanted to talk about it. They wanted to tell and retell it. And Rachel didn't help, you know. Because any time she was interrogated by anybody from the press she'd tell them 'I have nothing to say.' Well, when you say *that*, you imply."

Kell appeared mildly surprised that I'd talked with Joe Regan.

"I hear you found my old rowing partner. I haven't seen Joe much lately of course, but we were both very close friends when we were lifeguards down at the shore. He used to be a pretty wild guy. But once he got married he became very straight."

My host shook his head sadly.

"I think Joe's very down on me that I'm not living the perfect Catholic life. I know he disapproves of my actions. So, as I say, he did the things years ago that I'm doing now. That's the difference."

29

THEY LOVED HIM
IN LOUISVILLE

FOR WEEKS I'D BEEN UNSUCCESSFUL IN MANY ATTEMPTS TO
see Jack Edelstein, reputed to be one of Kell's best friends. The
other is restaurateur Stanley Green. But Edelstein was spending
his time traveling and I never could catch up with him, that is,
until recently, on a flight to Philadelphia from Los Angeles. I
wondered who my seatmate would be, naturally hoping for a
pretty girl. Instead, it was Edelstein. Out came my tape recorder
and over drinks, dinner, a horrible movie, and haughty unsmiling
hostesses who kept bumping their tight little behinds into my
armrest, I listened to another version of John B. Kelly, Jr., from
the tall, handsome, balding gentleman and occasional visitor to
Monaco.

"I saw Kell back in 1946," recalled Edelstein. "I was a navy
pilot on the carrier *Saratoga* and got shot down off the Philippine
Islands. They stationed me at Bainbridge, Maryland, to get ready
for my discharge. I was assigned to the camp newspaper probably
because I'd never been a newspaperman. I was sent to cover a
story of some world-famous rower who was coming through the
camp, and took a photographer with me.

"Well, the world-famous rower turned out to be Kell and
we recognized each other from the shore. He was in boot camp
on the V-12 program. The war was over at that time. So we posed
Kell sitting on a bench with his boots on and using a pair of mops

for oars. It was a good picture and made practically every paper in the country.

"We kept up the friendship ever since. I went down to Washington for his wedding. As you know he was married at Walter Reed Hospital where Mary's father was an Army Colonel. All the guys went down, Joe Flanagan, Dave de Filipo, Buddy and Felix Spatola and Joe Regan. I think Joe was the best man."

(Joe had told me he wasn't.)

"Well, so much for Kell's wedding. Kell still stayed in shape. He was always in training and could date only up to twelve o'clock at night. On weekends we used to wait for him to go home so we could steal his girls. He lived at 2601 when he was first married and then after Annie was born, he moved to Wynnewood and became very prolific."

I asked Jack if Harry Jay Katz or Kiki were among The Fast Folks. His answer was no, that the only ones close to Kell were Tommy Foglietta and Stanley Green and himself.

"*Not* Harry Jay Katz," Edelstein said with some emphasis. "Kell does have out-of-town friends, associates of his from being in the Olympics.

"*Not* Harry Jay Katz," Edelstein repeated. "If you remember the Kelly Roast, I did a simulated newscast which went like this:

"Harry Jay Katz asked me to mention his name here today, so here goes. Harry was in an automobile accident and fortunately somebody came by and saw his medical alert: 'In case of an accident, call a press conference.' "

I mentioned Sigrid and asked if Jack knew her well. He nodded. "She was a nice girl, came here and wanted to get married. She got a job and she was no dummy. Very quiet. I got along with her tremendously. At the mayor's inauguration held in the Academy I brought Sigrid there and hid her up in the press headquarters where we were watching the ceremonies. Evidently Mary saw her; I don't know how, but knowing Kell, he probably told her Sigrid was there.

"Then that night I went with Sigrid to the Inaugural Ball at the Spectrum and went over to Kell and Mary, not knowing Mary knew anything about it. Mary got really upset and ran out of the building.

"When Grace was in town for that Library Gala, we all went to Kell's afterward for a party. Grace said to me, 'Who's that girl with Kell?' and I answered with that old line, 'If this is Friday, it must be Sharon.' Grace laughed and said, 'I've got to go back and tell that to Rainier.' "

Edelstein's ginger ale and my martini arrived.

"I've got to tell you about Kell's fear of ever admitting he's sick. I've spoken to him many times when he's been deathly ill. I know because I've put a thermometer in his mouth and he's running a temperature. He might have a touch of flu or something but the guy will *not* get into bed and rest. He wants to stand on his record that he's never missed a day."

Jack laughed.

"He absolutely believes it, you know. Recently he came back from California. I picked him up at the airport and he couldn't talk. So I said, 'Kell, you go right to bed. I'll drop you off at your apartment.' He refused; he had to go to a 'meat market opening.' He just will not take it easy."

Edelstein considers himself almost a part of the family and with good reason.

"My parents passed away shortly before their fiftieth wedding anniversary, nine months apart. It was loneliness because they couldn't stand being apart. John B., Kell's father, unknown to Kell, called me up and asked me to come over to his house to meet him. He said, 'Look, Jack, I know your parents passed away and maybe you'd like to move into our home until you get yourself situated. You are *so* close to our family.'

"Mr. Kelly, himself, was getting very sick at the time. What he said to me I thought was fantastic. But I told him while I appreciated his offer very much I had to learn to live on my own."

Edelstein chuckled.

"My mother was always wanting me to get married. She'd keep bringing girls over to the house all the time. Finally she got so desperate she put up a sign on our house on the front lawn. It

read: 'THE LAST SINGLE JEWISH BOY BEFORE YOU HIT THE EX-
PRESSWAY.' "

Our second drinks arrived.

"Kell and I were in Lucerne, Switzerland, a couple of years
ago," Jack went on. "We decided since we were that close we'd
go to the Palace. Kell called Grace and said he'd be there the next
day. Kell and I both like practical jokes so he didn't mention
that I'd be along. Instead he told his sister he'd met the world's
championship diver, who was Japanese, and could he bring him
to Monaco.

"Grace said, 'Sure, of course.' So I went out and bought a ridic-
ulous swimsuit. I had a pair of extra-large kind of Japanese teeth
made by my dentist. Oh yes, and I was wearing a big pair of
dark glasses which covered my face. So Jack told Grace and Rainier
we were fortunate to have this Japanese with us because he was
willing to give a diving exhibition in the Palace pool.

"Well, Kell brought out Grace and Rainier and there I was
standing up on the diving board looking completely ludicrous,
waving my arms and nodding my head in a kind of warmup. Kell
didn't crack a smile while he was telling about my diving ex-
ploits."

Edelstein has a great flair for both mimicry and double-talk
and as he stood on the board preparing to dive, he put them both
into use.

"I looked over at Rainier and Grace watching me. In a Japanese
accent I informed them quite seriously that I was a 'Jupe,' that
my mother was a Japanese and my father a Jew. I could see Grace
was trying hard to preserve her dignity. Well, after some double-
talk about what a famous diver I was, I stepped back to the start
of the board, took a run to the edge, and did a tremendous belly
flop. Then they caught on and howled; Rainier was hysterical.

"Talking about Rainier; he's a great guy with a wonderful sense
of humor. Kell and I took him to the Kentucky Derby last year.
So the three of us went into a nightclub, which was kind of a
strip joint. The local press had made a big deal about Rainier
being in for the Derby and his picture was plastered all over the

lot. Well, one of the strippers kept hanging around Rainier, telling him he looked familiar.

"So I told her he was a rich Jewish clothing manufacturer from New York and that his name was Irving. Seems like Rainier likes Jewish humor. I make record albums but with Jewish humor. His favorite is 'When You're in Love, the Whole World's Jewish.' I sent it to him."

Our tray dinners arrived; while we ate them Jack told me another practical joke he played.

"Some time ago I got hold of a human arm from a Philadelphia medical college which shall be nameless. That night I had to drive to Jersey over the Delaware Bridge and I took the arm with me. After I'd inserted the coin in the collector's machine I manipulated everything so that the guy at the bridge was left holding the 'other guy's' hand.

"As I pulled away I heard a scream and boy, they came right after me. My father had to take care of the problem. I gave the story to Kell, who got the biggest kick out of it. He told it to students at Hahnemann Medical College, where he was giving a lecture. And I said to him that all of them would be pulling off cadavers' arms and using them for practical jokes."

The movie was playing; Jack watched it but I fell asleep even though that tale of the bodiless hand rested heavily on my dinner. By the time I awoke, the "No smoking" sign was on and a few minutes later we were on the ground. The trip had been profitable. I knew why Jack Edelstein bears the title of "Monaco's Court Jester."

30

"I LIKE THE GUY BUT . . ."

IF I GAINED NOTHING ELSE FROM MY REGRETTABLY TANGENTIAL association with the Fast Folks, at least I gained a new use for an old word.

Webster defines *bearding* as 1. "A beardlike growth, 2. The cutting away of . . . a timber to fit a ship's angle, 3. The forward edge of the rudder or the corresponding edge of the sternpost." My authority for an entirely new and certainly different interpretation of *bearding* is Stanley Green, restaurateur, husband of Agnes, and friend of John B. Kelly, Jr., as well as Fast Folks member in good standing.

"Bearding," said Stanley, "is what I used to do for Kell."

I *know* I looked puzzled.

"Bearding is like the third person. Say Kell is going out with a girl and he wants to take her to the Milano or Drake Hotel. He's married to Mary; instead of scooting and going way out into the suburbs and killing the time driving, a third person, like myself, would be the beard."

It dawned on me finally, although I couldn't quite comprehend just why Kell needed a "beard," an escort for a woman who was really his date. John B., Jr., isn't the least hypocritical about anything. If I may mix a metaphor, he never tries to hide his girls under a bushel or needs a disguise. The subject of Kell's grand passion arose and to my surprise, Stanley did not agree this was Sigrid.

"If there was any real love or anybody that he would have ever married, if he could have, it would have been Carol Clay. And there's a girl he's been seeing in Detroit called Tammy, a model, and she's a darling.

"Lately, Kell's been on the Jewish kick. He's taken out a very nice girl, one of Mike Douglas' production assistants, and a few others."

Stanley, who seemed quite pleased with his friend Kell's lack of prejudice told one on himself.

"You want to hear something, the funniest story in the whole world?"

I nodded vigorously.

"Well, when Sigrid broke off with Kell and even a while after, I was single at the time and I said, 'Sigrid, I would like to take you out.' She said, 'There's only one person in the whole world I wouldn't go out with.'

" 'Who's that, Sigrid?'

" 'You, Stanley.' "

I think it's time we heard a few words about Kell from his friend Harry Jay Katz, columnist, author, reporter, wit, and certainly the Quaker City's most famous man-about-town.

"You know," he said, "the other day I noticed them building a new stand on the Schuylkill, I guess for some national regatta. And I often thought, would they do a statue of Kell? And if they did, would they place it in front of his Dad or next to him? I finally decided it would have to be three steps behind his father."

Not long ago I spent an evening with Kell. It began in Kell's breathtaking twenty-seventh-floor penthouse overlooking the river he loves just as much as his father did. The place is comfortable, furnished in masculine fashion and filled with the medals Kell's won in national and international sculling events. Then, in the company of an attractive, intelligent blonde, we made our host's nightly rounds, self-appointed chores he handles with great dignity and no feeling of condescension.

We went to a student art exhibit, a school orchestra concert, a charity flower show. Everywhere we went Kell was greeted with considerable affection. Kids scrambled all around him, their parents pushed their way through crowds to shake his hands. Like many others who live in the Quaker City, I just wish he would use his popularity for some greater good.

I think Kell's oldest child, green-eyed Anne, understands her father better than anyone else and I know loves him deeply.

"I have very good feelings for my father," Anne said. "I know I could do anything because he doesn't love me for what I do. He loves *me*! He couldn't care less as far as my career is concerned or anything else as long as I'm happy. That's what matters to my father.

"My mother put a lot more emphasis on academic achievement and gave me the intellectual freedom to read whatever I wanted, no matter what. I was reading constantly, Edgar Allan Poe when I was nine. I was reading books the other kids in class weren't allowed to. Even books, you know, like *The Godfather*. My mother figured what I couldn't understand I'd skim over and when I reread it at an older age, I'd understand.

"So I was given a lot of leeway and was taken out of Catholic school where too many restraints are put on you. By that I think my mother meant prejudices. During the Cuban missile crisis I went to a Catholic school. My mother was really upset then. The attitude of the nuns was—I was seven years old at the time—that when the Communists came and asked you if you were Catholic and if you said you were not, they'd let you go."

Anne smiled bitterly.

"On the other hand, you would go straight to hell right after you died because you denied your religion. You had the choice of going to hell the minute you died or dying right away."

Anne's major interest is the care and training of the mentally retarded.

"I guess I got interested in that field because of my sister Moira. I'm taking courses at Penn now, night school, because during the day I'm a waitress at Stanley Green's restaurant. And on weekends and when I have time free I work as a recreational therapist for retarded adults at the Elwyn Training Institution.

"Moira's had fantastic teachers in the past. She is not Mongoloid as far as I know but this was something that my family never discussed. I can look at Moira almost objectively as a professional. I feel she's educable, that she'll be able to work in the community sometime, as long as she has a 'Citizen Advocate'—that's someone to watch over her.

"My sister Moira probably will be able to work in an institutional kitchen; she's studying dietary training now and she's eighteen. As far as marriage and children are concerned, I don't know. It's something that depends completely upon her maturity and intelligence. My own long-range plan is to open up a day camp center for normal or retarded children, although I can't train my sister. That would be like a doctor practicing on his own family."

Anne told me she's been working since she was fifteen years old.

"I've always liked to be able to do and have things but not on the allowance I would get, if I got one."

Anne paused and smiled.

"Well, what my father would call adequate; ten dollars wouldn't keep me in cigarettes for a week. So I work. He is good about school and pays tuition, that's when I can't work full time. I wouldn't know what to do with myself if I didn't work. I'm not the country club type and I'm not a good athlete.

"So, as I said, my major interest is in mental health and I'm keeping files on legislation. I'm trying to get a foster child but it's not easy as a single person. I had a little girl for a while last summer, a three-month-old baby who weighed only six pounds then. Her mother is an alcoholic who had given the baby to a friend who in turn 'gave' her to me. I had her for a month.

"I wasn't really equipped and for a while she was sleeping in a trunk at the end of my bed. But the mother eventually turned up again so I had to give her back the child. It's so sad; the little girl's name is Charleen. She's black and the last time I heard she was at Temple Hospital suffering from malnutrition. She was a darling!"

Anne sighed.

"I wish I had my own little family right now. I guess I miss the atmosphere. We have six children in our family but I'm not real, real close to them. I go out for holidays and things like that. I have more in common with my father than my mother. I think our personalities are closer."

I asked Anne if she knew why her parents separated.

"As far as I know it was another woman. I don't know whether I'm supposed to say that or not but it *was* another woman. You know I have four sisters and one brother. They're all intelligent and each has a different personality. But we're not just a warm, huggly family. I just don't know how my parents mated up.

"They're both so busy and the two, together, seemed incongruous. My mother is very intellectual and my father"—Anne laughed—"well, you know he is not. The only thing they had in common was sports. Other than that, nothing."

Anne described her siblings.

"My little sister Liz, who's seventeen, is a real fighter, and has great ambitions; mine are mediocre compared to hers. She wants to be a doctor; she's very engrossed and how she works! And she's a good little athlete. There's my sister Susan. She's nineteen and goes to the Pennsylvania Academy of Fine Arts night school. During the day she works in a photography shop, trying to finish art school.

"You know about Moira. My brother J.B. is quiet; it's hard for me to say if he's more like my mother or father. The poor guy, he's had so many girls around him all his life, all these hopping, chattering women. So he's quiet and smart, nice kid. He's sixteen.

"Buttons! Margaret Christiana, is our little show girl. She's nine, a very sensual little girl. She looks very much like a Kelly, my father. She's a real cutie pie. She's a combination of both her grandmothers, for whom she's named. I'm not tall, five feet two, but the rest of the family is. Liz is over six feet, Susan, five ten, my brother is over six feet also, and already Buttons comes up to my chin."

Anne reached legal maturity this past summer.

"Councilman John B. Kelly, Jr.," wrote Bill Curry (member of the Fast Folks) in the Philadelphia *Inquirer* on June 24, this past year, "helped his lovely daughter, Anne, celebrate her twenty-first birthday this past week at his penthouse bachelor pad in the Plaza overlooking the Benjamin Franklin Parkway."

I close the book of Kell with a one-liner from Charles Kelly, Sr.

"My father," said Charles Kelly, Jr., "told me Kell was a good bricklayer; there is no higher accolade."

31

"YOU *NEVER* PUT THESE THINGS IN WRITING"

BASED ON WHAT OTHERS HAD TOLD ME I WASN'T PREPARED FOR the kind of woman Mary Kelly was nor her physical presence. Of course I'd seen her photographs in swimsuits, leisure and formal attire, in the press, and a framed portrait of his wife on Kell's desk. But the image in my mind certainly was not the tall, stunning, beautifully groomed lady who greeted me with poise at the Art Alliance, where we had dinner. I'd been with Kell only a few hours before and I thought to myself what a handsome couple they must have made. Mary suggested we start out on a first-name basis and that's the way it was.

Of course Mary knew why I wanted to talk to her but she possesses so much natural dignity I didn't know how, or maybe didn't have the nerve, to begin probing into the marital life of this very reserved person. In fact, I wondered why she'd been willing to see me at all and that was the first question I asked as we sat in the Member's Room having a drink.

She smiled slightly and said she'd been urged by her daughter Anne, whom she loves and whose opinion she apparently respects. Since Mary promised to see me again the following week I thought it might go easier for both of us this first time if I left the recorder in its case so that what was said wouldn't go on tape. My guest agreed and, as a consequence, while my recollections of that initial evening we spent together are reasonably accurate they are not verbatim and hence are unquoted.

Mr. and Mrs. John B. Kelly, Jr.

For a long while, through cocktails and dinner, we spoke of almost everything and skirted the topic that brought us together. I don't think Mary is shy. I believe she's a private person and, except for her athletic activities, is almost the exact antithesis of her husband. We talked about books—Mary's an avid reader—theater, politics, education, housing, racial issues, and I freely admit that my guest was far better informed on those subjects than I.

Finally, near the end of an evening, pleasant and slightly uncomfortable for me and, although she didn't show it, a bit tense for Mary, she did speak of her present unhappy situation at home. She told me it was still almost impossible for her to believe Kell actually walked out and left her with six children. Never for a moment did she display signs of self-pity or the attitude of a "wronged woman." Rather I thought that, after eight years of abandonment, she still was bewildered by the fact that the man she loved (and probably continues to love) acted as he did.

One of the tragedies of the separation, Mary said, was the difficulty their son, John B. Kelly, III, has in adjusting to his father's way of life, which he reads about almost daily in the press. The other children who are at home, with the exception of nine-year-old Buttons, cannot comprehend why their parents are not together. Anne, Mary says, is adjusted to life, is ambitious, has managed to resolve any differences she had with her father, and is able to live with them.

Kell's association with Harlow and its subsequent notoriety appeared to horrify Mary more than anything else her husband did. For her mother-in-law's handling of the political situation that evolved from the association between John B. Kelly, Jr., and Rachel (née Richard Finocchio), Mary had nothing but praise and expressed her fondness and respect for the widow of John B. Kelly, Sr.

Another cause for Mary's astonishment at Kell's actions is the fact that frequently, when he returns to Philadelphia after AAU trips, he telephones her and discusses mutual friends he'd met on the road. Her husband's conversation, Mary said, is as though she and Kell were still living together; that he'd soon be home for dinner and that life would go on as usual between married couples who are briefly apart.

On my way home from dinner with this gracious, poised woman, I had difficulty reconciling my own impressions of Mary Kelly with those of others who'd known her longer. Mrs. William McKenna, for example.

"From my earliest recollection," Kathy said, "even when I was a teen-ager, and the Kelly women were well dressed always, to put it nicely, Mary Kelly was a kind of tacky-looking person. If she and Kell were going to a black-tie affair, she'd be in street clothes. Mary was the one who had a run in her stocking."

Kathy laughed.

"It wouldn't have been so bad if she didn't have to stand beside Ma and Grace Kelly, who were always done to the nines—hat made out of the same fabric as the suit—everything went together. And—there was Mary! It's something which would really not bother Kell. He just doesn't know. I'm very fond of Kell; he wouldn't notice and might not *care*. It's not important to him at all. I don't want to say he doesn't know 'good' but it doesn't concern him much.

"When Kell was inaugurated into Council this session, Anne Kelly attended. It was at the Academy of Music and wintertime. People were wearing fur coats, mufflers, and galoshes. And Anne had on a gray cotton dress with a bare midriff and a coat over it. This is wrong. It's bad! It gives a terrible impression. I assure you I've never been able to say to him, 'Kell, why do your children look like street urchins? Why are they so badly dressed? Why does their hair need washing? Why is Moira's neck so dirty?' It's not my business, they're not my children. But, I tell you if they were, they wouldn't look like that.

"I understand from Kell that during the years he and Mary were married, his sisters and father were thoroughly critical of Mary. And yet, at the time of the separation, they went over to her side."

Kell's administrative assistant chuckled.

"Let me tell you about waffles. Waffles! Mary and Kell were going to have them for breakfast. Something happened whereby Mary lifted the top of the iron and the waffles stuck to both sides and weren't done. She got totally hysterical. Poor Kell said, 'Oh well, Mary, we'll have pancakes or we'll have eggs.'

"But to Mary, this was a *terrific* problem. I think she'd been accustomed to being criticized and so everything weighed on her mind. She said, 'I can't do anything *right*. I can't even make waffles.' "

I asked Kathy who had been picking on Mary, whether it was when Mary had been a child.

"Oh, no," Kathy answered, "not when she was a child. It was by his family. During the early, latter, and entire years of their marriage she was subjected to great criticism and I think she became resentful of it but I don't think she was willing to heed any of it. Clearly, she must have thought she looked fine because now she looks worse than she ever did before.

"I don't know how much younger she really is than Kell, who's going to be forty-nine this month. She's probably forty-five. And now, as I understand it, and have seen, she's in jeans and tee shirts and stringy hair, which she loops on top of her head with some kind of woolen beret. Big on macramé and a scrubbed face and she's just a little too old for this number.

"But after all, who sees her? Who would *want* to? She's not seen Kell nor has he seen her in the entire years they've been separated. Not laid eyes on each other. They talk on the telephone. That's it. If he comes to the house, which is frequently to drop off the money, if she's there outside and the car pulls up, she goes inside. If he should come into the living room, she goes out the back door. She'll go anywhere but face him."

Kathy frowned.

"Where I understand the problem began is of an intimate nature."

Kathy smiled.

"Mary kind of figured out what was causing all those children. It finally came to her and she was unwilling to take the obvious precautionary measures. She took a real good one on her own [Kathy laughed] not to get pregnant. It's surefire; a *real* good way!

"This was all about the time Kell retired from active competition, the same year his father died. And he had all this pent-up energy."

"Sexual, you mean?"

Kathy nodded.

"I know he began to look for an outlet and he didn't have to look so hard. As I understand from Kell, he proceeded to see a girl whose name I do not know and don't think I ever did.

"I don't think Kell was seeing her frequently but he *was* seeing her. He did *not* know she was married. What happened is that her husband found out, then called Mary. And he then followed up with a letter containing a note or postcard which Kell had written [to the man's wife]."

Kathy frowned.

"Which was one of the stupidest things I ever heard of and I told him so. 'Good grief,' I said, 'you *never* put these things in writing.' Well, he learned. Now I don't know what it was, but it was in his handwriting and clear proof of the pudding. He wouldn't lie and he didn't. And therein is the crux of the whole matter. He denied nothing. Yes, that's right; that's what had been happening and why.

"They saw attorneys. His family persuaded Kell to see a psychiatrist because they were convinced he was crazy. And he did! He told the man the truth. 'Look, I'm not going to do this [what his father had done]. Perhaps I'm wrong and that may be. But I've spent my entire life doing *everything* that *everybody* wanted me to. And I won't go on anymore.

"And, Arthur, he hasn't," said Kathy.

I thought of Kathy's words when Mary met me, tape recorder in hand, the following week for dinner at the Peale Club. She looked as stunning ("smashing," the English say and it's a good adjective) as she had the last time. Offhand, except for Kell, I can't think of any male past the age of twenty who wouldn't be flattered to be seen in Mary Kelly's company.

This time there was no hesitation about the tape recorder.

"Kell and I met at the 1952 Olympic Games in Helsinki, Finland," Mary said. "People say we met on the plane but that's not so. In those days, I guess even today, sports teams went over on separate planes, the swimmers on one and the oarsmen on another. I didn't know him at all but he did know one of the girls on the swimming team, a girl I was rooming with.

"I was with her, Gail Peters, standing in front of the Olympic Village in Helsinki. He kept bounding across the street and started talking to Gail, who didn't introduce us. But I recall seeing him and I did know who he was. A couple of days later he and some others from the rowing teams came over to the girls' dormitory where we were staying and called up to ask if some of us would like to go to the circus.

"As it happened I felt ill that night and didn't come along. He told me much later this was, in a sense, when he became interested in me. But it didn't work out that particular time. He was stationed at the Naval Academy following the Olympic Games and in the fall he called me from Annapolis."

Mary was then living in Washington. Her father, a biochemist who'd been a professor at the Universities of Arizona, Maine, and Massachusetts, was stationed at Walter Reed Hospital doing toxicological research for the U.S. Army. He held the rank of colonel. During World War Two, Colonel Freeman was first stationed in England, after which he went to France.

I asked Mary if she were close to her father. She hesitated a few seconds before answering.

"It's very difficult for a young person—I was going on eight when he left for Europe and almost thirteen years old when he came home. And I think that's a tremendous gap to have a father away."

Mary paused. At this point I do think she was recalling that Kell had been away from his children for over seven years. During the past and in subsequent conservations Mary rarely referred to her husband by name; it was almost never Kell or Jack, merely "he."

"I have a brother three and a half years younger than I. I'd say we had the normal jealousies and fights. Looking back now, it must have been difficult for Monroe—we call him 'Mike'— when we were both teen-agers because I was very good at swimming and he wasn't. I was a national, although not a world champion and represented the United States in the Olympics. There are four categories in swimming—free-style, breaststroke, butterfly, and backstroke. The last was mine.

"This was in 1952 and the South Africans won the backstroke. Generally, European girls were stronger than those from the United States. Today it's another story, American swimmers are the best in the world. As I said, I represented the United States but I didn't make the finals. It was a very big thing in my life. I think it was difficult for Mike to come up behind someone like me and I wasn't much help, I must say. He's very, very bright and I think he's now a more whole human being than I ever was.

"My mother was a lovely person, feminine and very much an individualist. Neither my mother nor father is living. They were in Washington after I was married. I wasn't close to them in the sense that one might be close to one's parents if you were in the same town."

I asked Mary when her father died.

"Four years ago. I never talked to my parents about the problems leading to the breakup. I didn't talk to anyone."

Mary hesitated again.

"Yes, I guess I did. There was one person that I talked to. It wasn't someone whom I knew terribly well and it wasn't someone that anyone would know. It was a person who'd been very kind to me when my last child was born. She was a nurse. The baby was premature; she's as hale and hearty as can be now but she stayed in the hospital because it was a difficult birth. This particular nurse was very kind, stopped in to see the baby every day.

"It was really devastating for me to come home from the hospital without the baby. In fact, I wasn't allowed to see her there until the very day I left because I had a bad infection and they were afraid the baby would pick it up. I talked to this nurse because she was so understanding, was removed from the scene, and didn't know anybody else. I guess I felt free to confide in her simply because she had no connection with anyone I knew."

I asked whether there was any specific action on Kell's part that precipitated the break between them, a woman, for example. Mary stroked her forehead with her hand several times, deep in thought, and was silent for perhaps a minute.

"You know, it's awfully hard when you look back. It might have been a hint or a clue that things weren't going well. Perhaps there was an underlying difference in assumptions, on both our parts, assumptions so deep-seated that they are, perhaps, at the bottom of the whole thing."

Mary seemed to be going through such painful self-appraisal that I thought to myself, "The hell with putting her through any more." I reached over to disconnect the recorder; she saw my

Prince Rainier and Princess Grace leaving Kell's home in Wynnewood with his twelve-day-old daughter for the latter's baptism. Mary Kelly, the mother, is to the right of the Princess, and the grandmother, Mrs. John B. Kelly, Sr., is in the background.

action, shook her head, and smiled as though to imply she'd gone this far, she might as well finish.

"Well, I'm talking about the assumptions I meant about marriage and perhaps what were the premises on which he saw our marriage."

Was she referring to monogamy?

"Yes. Yes. But more than that. I don't think he ever would have said that his attitude was monogamistic. For me, a marriage or at least I believed at the time, you gave yourself wholly and completely."

Did Mary mean sexually?

"Oh, *more* than sexually. I don't think that was the cause of our break. I think that underlying all of that is the different expectations of marriage. Going beneath sexual compatibility or sexual needs or anything like that.

"I think it goes somewhere along the line—I had made the assumption that marriage meant a *total* sharing of your entire selves, your spiritual self, as nearly as possible, your whole being is shared with and a part of the other person. And I don't believe that was *really* part of his thinking. I sound indefinite because I'm not exactly sure how he felt about that.

"And therefore, in my thoughts of sharing, I gave of myself and even of my weaknesses. So that, whether it was a mistake or not, certainly in *our* marriage it was a mistake to share my weaknesses so easily."

"What were the weaknesses you refer to?" I asked.

"Well, for one thing a lack of confidence in myself. [This is probably what Kathy McKenna referred to as Mary's sense of inferiority.] I mean in my dealings with other people. For example, we'd come away at times, say from a family gathering of all the Kellys. Suddenly, I'd be horribly depressed and perhaps cry a little because I just felt overwhelmed by the competence and talent and good looks . . . everything. This was something, my weakness in failing to recognize he could not understand and cope with. It didn't enhance me in his eyes.

"And that was a mistake on my part. In other words, I'm afraid that I made him a receptacle for whatever feelings I might have had. And perhaps I was looking for some encouragement or some . . . This was something I don't think that he . . . Well, it didn't enhance me. It made me seem less in his eyes."

I asked Mary how she could be so sure.

"Because he was annoyed any time I felt uncertain of myself, or not very strong, ready to take on the world. You see, he *never* had those feelings of insecurity or if he did, he never showed them. I marveled at him always because he never appeared to be unsure of himself and, in a way, I used to regret that.

"I also thought that on the other hand, I wished that he needed *me* a little more. I felt that I needed him *so* much and yet I never *really* had the feeling that he needed me. Of course, I admired that sureness in him."

Again I made a gesture of putting away the tape recorder and again Mary shook her head.

"I think I'm losing my train of thought. Except that looking back I think that the underlying difference was in our points of view of what a marriage meant. And so, when you see I've gone through my life being pretty careful to cover up my weaknesses in front of people, I'm pretty reserved usually and I guess a lot of me is spilling over now. You know, even with my own parents, I've never revealed myself with anyone as I did with him. And that wasn't good as far as our marriage was concerned.

"There wasn't any one incident, a last straw. I can't go into what went on in those last months. He left home on the eleventh of March, 1968, and I couldn't begin to tell you what went on in the months preceding that."

Mary laughed and not bitterly.

"The tape's not long enough for that; I wouldn't be able to be selective."

Was there any particular woman?

"Oh, yes . . . yes. I saw her once although I never met her. My thinking, or what I'm describing is somewhat colored by what he told me during that period of time; things that I never had any idea or even imagined. You see there was so *much*. How *many* other people [she meant women, I'm sure] there had been and the fact that he was absolutely amazed. He'd assumed that I'd known all of this and just had been discreet and not said anything."

Having heard Kell's point of view I'm sure he never deliberately concealed his infidelities from Mary. I think that if at any time during their marriage she had asked him about the philandering, he would have told her, not in the form of a confession but rather as a fact of which he was not ashamed. This was the difference between John B. Kelly, Jr., and John B. Kelly, Sr.

In no way am I defending Kell for his adolescent approach to marriage even if I am not a practitioner of the Elsie Dinsmore philosophy. This, if I recall correctly, barred poor Mr. Travilla from even embracing Elsie until they'd had their second offspring without a satisfactory explanation of how they began their first. Too many innocents have been wounded by Kell's hedonistic existence. Furthermore, I do admit that my attitude toward John B. Kelly, Jr., is tempered by my fondness and respect for Mrs. John B. Kelly, Jr. (Mary still bears that title; divorce proceedings, instituted by her on September 4, 1968, were dropped subsequently.)

If there is any defense of Kell's actions, it must be found in the fact that he is merely the rebellious, unfortunate, highly visible product of a generation that placed more emphasis on the appearance of conformity than conformity itself.

Mary smiled ruefully as she ended the evening.

"Of course, my children accuse me of being very naive. They say I'm the easiest person in the world to pull the wool over. I suppose that's true. I do tend to take people very much at their word and have an inclination to believe what people say to me the first time around."

32

"WE COULDN'T SELL GRACE"

SO MANY PEOPLE (MOST RELATIVES EXCLUDED) HAVE EXPRESSED such wretched opinions of Grace, Rainier, the entire Grimaldi clan, and the Principality of Monaco, to say nothing of the gambling joint that supports it, that it is a pleasure to open this saga of their Serene Highnesses with kind words from someone who loves them both.

I refer to Mr. Dore Schary, my friend of long standing and my authority on the movie industry. Mr. Schary is a gentleman, wit, author, playwright, Academy Award winner, producer, director, after-dinner speaker and, what is of more importance to the subjects under discussion, Metro-Goldwyn-Mayer's chief during Hollywood's good old days.

Coevally with his song of praise for the noble couple, Dore spoke of the fluke that led Miss Grace Kelly to such international film fame that her hand in marriage was sought and won by the compelling combination of a Papal Emissary and a Prince of the Blood.

"The first time I saw Grace Kelly was in a picture that people have forgotten she made," recalled Schary. "I say they've forgotten because she was absolutely ignored afterward. As a matter of fact, she couldn't even get a job."

The film that Dore referred to was *High Noon*. He did not mention it to me by name because he knows I have seen it so many times that I can rattle off all the actors' names from Gary

Princess Grace, 1970.

Cooper and Katy Jurado down to the last bit player. Naturally I remembered Grace Kelly's role and how I fell in love with her rather than the more effervescent Miss Jurado. Had Grace given me a tumble I might have responded in kind even though, in 1952, when *High Noon* was released, I had already been happily married for twenty-two years. By the time I finally did meet Grace some twenty-four years after that she already had her Prince.

Dore interrupted my thoughts.

"We didn't know about Grace not being able to get a job because nobody in the picture business was that impressed with her. It was a namby-pamby part as you remember. Cooper was so wonderful and the picture such a marvelously suspenseful one that everybody paid *no* attention to Grace.

"Then, some time later, we at Metro decided to do a picture called *Mogambo* starring Clark Gable and Ava Gardner. We had in mind getting an English woman actor. Well, we 'lost' her and so we had to get somebody who had style. As the custom was then, you could excavate tests of people you had decided not to sign, which we did. So we asked Fox if they had some stuff.

"And we ran film of Grace Kelly acting as an Irish biddy for a test in a picture called *Taxi* with Dan Dailey. She didn't get the part. But there was something very nice about her. We all thought so and by *we* I mean Sam Zimbalist, the producer of *Mogambo*, John Ford, the director, and myself. We felt she was badly miscast to be playing a kind of dowdy nanny coming from Ireland, you know, with a broad brogue and all that. So John said, Why don't we make a nice color test of Grace?"

Metro-Goldwyn-Mayer made the test.

"Grace looked ravishing; forgive me for saying it but she had so much 'grace.' So we signed her and negotiated a contract which, in those days, was a little unique. That was because long-term contracts were beginning to be passé. But we insisted; we'd given her this role; we knew it was going to be a big part.

"We made the picture, *Mogambo,* and it was very successful. Before we made that there were other pictures we were trying to cast her in but we had Ava Gardner, Lana Turner, Greer Garson, Jane Powell, June Allyson, Deborah Kerr, and a host of others. So the producers say we don't want anybody like Grace; we want someone we know about, Elizabeth Taylor, for example. We couldn't sell Grace.

"Hitchcock asked us about her and put her in *Dial M for Murder.* That one was with Ray Milland. Then Grace made *Rear Window* with James Stewart and by the time *Mogambo* was moving on, Grace Kelly was a big star. And we'd made commitments with her."

Miriam, Dore's wife, interrupted to bring in a concoction called "strawberry tea," which was not nearly as bad as the name led me to believe. My host went on.

"When it was announced that Grace Kelly was going to marry a Prince, Charles Vidor came to me and said, why don't we make *The Swan.* I said, 'Great' and I produced it."

Dore laughed.

"Here's an interesting thing which kind of proves that sometimes truth is better than fiction. We thought *The Swan* was a good picture—a *really* good one. And we thought it was going to be an absolutely *tremendous* success. Here, we're dealing with this fairytale which turned out to be true.

"Then the marriage took place, with whole newsreels covering it. *Everybody* went to see the newsreels, then didn't bother going to see our film, *The Swan.* They said, 'Yeah, we know about that but here's the *true* story."

Dore downed his strawberry tea with evident relish.

"Grace invited Miriam and me to the wedding but I had other commitments and we couldn't go. I sent her a very beautiful silver bowl properly inscribed with the crest. I'd had lunch with Rainier one day while we were doing *The Swan.* I got to know him, he was a darling and Grace was always very sweet and ladylike.

"I forgot to tell you we put Grace into a picture before *The Swan* and it was a *dog*. It was called *Green Fire*, which we never should have made. It was terrible, with Stewart Granger. But we thought it would do well, that it would bring some money in. It didn't.

"Grace was very dear about the whole thing; wasn't the least angry. But *The Swan* she loved. Of course, it had a great cast— Louis Jourdan, Alec Guinness, Agnes Moorehead, Jessie Royce Landis, Brian Aherne, Leo G. Carroll, and Estelle Winwood. So we had a warm and pleasant relationship. She was very nice—we increased her contract salary—but she never bothered us, never tried to make any alterations."

It was *Mogambo*, my host recalled, that catapulted Miss Kelly to fame.

"Grace knew that this was true to a great extent. So then, when the Metro blowup took place [Dore was "released"], Miriam and I decided to take our two kids to Monte Carlo. I had written to Grace that we were going and that if there was an opportunity to see her, we'd be staying at the hotel.

"When we arrived there already was a note waiting for us asking to call her. We did. Her secretary said that the Princess was out but that she very much wanted to see us. Then Grace telephoned and asked if we could come to the Palace for tea. We told her we had our two children with us and she said, 'I'd love to see them.' So off we went, the four of us to see her and her new baby.

(The new baby, Parisian boulevardiers claim today, is "some baby!"—the Princess Caroline.)

"Grace then did something that I think was especially charming and thoughtful, and to me an indication of not just good manners," my host said. "By this time she knew I was no longer at Metro and that I was not doing anything, ostensibly, except writing a play about FDR.

"So there was no need for her to ask us to the Palace. But there was another little thing she did. On the table in the room where we sat, was the bowl we had sent her for a wedding gift. I don't want you to believe it was so precious or so extraordinary that she would do that. I'm inclined to think that when she knew we were coming she said to herself, 'Well, it would be nice to have it there.'

"I looked at it and Grace said that she and Rainier loved it. That was very special of her and to me very significant. I wrote her a note afterward and thanked her. But that afternoon she was charming; she teased about her French, which she said was improving although still 'indecipherable.' She added that most of her staff thought it was atrocious but that Rainier was doing his best to improve it.

"You know, Arthur, as I sat there and saw this, I kept thinking of *High Noon* and her total disappearance from the scene afterward and that *awful* test on the Irish biddy. Then, to see that within a period of just a few short years there she was, that beautiful and quite charming Grace Kelly, the Princess in a Palace."

Dore sounded a bit rueful.

"I guess that's why nobody came to see her in *The Swan*."

Nothing could be further from my mind than a dissent with Dore about *anything* pertaining to the industry. Yet I do wish he would scan those few words with which the New York *Herald Tribune*'s esteemed critic, William Zinsser, dismissed Miss Kelly's accomplishments in *The Swan*.

"Miss Kelly," said Mr. Zinsser, "is stately, but utterly colorless. She is supposed to be a very shy girl, of course, but enough is enough." I was reminded of Dorothy Parker's classic *New Yorker* comments on Katharine Hepburn's performance in *The Lake*, something about this actress "running the gamut of emotions from A to B."

In a way, I suppose, it was just as well that Dore had commitments that prevented him and Miriam from attending the wedding. I'm sure he'd have been disappointed in the production which, in the opinion of one guest, turned out to be a gigantic bar mitzvah.

"It really was schmaltzy," this guest said, then smacked his lips at the memory. "The only thing missing was chopped herring and bagels, which I think old Jack Kelly should have provided, knowing Ike Levy was there. But they did serve lox, Nova Scotia at that or I miss my guess, although they called it 'smoked salmon.' "

From what I read in the press and what was told to me by Miss Rita Gam, bridesmaid, actress, and former roommate of Grace Kelly, there was another difference between the Grimaldi nuptials and a super-de-luxe bar mitzvah. At any rate, in some of the very special weddings I've attended—those with two orchestras, two rabbis, and a cantor—doves, trained to be on their best behavior, are released to flit over both friends of the bride and friends of the groom.

However, in Monte Carlo, at those special nuptials that I did not attend (nor, in fact, was invited) countless millions of rose petals fell from the sky, courtesy of guest Ari Onassis and his helicopters, showering streets, rooftops, Monégasques, and foreigners in glorious profusion. Miss Gam did advise me that, although she saw it with her own eyes, I should get official confirmation of this Aristotelian gesture from the Monacan Director of Publicity. I did not; for me Miss Gam's word is sufficient.

There are many episodes in the lives of the twenty-seven-year-old bride and her thirty-three-year-old groom that ought to be touched upon, if only lightly, before that great Monégasque wedding bash. An appropriate beginning might be the birth of our Princess, who first saw the light of day, "The Twelfth Day of November, A.D. 1929" in Hahnemann Hospital, the same institution where Brother John B., Jr., was born.

An interesting footnote—no pun intended—is that Grace's left foot measured two and seven-eighths inches from the tip of the center toe to the bottom of her heel. I do not attach much significance to the fact that Kell's left foot was shorter by a full quarter of an inch. Another observation I made is that Her Serene Highness's right foot was one-sixteenth of an inch longer than the left or it could be that the ink on the official birth certificate was smudged.

The next item I wish to record is a copy of the letter the polite four-year-old Grace wrote to Santa Claus; I'll bet she got every single thing she asked for. I do not intend to introduce Virginia (the girl, not the Commonwealth) into the picture, but in view of all those goodies Miss Kelly received in later years one simply must keep the faith.

The note to Santa follows:

PENN ATHLETIC CLUB
Rittenhouse Square
PHILADELPHIA

Dear Santa
I want a sled
and a scotter.
Grace Kelly
Coalter and Henry
thank you

I will now move eight years ahead. Grace's education has been in Roman Catholic private schools, her deportment excellent, and her marks better than average. I wouldn't claim her home life was particularly happy. Ma Kelly was possessive and demanding; Pa Kelly was absent much of the time and when he was home, scarcely concealed his favoritism for Peggy. Grace's sisters and brother were extroverts and sports lovers while Grace was shy, retiring, and too myopic for athletics. I wouldn't doubt either, that she was the brightest of the four Kelly children.

At age eleven Grace began her stage career with The Old Academy Players, an East Falls little-theater group. As far as I could learn, Miss Kelly did nothing outstanding there but was respected as a quiet, dependable member of the cast.

Since reams have been written about Grace Kelly's rise to fame,

*Princess Grace's younger
sister, Lizanne.*

which was topped by an Oscar for her performance in *The
Country Girl*, I don't intend to devote any more space than I
already have to this aspect of H.S.H.'s life—with one exception.
This comes in the form of a note written to me recently by
B.A. Bergman, who, after a checkered career that included edi-
torial stints on *The New Yorker* Magazine, the Jewish *Exponent*,
the Philadelphia *Record*, and other publications, is now Book
Editor of the Philadelphia Sunday *Bulletin*.

"Dear Mr. Lewis," Bergman writes. "For three years I was
President of the Philadelphia Public Relations Association. At
the close of the season we always had a party and in this, my first
year as President, which was in 1953, I selected dinner in Fairmount Park and a visit to the Playhouse in the Park. The Playhouse was the creation of John B. Kelly, Sr., and at the time,
Grace Kelly was starring in *The Moon Is Blue*.

"So I thought of crowning Grace as 'Queen of the Kellys'
with all the Kellys in attendance. It was quite a party. I have a
photograph of myself crowning Grace as 'Queen.' A little prophetic, I would say, for, as you know, three years later she became a Princess."

I can't think of anything else that might hold me back from

proceeding with those events leading up to and including the wedding. I mentioned previously that for Rainier to survive without working he needed a fructiferous wife. As for Grace, she'd gotten about as far as she could with what she had to offer the theatrical world. Besides, there apparently wasn't much future in continuing her romance with Mr. Oleg Cassini, a divorced non-Catholic, despite that gentleman's many and divers charms, plus an international reputation for female conquests.

Who is accountable for arranging the match, I don't know. Most authorities—Charles Kelly, Jr., to the contrary—give credit to the Very Reverend J. Francis Tucker, an Oblate Father and Rainier's personal Confessor. Others say the match was arranged, or at least aided, by old friends of John B. and Margaret Kelly, the Austins of Atlantic City, New Jersey.

My friend, Bill Hegner, a writer (sixteen published novels to date) got to know a great deal about the future Princess and takes a more cynical view of the marriage.

"I sometimes get the idea that maybe Grace and her advisors just went over a roster of what was available among the world's royalty; then said, 'Hey, Monaco! They're looking for a Princess; we'll get the two sides together and arrange something.' It was kind of like going through a stud book and checking for a cross-reference in *Who's Who*. So, if it all adds up together, 'Well, this is it.'

"I also have a feeling that Rainier sat around with his Palace staff saying, 'How do we find out about this broad?' And the staff responded, 'We'll write to MGM's publicity department and get an eight by ten glossy and a studio biography.' So the Prince answered, 'I like this.'

"Not bad, you know, an exchange of photographs. Then, they told Grace that old story about how it's every little girl's dream to grow up and marry a Prince. They said, 'Look at this lovely little kingdom.' I think they bought each other out of a catalog. When it came to putting them together they didn't quite match."

Despite the fact that this was getting me ahead of my story I asked Bill what he meant.

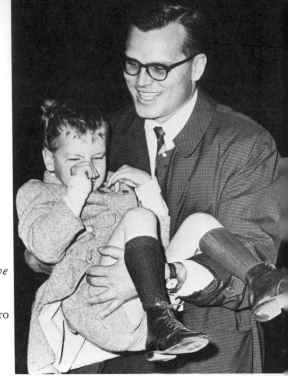

Uncle Jack Kelly with the young Prince Albert of Monaco.

AP WIREPHOTO

"Well, you see, Art," Bill explained, "they weren't really close to each other, Grace and Rainier, although that was hushed up, naturally. They started out having problems; she cried a lot and called her friends cross-Atlantic and said Rainier was terrible; difficult to get along with. She was homesick and he's a strong-willed person.

"They didn't communicate that well physically even if they've had three children. She fulfilled her commitment and they've stuck it out because it's mutually beneficial. Now she can live in Paris and meet her friends again. She travels a lot; you don't see pictures of them together so often."

Since it's unlikely that serious historians will give a damn about the wedding itself or the lives of their Serene Highnesses, who have done little or nothing to justify their existences, I can attribute the enormous world-wide interest in this very "royal" romance only to vulgar yet understandable curiosity. As for Monaco, all I can say is, while the paths of both lead to the same end, the road to the Monte Carlo Casino is a hell of a lot prettier than the Las Vegas strip. I know; I've traveled both trails.

33

ROMANCE HAS ITS LIMITS

THERE IS NO DOUBT THAT THE KELLY-GRIMALDI WEDDING WAS
a financial success. I speak not merely of the influx of new suckers
who lost their dough on Monte Carlo's green felt tables or end-
lessly dropped coins into His Serene Highness's one-armed ban-
dits that fill the "kitchen," a derisive Monégasque term for a
room devoted to slot machines.

There were no starry-eyed Graustarkians standing behind junk-
filled carts, or storekeepers who hawked plastic gimcracks outside the Palace gates. Nor were sentimentalists to be found among
the pragmatic manufacturers of such divers products as ladies'
underwear, aphrodisiacs, reducing pills, and toilet-bowl cleaners.

"Romance can extend only so far and after that, naturally,
comes sponsorship," wrote columnist John Crosby on April 10,
1956. "Prince Rainier has complained that he does not want any
commercialization of his wedding and everyone laughed heartily.

"Sponsors—in case you want to go buy the stuff right now for
the nuptials . . . will be Peter Pan Foundations, Maybelline,
Bourjois, Lanvin . . . Slenderella, Coty, and Purex.

"I can't remember anything so rich in comic possibilities since
the sailing of the Ford Peace Ship during World War I. The
press releases alone are full of wonderfully unexpected sentences.
Says the United Press: 'UP columnist Gloria Swanson already has
checked in at Monaco to cover the modern fairytale against the
backdrop of her Riviera memories.' "

Other networks were not far behind.

"CBS," reported Crosby, "has assigned Malcolm Johnson, news editor of the Washington Bureau, Don Hewitt, director, and Dave Schoenbrun and Blair Clark, of their Paris bureau, plus five cameramen, and three special assistants. From NBC, Jinx Falkenburg and Arlene Francis and practically everyone else except the telephone girls are going."

Nobody made an actual count, but Walter Ruch, who used to write for *The New York Times*, the Philadelphia *Inquirer*, and other newspapers, reported his estimate was more than thirteen hundred members of the media from all over the world. Most of them, he said, were from the United States, with France and England running second and third. I enjoyed Dorothy Kilgallen's appraisal of the English press's modus operandi.

"The only really bright chaps here," Miss Kilgallen filed from Monaco, "are the journalists for the sensational British papers. They solved the whole problem and haven't a care in the world. They just make up their stories, and believe me, they are a lot better than the stuff we conservative toffs are sending back home."

It's doubtful that Miss Kilgallen ever found out how close she came to being numbered among the uninvited. However, according to Hegner, who was in a position to know, Dorothy was on Miss Kelly's shit list.

"I got involved with Grace in terms of Dorothy Kilgallen. I better back up a bit to explain. In the early Fifties I represented Gant Gaither, who at the time was a Broadway stage producer. Gant was then and still is one of Grace's closest friends, one of her confidants. They had an almost daily relationship, telephone calls, and so on. They lived only a couple of blocks away from each other.

"I was planting stories in Winchell's and Kilgallen's columns on Gant and Grace, especially on Gant. In fact, Bob Sylvester once said in 'Dream Street' at the time of the wedding that he wasn't sure who was getting married, Gant or Grace. Well, to get back to that wedding tally sheet and Dorothy.

"We were trying to establish a list of guests selected from an enormous amount of suggestions and cut it down to a reasonable size. As far as Kilgallen was concerned, Grace was dead set against inviting her. 'I hate her guts. I despise her as a person,' Grace told us."

According to Hegner, Gant finally succeeded in persuading Grace to change her mind.

"She held out for a long while. Gant told her that Dorothy was the Number One Eastern Woman Columnist and *had* to be asked to the wedding. Finally, Grace granted her okay but only if she would be kept a deck apart from Kilgallen so that at no time would there be any opportunity for them to bump into one another. So it was worked out that the only time there'd be even a chance of their meeting would be at public functions. Dorothy, then, to her great joy, was a guest."

My favorite comment on the wedding came from Edward P. Morgan, ABC's distinguished newscaster.

"It was announced at the White House," reported Mr. Morgan, "that President Eisenhower in all probability will designate a personal ambassador to represent him. I'd kind of like to suggest that Mr. Eisenhower designate Walt Disney. In one gracious gesture that would confirm what so many people suspect, that we Americans—the public in general and the administration in particular—prefer fairytales to the stark nonfiction of everyday life."

Pickpockets abounded. However, I'll bet there was none so polite as the Spanish thief who once stole my wife's wallet, removed only the cash, and left everything else, including such memorabilia as grandchildren's snapshots. Then "our" pickpocket added a note, which we found when police retrieved the missing wallet dropped in a mailbox. *"Lo siento mucho. El Ratero."*

The presence of jewel thieves was noted almost as soon as the first guest arrived. Mrs. Matthew H. McCloskey, whose husband at the time was Treasurer of the Democratic National Committee, reported a loss of fifty thousand dollars in precious gems from her room in the Hotel de Paris.

Another victim, also a guest at the Hotel de Paris, was bridesmaid Mrs. A. A. Pamp, of suburban Philadelphia, one of Grace's schoolmates. Mrs. Pamp's loss was ten thousand dollars.

Unquestionably there were other thefts but by the time Mrs. Pamp's loss reached the ears of Grace's press agent, Morgan Hudgins, on loan to Miss Kelly from MGM, a clamp was put on these unromantic news items. Mr. Hudgins, it may be recalled, used to be in charge of Philadelphia Evening and Sunday *Bulletin* photographers and with *such* a background, was highly competent to deal with practically everything.

Mr. Art Buchwald had his own remarks to make.

"Prince Rainier II," wrote Buchwald on April 17, 1956, "is so furious over the jewel robberies that have taken place at Monaco during the last week that he has decided to ban all jewel thieves from the wedding. This drastic measure has raised a howl of protests from jewel robbers of every nationality who were sent there to cover the wedding.

"A top-flight jewel thief, who asked that his name not be mentioned, told us in the lobby of the Hotel de Paris, 'I am shocked at the Prince's attitude. We have only stolen jewels from Philadelphia people and we haven't even bothered the Aga Khan. The right of jewel thieves to operate on the Riviera is older than the Magna Carta and Prince Rainier has no right to bar us from the wedding.' "

His Serene Highness, with much at stake, took a more serious view of the thefts than did Mr. Buchwald. According to Joe Hyams of the New York *Herald Tribune*, the Prince brought in outside help.

"Instead of Scotland Yard," reported Hyams, "it was a member of New York City's Police Department who was called in to help solve the second jewel robbery in Monaco within two days. Detective Frank Cresci was one of the first policemen to reach the room of Mrs. Marie Pamp, after she discovered her gems had been stolen."

From newspaper and oral comments of those who were present, it would seem that the Kelly-Grimaldi affair was just too much for the little Prince. Notwithstanding the presence of Mr. Hudgins, H.S.H. had an open quarrel with the press and appointed a totally incompetent local public relations counselor whose only "experience" in the field was as a small-time actor. In general even his Father Confessor, the Very Reverend Tucker, admitted Rainier "behaved like a spoiled boy."

As a spectacle the nuptials must have been great fun; but as a royal wedding in the traditions of Europe's remaining aristocracy, it was not. From what I gathered, the Annual Bean Soup Rally in McClure, Pennsylvania, and the Philadelphia's Mummers' Parade are handled far more efficiently. I think that even Bert Parks would have been an improvement.

People were not likely to accuse the late Dorothy Kilgallen of sentimentality. Rather, this reporter, known to millions of TV fans for her role in "What's My Line?" and millions of others who read her column, was famed for biting wit, an acerbic tongue, and scorn for pomp. So I find it rather out of character for Miss K. to write glowingly about the wedding, which for prior weeks she had debunked, flaying principals, guests, and Monaco with equal disdain. Yet, of all the stories, at least those I perused, I found hers the most romantic. Hence I quote from a column she filed on April 18, 1956:

"Wide-eyed and trembling with emotion, actress Grace Kelly played the most important role of her life today when she stood at the candlelit altar of the Cathedral of St. Nicholas and vowed to 'love unto death' Prince Rainier III of this Riviera fairyland . . .

"Then in a moment of high drama, the golden girl of the films made a pilgrimage to a tiny peach-colored church under the railroad bridge of Monte Carlo, knelt in the dust in her gleaming wedding gown and begged the martyred St. Devote, patron Saint of her new land, to bless her marriage. It was a poignant scene as the young Princess, her fair hair veiled in cloudy tulle and precious lace, kissed the relics proffered to her by robed priests and laid her bridal bouquet at the feet of the virgin saint who brought Christianity to Monaco.

"The Prince, wearing a ribbon-sashed uniform heavy with medals and gold braid, and carrying his plumed helmet, watched with serious eyes. The sun for which Grace had prayed to St. Claire

Her Serene Highness the Princess Grace of Monaco about to receive the "Woman of the Year" award for 1965 of the Philadelphia Council Ladies Auxiliary, Jewish War Veterans.

shone brightly . . . Now, the American girl who sky-rocketed to fame as a Hollywood motion picture actress is not only her Serene Highness, but truly the wife of Rainier in the eyes of her God."

It is not easy to conceive that this is oozing from the normally poison-dipped pen of Miss K., but as she goes on, it gets even stickier. I can attribute this only to a common belief that all women cry at weddings even when they loathe the major participants.

"White lilacs banked the high altar of the cathedral and hung in great golden baskets from the chandeliers as the Prince and Princess repeated their solemn vows before Bishop Giles Barthé. Grace was a breathtaking vision . . . Her dress, with its pearl-studded Brussels lace bodice and big skirt of peau de soie, was regal yet girlish, emphasizing her slender waist while giving her a queenly stature. A short face veil fell over her chiseled counte-nance, but it did not conceal her beauty. Her skin shimmered through it and her eyes were darkly blue.

"They did not kiss at the altar. When the last benediction had been given, Grace and Rainier rose, genuflected at their prie-dieu, made the sign of the cross, and turned toward the congregation for the recessional. Grace gazed at her groom with an expression that asked, 'Now?' and he offered his right arm. When she had slipped her lace-sleeved arm through his, they proceeded down the aisle, unsmiling, past the smiling faces of their guests and outside to the smart salutes of the honor guard facing the cathedral and the joyous shouts of the crowd."

This, from Dorothy Kilgallen? Yes, and *still* more.

"They finally broke into smiles—at first, just for each other . . . when they reached their waiting car, Grace turned to her husband and said something that made him grin.

"As the open Rolls-Royce moved away to take them on a tour of the city, their cheering subjects saw them talking affectionately and animatedly as if they were the only two persons in the world."

All the Kellys, and there were scores of them present, adored the wedding; there were no exceptions. Another fun-loving mem-ber of the party was the Princess Ghislaine, Rainier's grandmother. For interesting, albeit brief, data on that cheerful nuptial guest, I turn to my friend Jules Lavin, the courtly gentleman who cur-rently is Ma Kelly's escort.

"I attended the flower show in Monaco on May 4, 1974." It is obvious that Mr. Lavin has a precise memory.

"This," continued Mr. Lavin, "was the celebration of the

twenty-fifth anniversary of the accession to the throne of Prince Rainier. I was driving in one of the Palace cars to the hall.

"On my right," Jules went on, "was Princess Ghislaine, Rainier's grandmother."

Jules smiled.

"Perhaps it would be better to say, 'step-grandmother.' She was a rather young woman. I found out she was only fifty-one. And upon further inquiry I learned that originally she had been the mistress of Rainier's grandfather, Louis II, and after the death of Louis' original wife, he married Ghislaine, his mistress."

So I commented to Mr. Lavin, "That would make Rainier older than his grandmother."

"Louis II and Ghislaine had a very, very happy life from what I understand. Louis' eventual successor would have been Rainier's father, Prince Pierre. However, Pierre (Rainier's father) was noted as the playboy of Europe while married to a very lovely woman, a beautiful woman, Princess Charlotte [Rainier's mother].

"Well, Princess Charlotte put up with his shenanigans as long as she could. When the question arose as to who would succeed him after Louis abdicated, he attempted to turn the throne over to Charlotte.

"Being the person she was, she told her father-in-law, 'For years we have schooled Rainier to take over the job someday. My honest opinion is that he is now ready to take your place. I don't want it; I don't want any part of Monaco. I am through with Pierre!' "

I felt a little sad about the treatment given Pierre at the wedding. Newsmen said he wandered about Monaco, a lost soul.

"I'm like the father of an orphan," he told Washington reporters shortly before his son and Grace were joined in holy matrimony. "But I do hope Miss Kelly will make a happy home for Rainier."

34

"THEY TAKE THEMSELVES SO SERIOUSLY"

To a large measure, I would say that Papa Pierre's hopes for his son were fulfilled, that Grace and Rainier have had a passably successful marriage these past twenty or so years and have suffered no more than most of us who have given "hostages to fortune."

Since the Société des Bains de Mer, a fanciful name for the organization that operates the Casino, keeps paying off His Serene Highness regularly, I would guess that lack of ready funds never troubles this branch of the Grimaldis despite the fact that Rainier III is not in the same fiscal category as, for example, the Aga Khan.

"Some accounts labeled Rainier as a member of 'one of the oldest royal families in Europe,'" wrote Cholly Knickerbocker. "That's so much rot, of course. There are hundreds of princely families in Europe older than Rainier's and certainly quite a few of them with more money.

"Rainier's forebears, the Grimaldis, were buccaneers. They took Monte Carlo by assault some seven hundred years ago and have occupied the place ever since, more or less undisturbed."

There are some who say that lately His Serene Highness is beginning to overestimate his international stature.

"When Rainier sent an unofficial emissary to the vital SALT talks at Helsinki, Finland," wrote a Philadelphia *Inquirer* reporter recently, "there were mutterings that the Prince's sense of his

Prince Rainier and Princess Grace arrive with their daughter Princess Caroline at the annual Red Cross ball, Monaco, 1975.
AP WIREPHOTO

world importance was getting out of hand. And now Monaco has grandly joined with France and Italy in a program to clean up the Mediterranean coast. For its part, Monaco will ban washday detergents. Carping critics point out that recent hotel and casino construction on Monaco landfill sites has done more to harm the beautiful coastline than a hundred years of detergents."

And how is the Princess comporting herself these days? For this information we go to Ms. Leslie Bennetts of the Philadelphia *Bulletin*. It should be remembered that Ms. Bennetts is the same sharp-tongued young blond reporter who did such an intimate portrait of Kell for her newspaper.

"It's so funny," Leslie told me, "you come up to this Palace and you see what looks like some little pink thing on top of a cake. And those soldiers outside in their funny, funny uniforms! They take themselves so seriously. There's a changing of the guards and they're all carrying bayonets. They also take their security very seriously.

"I presented myself at the door. It took an hour. I don't know what they were doing, maybe running around the hallways. Finally, I was admitted to the tower where Grace had her office. My recollection of that office is a lot of cool and subdued colors like celery green and icy lemon yellow. At ten o'clock she is dressed in a Dior suit, looking perfect, not a hair out of place.

"She is quite beautiful although not breathtaking. Not the way she was when she was twenty-five, when she really was exquisite. Now she has age spots on her hands but she *is* a beautiful woman."

Leslie and I were having predinner cocktails at the Peale Club and I must say my guest looked as stunning as any of the Kellys. She went on.

"As to her personality, she had less warmth and less spontaneity than anyone I've ever talked to. And I don't think this was because of me. After all, I had entrée there, I was a good friend of her brother's and a reporter from her hometown. But she is an awful stick.

"With Kell I always had the feeling—it's really funny—that he really knows only a certain number of things to say. Grace is exactly the same way, although I think she's brighter than he is.

"Before I went I had, of course, read all those interviews going back twenty-five years. I realize she'd been interviewed to death ever since she was about nineteen. Nevertheless, no matter how unusual a question, she reverts to something familiar and non-controversial, something that doesn't require thought."

I asked Leslie if she discussed politics with the Princess. My guest shook her head.

"She appears to have no political opinions whatsoever. The most controversial stand she has ever taken in terms of causes is being a member of *La Leche League,* which is in favor of breast-feeding children. Other than that she's strictly for garden parties and charity balls. Her life revolves around the rituals of her position.

"You can't believe that this girl from Philadelphia—not even Main Line Philadelphia—has developed the most astonishing accent. People who knew her when she was a child are shocked when they meet her. She has this stilted, vaguely bastardized French. It's the damnedest thing you ever heard, in this incredibly affected voice.

"We talked and then she took me on a tour, walking through the Palace. My time was limited to that one day. Rainier was away and Caroline was in school in Paris; the younger daughter was at school in town. That day I met Prince Albert, sitting with his tutor in the schoolroom. He was a well-behaved mannerly young man, who jumped up and shook my hand.

"Grace was very cordial but in a completely surface way.

"I think she's a woman of very rigid opinions, one who doesn't question a lot of things. It's beyond me how someone can grow up in America and feel comfortable having other people bow and curtsy and scrape to you and call you, 'Your Highness.' But this doesn't faze Grace in the least. She won't confess 'getting off on it.' I don't know if she does or doesn't enjoy that kind of thing. But it would make most Americans profoundly uncomfortable, the undemocratic set of rituals they go through over there."

Leslie shook her head.

"It's preposterous for a little postage-stamp kingdom. But she loves it; I think she loves all the trappings of royalty. And I *don't* think she thinks about the political, social, and moral implications of anything. She didn't talk about her mother or Kell or anything except in the most bland, innocuous, and totally uninteresting terms. It was really a *very* boring interview."

Leslie smiled.

"So I had to go back and write up a storm because what she had to say holds no interest. You never have a feeling of realness about her; that she's going to let her hair down and talk about what she really feels and thinks, what her kids are really like, whether she's worried about Caroline running around and getting into the headlines. Never in a million years would she do that."

In defense of H.S.H.'s reticence about discussing personal matters, I'm not sure that any woman in Grace's spot would have

Princess Caroline.

bared her soul to this astute Philadelphia reporter with a reputation for using a literary scalpel on her interviewees. It's also quite possible that before seeing Leslie, Grace had read some of Ms. Bennetts' *Bulletin* pieces sent to her by friends back home.

"I think Grace has an enormous amount of pride—and there's nothing wrong with that," Leslie admitted, "but her whole world revolves around artifice. You *know* she's a product of the image factory. That this is the extent of what she has to offer the world.

"In Grace Kelly's position, with the money and the social crowd that she carries, she could have done a lot of good in the world. When you ask her what she's interested in, she has a passing interest in astrology, needlepoint, and flower arrangement, although she has somebody else full time to arrange flowers.

"Grace is a very straitlaced woman; no emancipation from her husband. She's very Catholic and very puritanical. Kell told me once that the only one of the children who's gotten more Catholic through the years is Grace. The rest of them have strayed from the fold."

For those who subscribe to the belief that the Princess is a kind of nonperson, it's rather a pleasant shock to find that the former Miss Kelly may possess more than a veneer of emotional depth.

"She had her temper and her tantrums," recalled Hegner, the writer who handled some of Grace's P.R. "Gant was her buffer; she'd call him up, angry about someone, and he'd have to calm her down. Grace, you know, practiced denial by silence. That's her favorite trick. She was very much protected by everyone around her. Like, for example, Rita Gam and Gant and Sloan Simpson. She inspired that kind of loyalty.

"But Grace, in turn, didn't give anything of herself. I think she fritters away her time just doing nothing . . . being a public person. Telephone calls and figuring out what she was going to do that night."

Hegner smiled.

"Some afternoons, when Grace was feeling exhilarated, she and Gant and her other friends would play like children, roll around the floor. They'd be laughing and giggling as if they were at a kid's party."

For Her Serene Highness of Monaco, it must be a comfort to know that her party can go on forever.

INDEX